Biliterate Writing From the Start

Biliterate Writing From the Start
The Literacy Squared Approach to Asset-Based Writing Instruction

by

Sandra Butvilofsky, Ph.D.
Boulder Valley School District
Boulder

Kathy Escamilla, Ph.D.
University of Colorado
Boulder

and

Susan Hopewell, Ph.D.
University of Colorado
Boulder

Baltimore • London • Sydney

Paul H. Brookes Publishing Co.
Post Office Box 10624
Baltimore, Maryland 21285-0624
USA

www.brookespublishing.com

Copyright © 2023 by Paul H. Brookes Publishing Co., Inc.
All rights reserved.

"Paul H. Brookes Publishing Co." is a registered trademark of
Paul H. Brookes Publishing Co., Inc.

Typeset by Progressive Publishing Services, York, Pennsylvania.
Manufactured in the United States of America by
Versa Press, Inc., East Peoria, Illinois.

Literacy Squared and Lecto-Escritura Al Cuadrado are trademarks of Literacy Squared, LLC.

The individuals described in this book are composites or real people whose situations are masked and are based on the authors' experiences. In all instances, names and identifying details have been changed to protect confidentiality.

Purchasers of *Biliterate Writing From the Start: The Literacy Squared Approach to Asset-Based Writing Instruction* are granted permission to download, print, and photocopy the Literacy Squared Writing Rubric in the text for educational purposes. This form may not be reproduced to generate revenue for any program or individual. Photocopies may only be made from an original book. *Unauthorized use beyond this privilege may be prosecutable under federal law.* You will see the copyright protection notice at the bottom of each photocopiable page.

Library of Congress Cataloging-in-Publication Data

Names: Butvilofsky, Sandra, author. | Escamilla, Kathy, author. | Hopewell, Susan, author.
Title: Biliterate writing from the start : the literacy squared approach to asset-based writing instruction / by Sandra Butvilofsky, Ph.D., Boulder Valley School District, Boulder, Kathy Escamilla, Ph.D., University of Colorado, Boulder and Susan Hopewell, Ph.D., University of Colorado, Boulder.
Description: Baltimore, Maryland : Paul H. Brookes Publishing Co., [2023] | Includes bibliographical references and index.
Identifiers: LCCN 2023005175 (print) | LCCN 2023005176 (ebook) | ISBN 9781934000472 (paperback) | ISBN 9781681257303 (epub) | ISBN 9781681257310 (pdf)
Subjects: LCSH: Education, Bilingual—United States. | Literacy—United States. | Multiculturalism—United States. | Culturally relevant pedagogy—United States.
Classification: LCC LC3719.B8 2023 (print) | LCC LC3719 (ebook) | DDC 370.117/50973—dc23/eng/20230221
LC record available at https://lccn.loc.gov/2023005175
LC ebook record available at https://lccn.loc.gov/2023005176

British Library Cataloguing in Publication data are available from the British Library.

2027 2026 2025 2024 2023

10   9   8   7   6   5   4   3   2   1

Contents

About the Download vii
About the Authors ix
Foreword   *Allison Briceño, Ed.D.* xi
Acknowledgments xiii

1   **Literacy Squared, and Why We Need to Focus
    on Biliterate Writing** 1
    Key Terms 1
    Guiding Questions 1
    A Brief History of Literacy Squared 2
    Biliterate Writing 6
    Research Findings to Guide the Development
       of Literacy Squared 9
    The Need for a Book on Spanish–English Biliteracy 12
    Summary and Preview: Biliterate Children, Biliterate Writers 13
    Questions for Reflection and Action 14
    Chapter 1 Appendix: Literacy Squared Writing Rubric 15

2   **The Role of Oracy and Writing in Teaching
    Foundational Skills** 19
    Key Terms 19
    Guiding Questions 19
    Oracy and Writing: The Forgotten Components of Foundational
       Skills Teaching 22
    Sample Literacy Unit Incorporating Oracy: What Is a Refugee? 25
    Considerations for Developing Biliteracy 32
    Summary: Literacy, Oracy, and Writing 35
    Questions for Reflection and Action 35

3   **TheDictado Method for Writing Instruction** 37
    Key Terms 37
    Guiding Questions 37
    TheDictado: Definition, Purpose, and Implementation Basics 38
    TheDictado in Practice 41
    Summary: TheDictado 50
    Questions for Reflection and Action 51

4   **Nurturing Biliteracy in Emerging Writers in Kindergarten** 53
    Key Terms 53
    Guiding Questions 53
    Research Supporting Biliterate Writing Instruction
       in Kindergarten 54

Profiles in Biliteracy: A Nuanced Analysis of Early
    Biliterate Writing 55
Instructional Implications 61
Daily Writing Instruction in Both Spanish Literacy
    and Literacy-Based ELD 61
Paired Literacy Lesson 65
Summary: Biliterate Writing in Kindergarten 74
Questions for Reflection and Action 74

5 Cultivating Biliterate Writing in Grades 1 and 2 75
Key Term 75
Guiding Questions 75
Diego's Story: Biliteracy in Grade 1 75
General Trends in Biliterate Writing in Grades 1 and 2 77
Abel's Story: Biliterate Writing Potential in Grade 1 79
Instructional Implications 81
Summary: Biliterate Writing in Grade 1 91
Questions for Reflection and Action 91

6 Developing Biliteracy via Genre Studies in
Grades 3 to 5: Biography 93
Key Terms 93
Guiding Questions 93
Expanding Upon the Main Writing Genres to Develop Biliteracy 94
Backward Planning for Biliterate Writing 98
Sample Fourth-Grade Biliteracy Unit: Biography 100
Summary: Biliterate Writing and Genre Study in Grades 3 to 5 112
Questions for Reflection and Action 113

7 Furthering Biliteracy via Genre Studies in
Grades 3 to 5: Social Justice 115
Key Terms 115
Guiding Questions 115
Fostering Engaged Writing in Grades 3 to 5 116
Using a Bilingual Lens to Promote a Developmentally
    Appropriate Trajectory 117
Beyond the Common Core: Social Justice Standards
    and Humanizing Curricula 117
Sample Unit Sketch: Reading and Writing About Racism 121
Summary: Biliterate Writing in Grades 3–5 and Beyond 127
Questions for Reflection and Action 127

Glossary 129
References 133
Index 137

About the Download

Purchasers of this book may download, print, and/or photocopy the Literacy Squared Writing Rubric for educational use.

To access the materials that come with this book:

1. Go to the Brookes Publishing Download Hub: http://downloads.brookespublishing.com

2. Register to create an account (or log in with an existing account).

3. Filter or search for the book *Biliterate Writing From the Start: The Literacy Squared Approach to Asset-Based Writing Instruction*.

About the Authors

Sandra A. Butvilofsky, Ph.D., Boulder Valley School District

Sandra A. Butvilofsky, has been a bilingual/biliteracy elementary teacher and interventionist, instructional coach, researcher, and professor. She is coauthor of *Biliteracy From the Start: Literacy Squared in Action*. Her work in the Literacy Squared project involved assisting in program development, conducting research, and providing professional development to bilingual teachers and administrators. Her research interests include examining the biliterate writing and reading development of Spanish/English Latinx bilingual learners from preschool through fifth grade to demonstrate the potential of bilingual/biliteracy education.

Kathy Escamilla, Ph.D., University of Colorado, Boulder

Kathy Escamilla is a Professor Emeritus of Education in the Division of Equity, Bilingualism and Biliteracy at the University of Colorado, Boulder. Dr. Escamilla's research focuses on issues related to the development of bilingualism and biliteracy for emerging bilingual children in U.S. schools. She is a cofounder of Literacy Squared, a program dedicated to creating biliterate pedagogies with and for Spanish-speaking children and their teachers. She is a lifelong bilingual educator and has been a teacher, administrator, and professor in her 50+ years in public education.

Susan Hopewell, Ph.D., University of Colorado, Boulder

Susan Hopewell, coauthor of *Biliteracy from the Start, Literacy Squared in Action* and Associate Professor of Equity Bilingualism and Biliteracy at the University of Colorado Boulder, has spent her entire career working with, and learning from, bilingual learners. As the current director of Literacy Squared, Dr. Hopewell provides extensive professional development to schools around the United States to help them better design effective biliteracy instruction

Foreword

As a first-year bilingual teacher I was underprepared to support my students' biliteracy acquisition. But what I learned from them has stuck with me.

For example, Gloria, a quiet child, learned to read before she learned to write and would often use her favorite books as resources when she wrote. Another student, Brandon had a lot to say, and when I was able to direct his verbosity to a blank page, his strong oral language was the foundation for great writing. But he resisted reading for a long time. Citlali was diagnosed with developmental delays but learned to read beautifully, despite her special education teacher telling me I should direct my attention to the other kids, who were more likely to learn to read and write.

Other students, like María and Nicolás, made me look good, but they essentially taught themselves. While they needed some support with spelling, their strong oral language and the literacy skills they brought from home made them successful with minimal help from me. I was less successful teaching Edgar to read and write, and his lack of success haunts me to this day.

During my first year teaching I was also completing my teacher credential program. My credential classes were focused on English only, and I was primarily teaching in Spanish. I struggled this way for a number of years, as many teachers do, until I came across the work of Drs. Sandra Butvilofsky, Kathy Escamilla, Sue Hopewell, and the BUENO Center. Their ground-breaking research taught me many things, including how to teach through a holistic biliteracy lens, despite schools traditionally having monolingual curricula and assessment practices.

The authors also taught me that bilingual teachers do not have to struggle like I did; we do not have to sacrifice children's biliteracy while we (teachers) are novices. The research on effective biliteracy practices exists. In fact, some of the most significant biliteracy research of the last three decades was done by the authors.

Butvilofsky, Escamilla, and Hopewell's first book, *Biliteracy from the Start: Literacy Squared in Action* (2014) codified a biliterate instructional model and provided a set of evidence-based instructional practices that were tested and proven in bilingual programs across the country. I have been using it with preservice teachers for almost a decade.

Biliterate Writing from the Start builds on the authors' prior work and focuses on writing as a critical piece of the puzzle that is often missing from "science of reading" programs. It is also extremely timely, as many bilingual programs are feeling the pressure to apply English-specific "science of reading" literacy concepts to bilingual classrooms. Butvilofsky, Escamilla, and Hopewell demonstrate how to teach foundational skills —and broader literacy skills— in ways that are appropriate for bilingual students.

For many kids, writing is the first and most accessible entry point to literacy. The authors explain that writing is evidence of what students know and can do across languages; it is a fantastic window into students' understandings of how biliteracy works. We learn to use students' writing as a useful formative assessment and an opportunity to consider next instructional steps. Learning from our students' writing allows us to provide more targeted and strategic instruction and improve as teachers every day.

This is the book I wish I had years ago when I struggled to teach biliteracy. Butvilofsky, Escamilla, and Hopewell share evidence-based practices from Literacy Squared that have been proven to advance students' biliteracy acquisition. They open doors for all of us to engage in biliteracy through a social justice lens by identifying culturally and linguistically relevant practices that connect home language and culture to the classroom. Having done the research themselves, they make it practical and understandable for the reader. The authors excel at connecting research and theory to classroom practice, showing teachers what it looks like with real students and real writing samples.

Butvilofsky, Escamilla, and Hopewell's concept of "bilingualism as a first language" (p. 3 of this book) shifts our thinking from the monolingual norm to bilingual practices. It provides a better representation and understanding of many of our students. And, building on the idea of bilingualism as a first language, the authors advance a *holistic biliteracy framework* that enables us to approach bilingual classrooms through a lens that values the whole child, including their linguistic assets. While taking a bilingual approach to bilingual classrooms may sound obvious, many bilingual programs instead apply monolingual views of teaching, learning, and assessing in each language.

But, as the authors explain, bilingual people—bilingual brains—don't compartmentalize languages in their brains. Instead, we judiciously use the entirety of our linguistic knowledge and consider the task, context, and audience. Therefore, it is clear that an assets-based bilingual pedagogy must involve building cross-linguistic connections, developing metacognition, and integrating all aspects of literacy across languages. Students learn that they can write what they can say, they can read what they write, and they can do it all across two or more languages. The holistic biliteracy framework, therefore, supports both the teacher and the students as we all continue learning and developing our bilingualism and biliteracy.

This book brings the holistic biliteracy framework to life, showing how students' approximations are invaluable clues to us, their teachers. The authors consolidate the relevant research, break down key concepts, and provide lots of real-life examples to help us understand what we can do to support our students. They illustrate how to systematically analyze students' writing and how to use it as a tool for future teaching. They explain how to differentiate and how to implement in online settings. In short, the authors' holistic biliteracy framework is a foundation for increased educational equity. It provides a biliterate trajectory across the elementary grade levels, ensures greater access for students to grade-level content, and, as the authors' award-winning research has shown, results in more equitable outcomes.

The book is organized to ensure our success: the key vocabulary and guiding questions at the beginning of each chapter, the student examples, the useful summaries, and the reflection questions at the end of each chapter help us learn the key ideas and how to implement them. After reading this book, teachers will feel confident to use the strategies in their classrooms.

Butvilofsky, Escamilla, and Hopewell have been working with schools and educators for decades, doing the research, examining student work, and identifying classroom practices that effectively advance biliteracy. Together, they have close to a century of experience in bilingual education as teachers, literacy specialists, coaches, teacher educators, professional developers, and researchers.

This book sets the stage for teachers to have high expectations for all students. Due to housing segregation and other inequitable systems, Latinx students are largely segregated in schools across the country. I taught in such a school and was repeatedly told it was unrealistic to expect all students to learn to read and write. To overcome that belief, which permeates many schools with large populations of students of color, the authors have codified culturally and linguistically relevant research-based practices that advance students' literacy development. After using this book other teachers won't have to continue wondering, 20 years later, what else they could have done to teach their version of Edgar.

Allison Briceño, Ed.D.
San José State University
San José, California

Acknowledgments

We want to make special mention of several valued colleagues, all of whom actively contributed to the development of some of the lessons we share in the book: Khanh Nguyen Le (Chapter 2), Lucinda Soltero-González (Chapter 4), Adriana Alvarez (Chapter 4), Sandra Castor (Chapter 5), and Hilary Barthel (Chapter 6).

*Este libro se dedica a todos los aprendices bilingües y sus
familias para quienes la educación es más que un derecho, sino un acto de
justicia social; y para los maestros bilingües que dedican su profesión para realizarlo.*

1 Literacy Squared, and Why We Need to Focus on Biliterate Writing

"La escritura es importante en la escuela porque es importante fuera de ella y no al revés. Leer no es descifrar, escribir no es copiar."

—Emilia Ferreiro, 2017

Key Terms

Bilingualism as a First Language	**Metalanguage**
Biliterate pedagogies	**Metalinguistic development**
Biliterate writing	**Oracy**
Cross-language connections	**Paired literacy instruction**
Holistic biliteracy framework	**Trajectories toward biliteracy**
Literacy Squared	

Guiding Questions

▶ How does a **holistic biliteracy framework** differ from earlier versions of biliteracy instruction?

▶ How does a focus on quality of instruction shift the debate about effective practice in the bilingual education field?

▶ What are examples of deficit-oriented views of emerging bilingual (EB) children's writing, and how can we create more asset-based views?

About one quarter of U.S. children (10 million) speak a language other than English at home. EB learners often perform below monolingual English grade-level expectations, are twice as likely to drop out, and are less likely to attend a 4-year college. EB learners have been the recipients of many monolingual English reforms over the years, but research about their strengths and needs are rarely considered and built upon when literacy reforms are created and implemented. As a result, outcomes have been disappointing and perceived gaps have maintained.

This student population has not been served well by approaches to literacy instruction that are geared to monolingual students; in particular, approaches that emphasize foundational skills to the detriment of oracy and comprehension. This is not just an education issue but also an equity and social justice issue—we must do better by these students. We have a strong research base upon which to build effective literacy approaches for EB learners, and in this book, we intend to build on and utilize that strong research base to recommend pedagogical orientations as well as strategies and methods for teachers and schools to use that are both research based, and research tested. These include the **Literacy Squared** model, examples of assets-based orientations and teaching approaches for EB learners, and attention to all components of biliteracy instruction, with a particular focus in this book on writing.

A BRIEF HISTORY OF LITERACY SQUARED

In 2004, the authors of this book set out on an academic and pedagogical adventure that asked a seemingly simple question—how do we create school-based opportunities for Spanish/English EB children in the United States to develop, enhance, and value their language and literacy skills in two languages (Escamilla et al., 2014)? As with all excellent adventures, we have picked up colleagues, friends, partners, and critics along the way, all of whom have helped us to reflect, revise, and refine our thinking. This collection of colleagues originated in Colorado and Texas in 2005 with a small pilot program and over the years has expanded west to Oregon and Washington while also moving south to Texas and Arizona and east to Illinois. Our musings and experiences eventually spawned a formal project titled "Literacy Squared." In its totality, Literacy Squared has four components, including research, professional development, assessment, and instruction. Over the course of the past 18 years, this project has touched 450 teachers and 12,744 children in 7 states. We have also written 1 book, 18 journal articles, 12 book chapters, and 24 technical reports about the research results from Literacy Squared projects nationally, many of which can be accessed on our website (https://literacysquared.org).

From the onset, we argued the need for innovative approaches to the instruction of EB children that would include the following:

1. A deeper understanding of EB children in 21st-century U.S. schools, with an emphasis on viewing these children from assets-based perspectives

2. A broader definition of literacy to include **oracy, writing,** and **metalinguistic development** in addition to reading

3. Biliteracy instruction from the beginning of school, with more focus on the quality of instruction rather than the language of instruction

4. An approach to assessment that was built around a holistic biliteracy framework and building **trajectories toward biliteracy.**

Each of these concepts is explained briefly below, and each contributes to the focus of this book on writing assessment and instruction for EB Spanish/English learners. It is important to note that we view writing assessment and instruction not as a discrete and separate subject area, but as a part of an integrated approach to teaching literacy in Spanish and English that includes **cross-language connections.**

This book is particularly relevant at this time given the resurgence of a movement in U.S. literacy instruction that has waxed and waned over at least the past 50 years. Currently, this movement is known as the Science of Reading (SOR) (Ehri, 2020; Moats, 2020) and signals a renewed focus on teaching foundational skills, particularly phonics. A precursor SOR in the 1950s was a movement led by Rudolph Flesch, who wrote a book titled, *Why Johnny Can't Read*. Flesch argued that the reason that Johnny couldn't read was that he didn't know phonics (Flesch, 1955). Over the decades, how much time and attention should be devoted to teaching phonics and other foundational skills within school literacy programs has been hotly and laboriously debated. In 2000, the National Literacy Panel Report released findings of a synthesis of research that concluded that effective reading programs need to include five foundational skills: phonemic awareness, phonics, vocabulary, fluency, and comprehension. A $6 billion program titled Reading First (2008) took the findings of the National Literacy Panel Report and created literacy programs for U.S. schools, which were heavily focused on phonics and other foundational skills. Research results from Reading First were not positive. An extensive evaluation of the efficacy of Reading First was conducted by the Institute of Educational Research (2008) to determine its impact on student reading achievement and on classroom instruction. The report found that there was a significant impact on strengthening decoding skills among first-grade students. However, Reading First did not produce a statistically significant impact on student reading comprehension test scores in grades 1, 2, or 3, and there was no substantial improvement in student motivation and engagement with literacy.

The current SOR approaches are primarily based on the previous Reading First Program and the findings of the National Reading Panel Report. It is important to note that neither the National Reading Panel nor Reading First research and subsequent programs were created for EB learners. Proponents of SOR have argued that beginning reading instruction should focus on teaching five foundational skills of phonemic awareness, phonological awareness, phonics, fluency, vocabulary, and comprehension. As it relates to this book, it is important to note that we agree that the teaching of foundational skills is important in the teaching of reading, especially in alphabetic languages. However, we propose that the current focus on foundational skills in literacy instruction is insufficient in the creation of robust and effective biliteracy programs for EB learners.

Significantly, the five foundational skills endorsed and emphasized by SOR have excluded the teaching of oral language and writing (see Chapter 2 for a more detailed discussion of this issue). Further, SOR has been criticized as being monocultural and inattentive to issues of social justice and has been characterized as being "entrenched in Anglocentrism, and Eurocentrism" (Share, 2021, p. 5391), as being "confined to an insular, Anglocentric research agenda addressing theoretical and applied issues with limited relevance for a universal science of reading," (Share, 2021, p. 5391), "as needing to be reimagined to attend to linguistic, cultural and individual variation . . . to make it more robust and socially just," (Auckerman & Schuldt, 2021, p. 585), and as "neglecting to promote bilingualism and biliteracy which has mostly been ignored in debates over English only and bilingual education," (Goldenberg, 2020, p. 2).

We agree that the teaching of foundational skills is important, but insufficient for teaching EB learners in either Spanish or English. We would further argue that the teaching of foundational skills is different in Spanish than English. Most important, we would further argue that what our field needs is not another monolingual framework focused on reading; rather we need to build programs based on the most current research on developing bilingualism and biliteracy, in which the foundational skills of SOR are integrated and taught but expanded to include oral language, writing and metalinguistic development; these are *all* considered foundational skills.

To further understand the history and aims of Literacy Squared, let's turn to the four elements we identified above as being key to innovative approaches to the instruction of EB children.

A Deeper, Assets-Based Understanding of Emerging Bilingual Children

Over 85% of EB children of the 21st century are U.S.-born (U.S. Department of Education, 2018). EB children are simultaneous bilinguals for whom bilingualism is their dominant language. They represent a "new normal," and a demographic shift from children entering bilingual programs in the 1980s and 1990s who were clearly limited in their exposure to English and who clearly had a non-English language dominance. For this reason, Literacy Squared has maintained from the start that school programs need to be created in ways that develop Spanish and English literacy side by side beginning in kindergarten. Literacy Squared is one of the few programs in the United States that was created for EB children in Spanish and English who enter school with a language dominance that we label as **Bilingualism as a First Language.**

A Broader Definition of Literacy—Including Oracy, Writing, and Metalinguistic Development

As our adventures in biliteracy grew and developed, we created and continue to use a holistic framework for biliteracy laying out our vision for a more comprehensive approach to teaching biliteracy in Spanish and English. A holistic biliteracy framework is one that includes recommended teaching approaches and time allocations across the grades intended to foster development and learning in two languages through **paired literacy instruction,** in which students learn to read and write in two languages simultaneously starting in kindergarten. This holistic biliteracy framework intentionally and purposefully connects Spanish and English environments.

While this book focuses on writing, we cannot emphasize enough that the writing instruction in Spanish and English is an endeavor that should integrate and teach writing in tandem with other language arts skills. We would never advocate for the teaching of writing as an isolated subject area. In our framework, we decided to develop Spanish and English literacy at the same time and redefine biliteracy instruction to include oracy, writing, and **metalanguage** as well as reading. **Oracy** refers to the development of oral skills in formal education, while metalanguage refers to the language used to think and talk about language and, in biliteracy, understand the relationships between and within languages. Further, we decided not to delay English literacy instruction while children are learning to write and read in Spanish, as is commonly done in many bilingual and dual language programs. We also made the decision to discourage schools from ceasing Spanish literacy instruction once children reach some criteria for transition or redesignation as is also common practice in many bilingual programs.

Figure 1.1 is a visual illustration of our comprehensive holistic biliteracy framework. The pie charts presented under Spanish literacy and literacy-based English-language development (ELD) illustrate the need for oracy (the children talking to each other), reading (the book), writing (the pencil) and metalinguistic awareness (the child with the idea bubble). This framework emphasizes building trajectories toward biliteracy, with sustained language and literacy development in both languages. A trajectory toward biliteracy is a framework for documenting patterns of development and growth in Spanish and English for EB learners who are receiving paired literacy instruction. Children's achievement is expressed in terms of biliteracy development rather than by grade levels or other monolingual norms that separate the two languages. Spanish literacy outcomes may be higher than English literacy outcomes in this trajectory or vice versa.

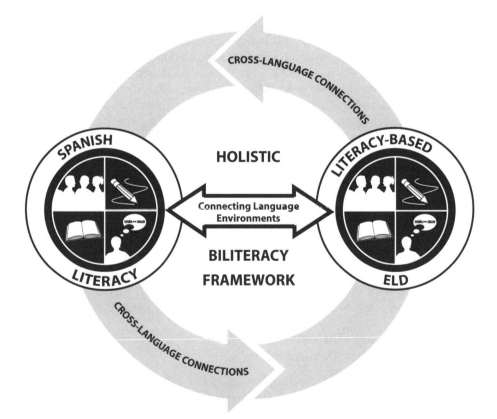

Figure 1.1. Holistic biliteracy framework. (From Escamilla, K., Hopewell, S. Butvilofsky, S., Sparrow, W., Soltero-González, L. & Escamilla, M. [2014]. *Biliteracy from the Start: Literacy Squared in Action*.)

While this book will focus on writing, it is important to note that we have developed Literacy Squared with a lens toward the following:

1. Giving equal attention to Spanish literacy and literacy-based ELD, with

2. Oracy, reading, writing, and metalanguage sharing equal attention within instructional blocks in Spanish and English.

Readers of this book should also note the arrows surrounding the framework in Figure 1.1, referring to cross-language connections, and the arrows within the framework, suggesting the need to connect language environments. Making cross-language connections is a strategic method a teacher uses to help students connect what they know in one language with what they are learning in another. Cross-language connections are particularly useful in **biliterate writing** development and assessment practices, and we will argue throughout this book that cross-language connections are particularly important components of **biliterate pedagogies**. Similarly, cross-language connections indicate the need to connect literacy environments to explicitly help children deepen their knowledge and awareness of how two languages work in ways that are both similar and distinct.

Bilingual Instruction from the Beginning, Focused on Quality and Bilingual Pedagogy

When we began our adventure in biliteracy work, we observed that the field of bilingual/dual language education seemed to be mired in a debate about minutes of instruction that we have come to call "language of instruction." These debates generally address how many minutes of a school day should be devoted to teaching in Spanish and how many in English. To be sure, these debates are over 50 years old and were created to define certain types of bilingual/dual language instruction as well as to ensure that non-English languages were included in instruction and given status in school programs labeled as bilingual and/or dual language. Language of instruction guidelines are present in virtually all textbooks related to teaching in bilingual/dual language programs in the U.S. including in Escamilla et. al. (2014), and *Guiding Principles for Dual Language Education* (Howard et. al., 2019) is the most widely used resource in the United States to guide the development and creation of bilingual/dual language programs. Recently, time allocation debates have included spaces and times students are invited or allowed to use both of their languages, or their full linguistic repertoires, in bilingual/dual language classrooms (García, Ibarra Johnson, & Selzer, 2017; García & Wei, 2014; Lewis et al., 2012).

In our early work, and after reading the work of Genesee and Riches (2006), García and Kleifgen (2018) and García et al. (2017), we proposed to our partner teachers and schools that perhaps the quality of instruction, including bilingual pedagogies, was equally, if not more, important than the language of instruction. To that end, we have encouraged teachers to use more explicit and direct instruction for teaching all literacy domains in Spanish and English and to consider giving children more opportunities to do more collaborative and shared oracy, reading, writing, and metalanguage development. Further, and far more controversially, we have advocated for bilingual pedagogies. This means developing methodologies to teach students bilingually and reducing the use of the ubiquitous methods and materials used to teach monolingual English students. Too often, these materials have not been translated into Spanish and/or have been poorly translated without attention to how languages differ and/or to how children use both of their languages to make sense of the world.

This high-quality bilingual instruction needs to be present from the beginning of a student's education beginning in kindergarten. Children coming to school with two languages are blessed with bilingual brains, and their schooling experiences should reflect and develop these assets. Social justice teaching in biliteracy programs has its foundation in biliterate pedagogies, which can possibly best be explained by the use of the metaphor of a tandem bicycle to illustrate. Imagine starting out learning to ride a bike, but with the caveat that you must do so while coordinating with another person. The process itself (mounting, balancing, coordinating, and communicating) would be substantially different than learning to ride solo. Certainly, much about riding a bike solo (pedaling, steering, etc.) overlaps with what one needs to understand about riding tandem, but the effect of two riders changes the experience in meaningful ways. Similarly, we propose that the effect of two languages changes the language acquisition and academic learning process in meaningful ways. Those changes are what we need to attend to as we think about conceptualizing bilingual pedagogies (Hopewell et al., in press).

A Greater Focus on Writing

Historically, research and practice for EB learners has focused on oral production and learning and to a lesser extent reading (August & Shanahan, 2006; Escamilla, et. al., 2014; Serrano & Howard, 2007). Further, assessment and testing for EB learners, no matter what their program of instruction, has been focused on achievement in English with little or no attention to developing bilingualism and biliteracy.

The role of writing in the learning of two languages has received much less attention in the research and literature and indeed in instruction in bilingual/dual language programs. The teaching of literacy in the United States in elementary schools has placed less emphasis on teaching writing than teaching reading, and moreover, bilingual curricula mirror monolingual English curricula, both in the overemphasis on teaching reading and on the pedagogical approaches to teaching writing.

The current high stakes testing practices that include writing assessment as well as reading aligned with the Common Core State Standards have outlined what students in the U.S. should know in English language arts and mathematics at the conclusion of various grade levels. In bilingual/dual language programs, this entails writing development in two languages, for which some states have not only created standards to accompany English but have also developed those same standards in Spanish. (See for example the Spanish Language Development standards page on the California Department of Education website, accessible at https://www.cde.ca.gov/sp/el/er/sldstandards.asp.)

The high stakes tests and their companion standards have provided much information but notably little guidance and direction in either the processes of teaching writing in two languages, or formative and summative assessment practices to help determine expected outcomes across grade levels for developing trajectories toward biliteracy. This lack of guidance leaves thousands of bilingual/dual language teachers, charged with developing biliteracy in their students, on their own to "figure it out."

BILITERATE WRITING

This book is about writing, specifically about biliterate writing when learned in early childhood in Spanish and English, and in contexts when culturally and linguistically diverse children are not always viewed as assets to schools and their families are not always viewed as assets to a community. In this book, we set out to challenge some of the deficit labels and perceptions that have been applied to the EB children, including but not limited to the idea that they "have no language," that they "are low in both languages," that "learning to write in two languages confuses them," that "Spanish causes interference in learning English," and that "their parents aren't involved [in their] education." We, like many others, have frequently heard the above perceptions in our professional development sessions and in other venues (Escamilla, 2006; Escamilla & Hopewell, 2010; Escamilla et al., 2014; Soltero-González et al., 2011).

To be sure, and in an effort to refrain from the all-too-common teacher-bashing so prevalent in current discourse about public schools, our teacher partners had evidence to support their statements. For example, when examining EB children's writing, teachers have often applied the term "interference" to children's writing when children write in the ways shown in Figure 1.2.

Since the approximations in Figure 1.2 relate to children's writing and to children using the Spanish phonetic or syntactic system to write in English, teachers interpreted these approximations as signs of cross-language interference and potential confusion. Through our work we have

Children write:	They mean:	Interference	Asset
eschool	school	Spanish beginning sounds cause interference.	Child hears sounds in words and can encode them.
Plei	play	Child does not use ay to spell letter sound for long *a*.	Child's use of sounds indicates a cross-language application of what is heard orally (in English) and how it applies in writing in Spanish.
Es not bery perti.	It's not very pretty.	Child does not use subject to start the sentence; use of letter *i* in *perti* is Spanish.	*Es* means "it is." B and v in Spanish sound alike. *I* makes e sound like y in *pretty*.
Mai favrit ting at rices	My favorite thing at recess	Child is confusing Spanish vowels with English.	Writing is rule-governed with regard to use of phonetic principles.
A duck wing is hirt we look for the doctor of the zoo.	A duck's wing is hurt and we looked for the zoo's veterinarian.	Spanish syntax interferes with English; child lacks vocabulary in English.	Child has knowledge of syntax and knows circumlocution as a communicative strategy.
Et tuc os o wal	It took us a while.	Child writes random strings of letters—unreadable.	This reflects the need to be able to interpret emerging biliteracy in context and with a bilingual lens.

Figure 1.2. Examples of "interference"/assets.

learned that it is not solely a matter of what children produce that determines whether we judge the writing to be proficient; it is a matter of interpretation by the person reading the work. In this case, teachers were interpreting the work through an interference lens rather than a cross-language lens or asset-based framework.

The writing sample of Manuel, a fourth-grade student in a Literacy Squared school in the early stages of the program, further illustrates the interference/asset contrast. The sample included in Figure 1.3 is further problematic in that the child's writing was assessed through his English writing alone, without the benefit of a Spanish sample, and assessed through the lens of what he could not do rather than what he could do.

As assessed by teachers at his school, Manuel's writing sample (as he wrote it) was scored as unreadable and unsatisfactory. Unreadable writing samples are thought to be those where the student writes random strings of letters and does not show that their writing is rule-governed. The reader is unable to discern that he has strategies to help him write words or thoughts. Further, scorers noted that he seemed to lack fine motor skills and control of his writing and he was likely in need of "special help." Notice, even though the readers determined that the message was unreadable (a matter of interpretation), we were able to use a bilingual lens to understand the message the student wished to communicate. However, in Manuel's case, deficit-based observations then become the basis for questionable interventions such as those described below, which teachers in the school offered, using the rhetoric that these are data-driven observations that come directly from Manuel's writing.

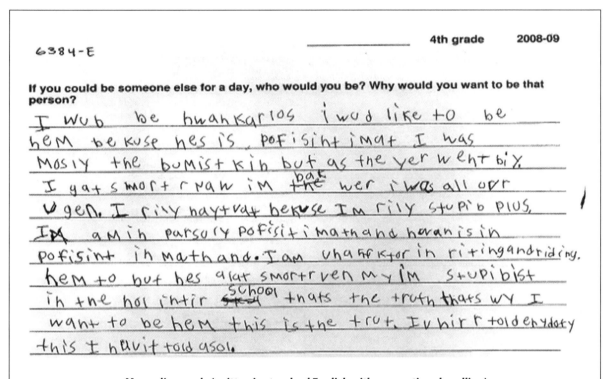

Manuel's sample (written in standard English with conventional spelling)

I would be Juan Carlos. I would like to be him because he is proficient in math. I was mostly the dumbest kid, but as the year went by I got smarter. Now I'm back where I was all over again. I really hate that because I'm really stupid, plus I am partially proficient in math and Juan is proficient in math. And, I am unsatisfactory in writing and reading, him too but he's a lot smarter than me. I'm the stupidest in the whole entire school. That's the truth. That's why I want to be him. This is the truth. I've never told anybody this. I haven't told a soul.

Figure 1.3. English writing sample for a fourth-grade boy.

Manuel: A Prescription for Remediation

A remediative, English-centric approach to Manuel's writing emphasized the following:

- Approximations like *kwankarlos* for *Juan Carlos*; *hem* for *him*; *rily* for *really*; and *ugen* for *again* indicated to teachers a need for more intensive *phonological awareness and phonics* instruction.
- Approximations of words like *proficint* for *proficient* might indicate to teachers a need for more *phonics* or *spelling*.
- Approximations for words like *bak/back; biy* might indicate *Spanish interference*, maybe bilingual instruction is too hard for him, and teachers felt the school should perhaps put him in an English only classroom—he needs to focus on English.
- All of the above are necessary *before* teachers look at the content of his writing.

From the above, we see the clarion call for foundational skills (phonics, phonemic awareness, etc.), but no attention to figuring out the content of the child's writing. Below, we offer a more holistic bilingual interpretation of Manuel's writing, unfortunately one that is often not taken up in schools with large numbers of EB learners.

Manuel: An Asset-Based, Holistic, Bilingual Interpretation

An asset-based, holistic, bilingual approach to Manuel's writing would emphasize points such as

- Manuel has a strong voice in his writing.
- He knows how to express himself in complete thoughts.
- He uses sophisticated phrases and vocabulary.
- His spelling is *not* Spanish interference but utilization of multiple strategies that come from both of his languages (e.g., HwanKarlos).
- He is quite aware of his status in the school.

To be clear, the above discussion is not intended to demonize the teachers in this school or their observations of Manuel and his needs. They have been taught and are using an English-centric language lens to assess his writing and to prescribe an instructional strategy. We have seen thousands of examples like this in Literacy Squared, and if we are to improve writing and writing assessment for EB learners, we need to improve not only children's writing, but the lenses through which educators observe, assess, and instruct children in two languages. We propose that if our observations are wrong or misinformed because of the utilization of monolingual frameworks, then the proposed instructional interventions are also not likely to be effective (Hopewell & Escamilla, 2014). Through our work, we have introduced the following ideas (Soltero-González et al., 2012):

1. Rather than interference, the above examples represent normal stages in the development of writing in EB Spanish/English children.
2. In fact, what they are doing is making cross-language connections that go from Spanish to English and from English to Spanish that we need to better study and understand.

Over time, we have worked hard to dispel the deficit notions described above, and we do not write about them here as a way of disparaging our teachers, for all too often these views are shared by school leaders, policy makers, and even some of our university colleagues. We do, however, hope through this book to illustrate the need to challenge these chronic misperceptions and replace them with more positive orientations for developing and assessing Spanish/English biliterate writing. Throughout the book, we present frameworks and assessment practices across grades K–5 that are aimed at normalizing the development of biliteracy in writing. We will demonstrate how we can use the formative assessment tools in our **Literacy Squared Writing Rubric** (Escamilla et. al., 2014; the rubric is provided as an appendix to this chapter) to engage in dialogues about children's writing that begin with observations of what children *can do* and how we can build on their strengths when teaching writing. We will also argue that students can and do have important information to share via writing if only we provide them with the opportunities.

Clearly there is a need for educators to understand more about how writing, when learned in Spanish and English simultaneously by EB children, develops and changes across time. There is a concomitant need to develop interpretive lenses that seek to understand this development from an asset-based perspective and to help policy makers and practitioners see potential rather than the problems.

RESEARCH FINDINGS TO GUIDE THE DEVELOPMENT OF LITERACY SQUARED

At its inception, Literacy Squared created a biliterate writing rubric for teachers in our Literacy Squared schools to use to assess children's developing writing in Spanish and English in a side-by-side manner. The side-by-side assessment was meant to enable teachers and others to see what children produced in each language and how children were using what they knew in one language to inform writing in another language. (See the Chapter 1 Appendix.) When creating this rubric, we intentionally created a system wherein the content portion of the rubric was weighted more heavily than the structural elements or spelling. We did so because we had observed previously that student ideas in both languages emerged before structural elements and spelling, and we wanted children to be credited with what they *can do*, again a focus on asset-based perspectives. The Literacy Squared Writing Rubric is provided as an appendix to this chapter, and it is explained in detail in our first book (Escamilla, et. al., 2014). The purpose of this book is to move from the assessment to applications of our assessment results to practice.

Our research efforts in emerging EB Spanish/English biliteracy have included descriptive aggregate results from technical reports from our school sites as well as empirical quantitative and qualitative studies. Findings from several of these studies include the following:

1. There are cumulative effects for teaching Spanish and English writing across time.

2. Significant information about what children can do in writing is lost if children are only assessed in English.

3. Learning to write in two languages simultaneously does not delay acquisition of English Literacy.

4. Literacy Squared enhances biliterate writing acquisition.

These findings are discussed in depth below, along with evidence that they provide for biliterate writing assessment and instruction.

Cumulative Effects for Teaching Spanish and English Writing Across Time

We hypothesized that for EB children coming to school from Spanish-speaking homes, their academic outcomes in Spanish would likely be higher in the beginning elementary years than their English outcomes, but that across time, and with consistent bilingual paired literacy instruction and focused attention on writing, their Spanish and English outcomes would more closely match.

The results in Table 1.1 illustrate an aggregate snapshot analysis by grade level for students participating in the Literacy Squared Research Project from 2009 to 2015. We aggregated data from 19 schools in four school districts (Boulder Valley School District [CO], Denver Public Schools [CO], Hillsboro School District [OR], and Salem-Keizer Public Schools [OR]) during this time. From first grade through third grade, students have higher mean scores in all constructs in Spanish when compared to English. In the fourth and fifth grades though, students have comparable scores in all constructs across languages. The line graph presented in Figure 1.4 illustrates this trend with the mean overall scores in both Spanish and English and includes a very healthy sample of 11,463 students.

Table 1.1. Aggregate snapshot analysis by grade level for students participating in the Literacy Squared Research Project from 2009 to 2015.

		Spanish					English				
Grade	n	Content	SE	Spell	Overall	SD	Content	SE	Spell	Overall	SD
K	2601	2	0.8	1.8	4.6	3.3	n/a				
1	2622	4.2	1.6	3.5	9.2	3.4	3.4	1.5	2.4	7.2	3.4
2	2412	5.1	2	4.2	11.3	2.5	4.7	1.9	3.4	10	2.7
3	2116	5.4	2.3	4.3	12	2.3	5.3	2.2	3.8	11.3	2.7
4	1500	6	2.6	4.5	13	2.4	5.8	2.6	4.3	12.7	2.7
5	772	6	2.7	4.4	13.1	2.6	5.9	2.8	4.4	13.1	2.6

Key: SE, Structural Elements; SD, standard deviation

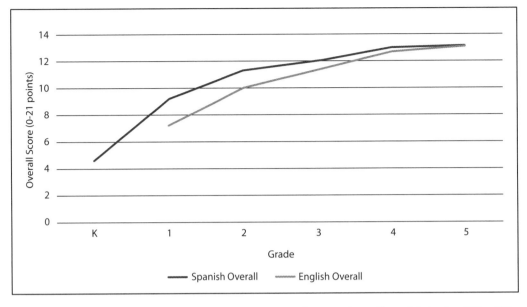

Figure 1.4. Mean overall scores by grade level for students participating in the Literacy Squared Research Project from 2009 to 2015.

Loss of Information If Children Are Only Assessed in English

Research conducted on Literacy Squared has illuminated on several occasions the limitations of English-only assessments to examine the writing growth and development of EB children on either formative or summative assessments. A study conducted by Escamilla et al. (2017) examined the writing skills of 44 EB fourth and fifth graders. All 44 of the study students had been determined to be unsatisfactory in their writing development as a result of the state's English only high-stakes writing assessment. The purpose of this study was to compare and correlate various writing outcomes as measured by the state's high-stakes writing assessment, English language proficiency writing assessment, and the Literacy Squared Writing Rubric. Results indicated that when students' Spanish and English outcomes are considered holistically, students' outcomes in Spanish surpassed English for the majority of students. In fact, these students were proficient writers but were not yet proficient in English. Findings indicate the potential for a writing assessment protocol that is intentionally biliterate and that displays Spanish and English together as a part of the assessment process.

In a recently completed study, we examined three different sets of writing samples for 29 EB children who had previously been tested on the Dynamic Indicators of Basic Early Literacy Skills (DIBELS) reading assessment (Good & Kaminski, 2002) and had been determined to be below or significantly below benchmark outcomes on the DIBELS (Butvilofsky et al., 2021). Using principles outlined in the Literacy Squared Writing Rubric, children's writing samples in Spanish and English were examined across an entire school year and each pair of samples represented three distinct points in time. It is significant to note that outcomes for these students on DIBELS did not change over the course of the school year. Despite this, an examination of writing in Spanish and English showed a great deal of growth across the school year. Through the qualitative analysis of children's writing, we were able to document how children's understandings grew in terms of how texts are organized, punctuated, expressed with standard syntax, as well as in terms of phonological and phonemic knowledge across languages. Essentially, their writing indicated that they were making progress in any number of skills that are ultimately relatable to reading (and foundational skills). The work suggests that assessment of biliterate writing provides a means of assessment that is broader in scope and is appropriate for assessing what children can do across languages as well as within languages in their literacy development.

No Delay in English Literacy Acquisition Due to Learning Writing in Two Languages

Hopewell and Butvilofsky (2016) examined the extent to which writing instruction in two languages delayed or advantaged students educated in paired biliteracy instruction as compared to those who only had access to English literacy instruction. In this quasi-experimental study, the authors used the Literacy Squared Writing Rubric to compare the biliterate writing outcomes of EB students who participated in Literacy Squared (n = 108) to those of EB learners who participated in English-only literacy instruction (n = 92). Findings indicated that learning to write in two languages simultaneously, as in the case of Literacy Squared, resulted in students becoming equally proficient in writing in Spanish and English by the fifth grade and that paired literacy instruction in Literacy Squared did not delay English writing acquisition. In fact, the English writing acquisition outcomes for Literacy Squared students were comparable to those of students in English-only classrooms. Notably, students in Literacy Squared had the added advantage of becoming biliterate.

In a similar study, Escamilla, Fine, and Hopewell (2019) examined the biliterate writing growth of students participating in one-way Spanish/English dual language programs using two different models. Literacy Squared was the treatment model, and a different biliteracy model was the control. The study utilized a longitudinal study design that examined growth in students' writing in Spanish and English in Grades 1–3 from a quantitative perspective (n=38 in the Literacy Squared group, n= 72 in the control group. Results of the quantitative analysis indicated a statistically significant difference between the Literacy Squared program and control group students in Spanish/English writing outcomes. Fortunately, students in both groups were becoming biliterate; however, in the Literacy Squared schools, students were outperforming control school students.

Results of these various studies indicate to us the potential of not only the Literacy Squared Holistic Biliteracy Model to successfully develop Spanish and English biliteracy in EB students, but also the Literacy Squared Writing Rubric as a formative and summative assessment tool to illustrate students' cross-grade level writing growth in paired literacy and other types of bilingual programs.

THE NEED FOR A BOOK ON SPANISH-ENGLISH BILITERACY

The need for this book is further demonstrated by the current state of the teaching of writing in U.S. elementary schools. This situation can best be described as a hodgepodge. In the over 50 school districts we have worked with in Literacy Squared, we have found that many districts do not have a writing curriculum at all, even for English-only classrooms. This is quite a contrast from the teaching of reading, which, in most districts, is highly prescriptive in both Spanish and English and, if not prescriptive, at least well-defined across grade levels with appropriate texts and other resources. The fragmented and poorly defined nature of writing curriculum in general becomes exacerbated in bilingual/dual language programs when there is also a poorly defined curriculum, and often no curriculum, in Spanish. In the same districts in which we have worked, it is quite common for teachers to be told to use the same curriculum in Spanish as they use in English to teach writing, including the same assessments, and often are told to just "translate" English to Spanish. Further, most bilingual/dual language programs do not include curricula or approaches to developing biliteracy, and rarely provide guidance for teachers on how to help students make cross-linguistic connections. In a very informal national survey, we recently posed a question asking bilingual teachers and program directors what curriculum they were using to teach writing in Spanish. There were only 44 responses; however, they represented several large districts in large states (e.g., California, New York, and Texas). Overwhelmingly, the responses indicated that English writing strategies were used to teach writing in Spanish and that teachers are expected to do translations or modifications with little or no support. They also expressed concern that this is extra work for teachers and that there is little professional development for teachers in teaching writing in Spanish. Spanish writing curricula that were named were translations or recreations from English, and some titles of programs had not even been changed from

English to Spanish. For example, one title was "English writing program en Español." Finally, it is noteworthy that many respondents say that they use readers' and writers' workshops to teach writing in Spanish and English. Workshop approaches are just that, approaches, and are not curriculum programs or materials, and likely best represent the dearth in the field of quality writing curricula and programs to guide schools and teachers in the teaching of writing in Spanish.

We, along with others, have advocated for direct and explicit teaching in oracy, reading, writing and the teaching of metalinguistic development (Escamilla et. al., 2014; Genesee & Riches, 2006). It is the intent of this book to give teachers insights via analyses of writing into how to view the writing of EB students as assets to be developed instead of problems to be remediated. We hope to also provide some suggestions for teaching writing at various grade levels, including not just the tools of writing but the use of writing to teach for social justice.

The importance of this book is even more pronounced when one considers exciting advances in policy in the field of bilingual/dual language education in the past few years. In 2016, with the passage of Proposition 58, the state of California lifted the ban on bilingual education, thereby creating new opportunities and challenges for teaching biliteracy and implementing new and innovative bilingual and dual language programs. Similar policy changes have occurred in Massachusetts and Arizona, creating similar needs for books such as this one. Finally, the Seal of Biliteracy is now available in 21 states (www.sealofbiliteracy.org). This Seal is offered to students who have studied and obtained proficiency in two or more languages by high school graduation. Proficiency in writing in Spanish and English will assist students and schools desiring to pursue this Seal.

SUMMARY AND PREVIEW: BILITERATE CHILDREN, BILITERATE WRITERS

This book is about developing biliteracy in Spanish and English with a focus on writing. Using an asset-based perspective, we begin from the assumption that, with the appropriate instructional support, children are quite capable of becoming biliterate beginning in kindergarten, and that the simultaneous learning of literacy in two languages provides a scaffold to learning, not a source of interference.

Chapter 2 of this book illustrates further the need for the creation of a biliterate pedagogy. This chapter looks specifically at the connection between oracy and writing and how the foundational skills promoted by SOR can be integrated into biliteracy units that include direct and explicit attention to teaching the expressive skills of oracy and writing. A sample literacy unit is included in this chapter that also demonstrates how biliterate pedagogies can include teaching for social justice.

Chapter 3 provides an in-depth examination of a strategy called theDictado, which we advocate using to emphasize foundational writing skills and cross-language foci. It is a strategy with usefulness at all grade levels. Following this chapter, in Chapter 4 we provide an examination of writing at the kindergarten level. We isolated kindergarten as we know that the developmental needs of kindergarten differ in important ways from the writing needs in first grade and beyond. Chapter 5 focuses on Grade 1, further demonstrating how writing samples are evaluated through the use of the Literacy Squared Writing Rubric and then used to inform instruction. Chapter 6 provides glimpses into genre-based applications of the Literacy Squared Framework for the intermediate grades utilizing the holistic biliteracy framework. Finally, Chapter 7 provides a look at how teaching for social justice can be part and parcel of biliteracy teaching and uses an example of a plan to develop biliterate writing and specific cross-language connections in the fifth grade.

The goals of this book are ambitious. First and foremost, we hope that this book and others like it will help to shift the current discourse from a deficit-based discourse about the problems of emergent bilingual learners to a more asset-based discourse. From an existential level, it is our hope that one day work like ours, along with others', will influence how biliteracy is viewed, to the point where monolingual word processing programs to no longer identify the word *biliteracy* as a misspelled word in the English spell-check system (accompanied by a suggestion to change the word from *biliteracy* to *illiteracy*) and instead recognize the word *biliteracy* as a legitimate word in the English language. On a theoretical level, we hope that our book helps to promote the theory that biliteracy is a higher form of literacy than monoliteracy, and that it is distinct from the literacy experiences and process of monolinguals (Bauer & Gort, 2011). Most importantly, on a practical level, we hope that this book will help teachers come to see the many strengths that their EB children have in their two languages, and to see the instructional and assessment strategies posed in this book as tools to create instructional environments to nurture biliteracy development.

Throughout our adventures over the years, we have created several slogans for biliteracy teaching. They include: "Biliteracy better not faster," "English earlier and Spanish longer" and a new slogan just for this book, *"never ever, nunca, jamas* speak or write about children in deficit terms." In this book we add a challenge to the field—"Juntos toward the creation of a biliterate pedagogy!"

Questions for Reflection and Action

- ▶ What writing curriculum or program does your school offer for EBs in Spanish or English? What do you consider to be the advantages and disadvantages of your current program/curriculum?
- ▶ List all of the professional development (PD) opportunities you have had in the past 2–3 years that specifically focused on the teaching of writing. How many of these PD sessions were either offered bilingually or were focused on Spanish?
- ▶ How might you use the research designs and/or questions posed above to implement and examine a biliteracy program at your school?

CHAPTER 1 APPENDIX

Literacy Squared® Writing Rubric

Quantitative Rubric Assumptions

GENERAL ASSUMPTIONS:
- The students' Spanish and English writing samples will be scored **side-by-side**.
- **Critical descriptors are cumulative**. To receive a 10 in Content, the student must exhibit all of the relevant indicators listed in the previous levels.
- All samples should be scored, but if the student **did not respond to the prompt**, this should be indicated at the top of the rubric.
- Samples written in a language other than the language of the prompt are scored as a 1 for Content. This score credits the child for demonstrating an understanding of the task and the topic. Additionally, it recognizes that bilingual students bring multiple linguistic resources to the learning environment. All other constructs are scored 0.
- Children are not penalized for nonstandard syntax (noun/adjective – *agua frio*; noun/article – *los serpiente*; verb/adjective—*están grande*).

CONTENT
- **"Descriptive language (use of adjectives/adverbs at the word level)"** – This includes more than basic adjectives such as *my blue bike*. Instead, to be considered descriptive language, the student must include more extensive descriptions. For example, *I like my bunny that is white and soft* contains adjectives but is not considered descriptive language. *Me gusta el perro porque me obedece cuando le digo siéntate. También porque está bonito, tiene pelaje y lo puedo vestir como quiera,* is an example of descriptive language.
- **"Varied sentence structures"**—Just because each sentence starts a different way, this does not necessarily qualify as "varied sentence structures." To be varied sentences, the composition should contain some combination of:
    - *Simple sentences*—independent clause, contains a subject and verb, includes a complete thought.
    - *Compound sentences*—two independent clauses connected by a coordinator: *for, and, nor, but, or, yet, so*
    - *Complex sentences*—independent clause joined by one or more dependent clauses, contains subordinators (*because, since, although, when*), relative pronouns (*that, who, which*), etc.

STRUCTURAL ELEMENTS
- **Structural elements** are those elements the writer uses to guide readers through the text. They include the use of capitalization, punctuation marks, and paragraphing. Punctuation marks include: periods, commas, question marks, *guiones*, quotation marks, exclamation points, apostrophes, hyphens.
- **Accent marks** are *not* considered punctuation—they are part of spelling.
- "Controls" in critical descriptor 3 means "mostly controls" (at least 85% or more).

SPELLING
- Children are not penalized in the spelling section for approximated code-switches.
- **Majority** = at least 50%
- **Most** = at least 85% or more
- Reversed letters are counted as spelling approximations if the reversed letter is a different letter (b/d). However, if the reversed letter does not represent another letter (reversed letter c) is not counted as a spelling approximation.
- Words that are written with hyper- (*con migo/conmigo*, snow man/snowman) or hyposegmentation (*ala/a la*, alot/a lot) are counted as spelling approximations.

Rater ID: _____

Student ID: _____

Not to prompt *(Circle)*

| Span | Eng |

Literacy Squared® Writing Rubric: Grades K, 1, 2, 3, 4 & 5
(Circle Grade)

SPANISH SCORE	CONTENT	ENGLISH SCORE
10	Focused composition, conveys emotion or uses figurative language, is engaging to the reader; clearly addresses the prompt; book language	10
9	Organization of composition includes effective transitions and vivid examples	9
8	Writing includes complex *sentence* structures and has a discernable, consistent structure	8
7	Sense of completeness—Clear introduction and clear conclusion	7
6	Includes descriptive language (use of adjectives, adverbs at the word level) or varied sentence structures	6
5	Main idea discernable with supporting details, or main idea can be inferred or stated explicitly, or repetitive vocabulary: may include unrelated ideas	5
4	Two ideas—*I like my bike* **and/because** *it is blue*	4
3	One idea expressed through a subject and predicate, subject may be implied (*I like my bike, amo,* or *run*)	3
2	Label(s), list of words. May communicate an idea w/o subject & predicate	2
1	Prewriting: Picture only, not readable, or written in a language other than the prompt	1
0	The student did not prepare a sample	0
	STRUCTURAL ELEMENTS	
5	Multiparagraph composition with accurate punctuation and capitalization	5
4	Controls most structural elements and includes paragraphing	4
3	Controls beginning and ending punctuation in ways that make sense and is attempting additional structural elements (commas, question marks, *guiones*, apostrophes, ellipses, parentheses, hyphens, and indentation)	3
2	Uses one or more of the structural elements *correctly*	2
1	Uses one or more of the structural elements *incorrectly*	1
0	Structural elements not evident	0
	SPELLING	
6	Accurate spelling	6
5	Most words are spelled conventionally	5
4	Majority of high-frequency words are correct and child is approximating standardization in errors	4
3	Most words are not spelled conventionally but demonstrates an emerging knowledge of common spelling patterns	3
2	Represents most sounds in words and most high frequency words are spelled incorrectly	2
1	Represents some sounds in words	1
0	Message is not discernable	0

From Escamilla, K., Hopewell, S. Butvilofsky, S., Sparrow, W., Soltero-González, L. & Escamilla, M. (2014). *Biliteracy from the Start: Literacy Squared in Action*.
Biliterate Writing From the Start: The Literacy Squared Approach to Asset-Based Writing Instruction by Sandra Butvilofsky, Kathy Escamilla, and Susan Hopewell. Copyright © 2023 Paul H. Brookes Publishing Co., Inc. All rights reserved.

Literacy Squared® Qualitative Analysis of Student Writing
Bilingual Strategies

	(Spanish → English)	(English → Spanish)	Spanish ↔ English (bidirectional)
DISCOURSE ☐ ***Rhetorical structures*** (first, next, last) ☐ ***Punctuation*** (signals awareness of code-switches—*me gusta* "basketball," or ¡Run fast!)			
SENTENCE/PHRASE ☐ ***Syntax*** (subject omission, word order- the bike of my sister) ☐ ***Literal Translations*** (*agarré todas bien*/I got them all right) ☐ ***Code-switching*** (*no puedo hablar* in just one language)			
WORD LEVEL ☐ ***Code-switching*** ☐ ***Loan words*** (soccer, mall) ☐ ***Nativized words*** (*spláchate*/splashed)			
PHONICS Spanish → English (*japi*/happy) English → Spanish (*awua*/agua) Spanish ↔ English (*bihave*/behave, *lecktura*/lectura)			

Developmental Language Specific Approximations

SPANISH	ENGLISH
Structural elements, syntax, spelling, hypo/hypersegmentation	Structural elements, syntax, spelling, hypo/hypersegmentation

From Escamilla, K., Hopewell, S. Butvilofsky, S., Sparrow, W., Soltero-González, L. & Escamilla, M. (2014). *Biliteracy from the Start: Literacy Squared in Action.* *Biliterate Writing From the Start: The Literacy Squared Approach to Asset-Based Writing Instruction* by Sandra Butvilofsky, Kathy Escamilla, and Susan Hopewell. Copyright © 2023 Paul H. Brookes Publishing Co., Inc. All rights reserved.

2 The Role of Oracy and Writing in Teaching Foundational Skills

"Frederick Douglas once said that once you learn to read, you will forever be free. We would add that once you learn to write, you will forever have a voice."
—(Escamilla et al., 2022) Literacy Squared is committed to developing these voices in two languages.

Bilingüe
Alma Flor Ada

Porque hablo español,
Puedo oir los cuentos de mi abuelita
Y decir familia, madre, amor.
Porque hablo inglés,
Puedo aprender de mi maestra
Y decir I love school.

Porque soy bilingüe,
Puedo leer libros y books,
Tengo amigos y Friends,

Disfruto canciones y songs,
Juegos y games,
Y me divierto el doble.

Y algún día,
Porque sé hablar dos idiomas
Podré hacer el doble de cosas
Ayudar al doble de personas
Y hacer lo que haga el doble de bien.

—*"Bilingüe." by Alma Flor Ada. Copyright © 2015. All rights reserved. Used with permission of Alma Flor Ada.*

Key Terms

Expressive language skills
Foundational skills
Oral language
Phonemic awareness

Phonological awareness
Receptive language skills
Teaching for social justice

Guiding Questions

▶ What is the difference between **oral language** and oracy?
▶ How does explicit teaching of oracy enhance the development of writing in both Spanish and English?
▶ How does the teaching of oracy and writing broaden and strengthen the teaching of **foundational skills**?
▶ How can inclusion of social justice standards in our literacy programs help achieve the goals of biculturalism in bilingual/dual language programs?

Over the years, many people have asked us why monolingual theories and practices are insufficient for EB learners. They sincerely want to know what is different about emergent bilingualism and biliteracy. As noted in Chapter 1, to introduce this difference, we have found it helpful to use a metaphor about learning to ride a bike. Biliterate pedagogy proposes that the presence of two languages changes the language acquisition and academic learning process in ways as significant as learning to ride tandem, rather than solo, would change the process of learning to ride a bike in meaningful ways. There is no doubt that we need to be informed by monolingual theory and practice, but these theories are simply not robust enough to completely inform and enhance biliterate pedagogies.

This chapter will focus first on how biliterate pedagogies incorporate monolingual pedagogies but will then explain how current monolingual pedagogies are insufficient to develop comprehensive biliteracy programs. The chapter will then focus on oracy, explain how oracy teaching is different from oral language teaching, and then focus on how oracy can and should be connected to writing in the development of biliteracy. A sample lesson is provided.

The history of the United States has been rife with movements condemning the way that literacy is being taught in public schools, in ways that are often hyperbolic and unwarranted. Examples of such movements include the 1950s' *Why Johnny Can't Read* (Flesch, 1955) followed by the 1980s' *A Nation at Risk* (Gardner, 1983), and No Child Left Behind (NCLB) (No Child Left Behind Act, 2002). A brief history and critique of these reform movements was recently chronicled in a white paper published by the National Committee for Effective Literacy (Escamilla et al., 2022) and is summarized below.

In the 1990s, concerns about a reading crisis in the United States fueled national research and policies that were aimed at closing achievement gaps. National policies focused on early literacy, seeking to ensure that all students tested as "proficient" on standardized English reading tests. The No Child Left Behind Act—with a strong commitment to equity and closing gaps (including naming English language learners, as they were labeled at the time, as a subgroup for whom schools had to report outcomes)—resulted in a mistaken reliance upon inappropriate English assessments for EB learners leading to the mandated use of unsuccessful, one-size-fits-all literacy curricula and instructional approaches (that weren't designed for second language learners) as the corrective action. The lowest-performing schools—which typically enrolled high concentrations of EB learners, among other historically underserved groups—were consigned to this "corrective action and program improvement." The NCLB Act ushered in a federal $1-billion-per-year campaign of professional development, school restructuring, and implementation monitoring known as the Reading First initiative as the means of holding schools accountable for ensuring that all students scored at state reading benchmarks by third grade. Reading First required schools to adopt "scientific, research-based reading programs" based in large part upon the research of the National Reading Panel which had summarized research on literacy instruction as a set of five components of reading instruction (phonemic awareness, phonics, fluency, vocabulary, and comprehension). These five reading components have since become widely known as the foundational skills to teach reading.

Reading First enthusiasts primarily emphasized the academic studies showing that phonemic awareness and phonics raised achievement on standardized tests. It was a narrow slice and loose interpretation of the National Reading Panel's work, with harmful consequences for the increasingly large emerging bilingual learner student population in the nation's schools. An extensive evaluation of the efficacy of Reading First was conducted by the Institute of Educational Research (2008) to determine its impact on student reading achievement and on classroom instruction. The report found that there was a significant impact on strengthening decoding skills among first-grade students. However, Reading First did not produce a statistically significant impact on student reading comprehension test scores in grades one, two, or three, and there was no substantial improvement in student motivation and engagement with literacy.

Furthermore, Reading First policies—and in turn, the literacy curricula and approaches that schools adopted—were not designed for emerging bilingual learners. By its own admission, the National Reading Panel had not considered research about literacy development for this group.

As stated in the introduction to the National Reading Panel's report (upon which Reading First was based) delineating the limitations of their work, "The Panel did not address issues relevant to second language learning" (NICHD, 2000).

In a 2006 report on literacy development research specifically for emerging bilingual learners, the National Literacy Panel on Language Minority Children and Youth came to different conclusions. This new report affirmed the importance of all five of the components of a comprehensive reading approach described by the National Reading Panel but found that these components are not sufficient for EB learners (August & Shanahan, 2006). It described the linguistic, cognitive, sociocultural, and academic variables that compound the reading challenges for emergent bilingual learners and how these students require additional specific instructional considerations. The report emphasized the role of home language; the uniqueness of the dual language brain; the importance of background knowledge, meaning making, scaffolds to support comprehension, and the foundational role of oracy. The report found that efficient reading comprehension depends not only on efficient word recognition skills but also on general language proficiency. In short, it made clear that effective literacy instruction for emerging bilingual learners was different in significant ways from instruction for monolingual students.

For EB learners in programs that emphasized foundational reading skills in the absence of meaning making (building background knowledge, integrating language development with learning content, effective expression, and metalanguage awareness), the so-called scientific reading approach embraced by Reading First was particularly problematic. The ability to sound out words in a language a child does not know is simply not sufficient to build literacy skills—and that emphasis likely explains the lag in reading comprehension and writing that was uncovered in the Reading First evaluation. Across the nation, gaps in literacy skills for emerging bilingual learners did not close. Indeed, the National Assessment for Education Progress (NAEP) confirmed Reading First's failure to reduce reading gaps for this population. It has been argued by many that the current Science of Reading programs represent a replication of the Reading First curriculum (Escamilla et al., 2022). Figure 2.1 below illustrates the narrowing of the literacy curriculum in Reading First and the Science of Reading.

Finally, August and Shanahan (2006) found that emerging bilingual children achieve requisite decoding skills at the same rate, in English, as their English-speaking peers, but they lag behind in comprehension and writing. They argued to widen the definition of language and literacy particularly for emerging bilingual learners. This finding is particularly troubling given the narrowing of the curriculum in Reading First and the Science of Reading.

- Narrowed a broad understanding of language and literacy development to focus just on literacy.
- Narrowed the focus on literacy to reading.
- Narrowed the components of effective instruction to primarily be about foundational reading skills.
- Within foundational reading skills, the focus was primarily on phonemic awareness and phonics (decoding).

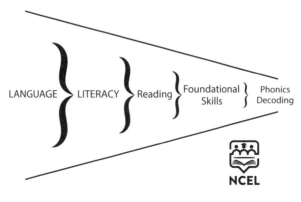

Figure 2.1. The narrowing of the literacy curriculum in the Science of Reading era. (From Escamilla, K., Olsen, L., & Slavick, J. [2022]. Toward comprehensive effective literacy policy and instruction for English learners/emergent bilingual students. The National Committee on Effective Literacy. www.MultiLingualLiteracy.org; reprinted by permission.)

ORACY AND WRITING: THE FORGOTTEN COMPONENTS OF FOUNDATIONAL SKILLS TEACHING

In this chapter, we propose to address the neglected components called for by August & Shanahan's research (2006) as represented by our comprehensive biliteracy framework (see Chapter 1). In that regard this chapter focuses on oral language development, specifically oracy, and its relationship to the development of biliteracy in writing, and the teaching of writing. We argue that oral language and writing are foundational skills and that their marginalization in the literacy program is harmful to the development of biliteracy.

Oral Language Development and Oracy

It has been well established that reading and writing are extensions of spoken language and therefore oral language cannot be separated from reading and writing. James Britton's research (2018) posits that oracy floats on a sea of talk, and yet with our current educational system where the pressure is on for students to pass written exams, oracy is all too easily left adrift. Gaunt & Stott (2018) go a step further and ask how, as teachers and educators, can we turn the tide and harness the power of talk in our classrooms? They assert that this is not just an educational choice but rather, given students' vastly different experiences with language, a moral imperative. We agree and provide guidance to teachers in this chapter about how to ensure that oracy in two languages might be taught in biliterate settings, and how critical it is in the teaching of writing as well as reading and metalinguistic awareness.

Think about your own experiences teaching literacy—how much time is suggested to devote to the teaching of oral language either in Spanish or English as compared to reading? We know that oral language is developed in the home and community before young children go to school, and we know that the homes and communities of EB learners are rich ethnolinguistic environments for oral language learning. However, schools are places where oral language repertoires and registers of EB learners are enriched and expanded in both of their languages.

Further, most bilingual/dual language teachers are very familiar with the term *oral language*, but not as familiar with the term *oracy*. What is the difference? Oral language, sometimes called spoken language, includes speaking and listening—the ways that humans communicate with one another. Oral language skills *provide the foundation for word reading and comprehension.* They are at the heart of listening and reading comprehension, serving as a predictor for both. In Literacy Squared classrooms, children develop oral language skills in both Spanish and English, however, in different ways. In Spanish, for simultaneous bilinguals, oral language skills are necessary so that the language students bring to school does not atrophy and get lost. In our framework, the linguistic repertoires that children bring from home are linguistic and cultural assets to the school and classroom. Moreover, for these same children, learning English oral language skills is critical because they are being asked to learn to read and write in English at the same time as they are learning to understand and speak basic English. Without a solid foundation in oral language skills, reading and writing will be that much more challenging for them.

For emerging bilingual learners, oral language development is not the same in Spanish and English as we must strive to respect the internal structure and discourse patterns of each language, and it is *not* the same for emerging bilingual students learning English as it is for native monolingual English speakers.

For example, the state of Colorado has the following standards in first and second grades to develop communication (oral language) skills:

- **First Grade:** Identify specific sounds in words and experiment with those sounds (changing *ch* in *chip* to *sh* for *ship*). Expand spoken vocabulary and demonstrate how words, gestures, and actions are used to give and receive information. (Colorado Department of Education, 2020).

- **Second Grade:** Learn new information, expand understanding and engage in better conversations by listening actively (eye contact, asking questions, body posture) (Colorado Department of Education, 2020).

While these standards may be fine and sufficient for monolingual English students, they are insufficient for students learning English as an additional language as they do not specifically address the teaching of English.

If we are going to develop adequate guidance for teachers to plan and teach oracy, we need to begin by having a clear understanding of what oracy is. Oracy is a subset of oral language. Think of oral language as being the big umbrella (Figure 2.2)—it entails all the oral language skills that children use as they are growing, experiencing, and developing understandings of the world. It is the language they use to make friends, to learn and develop thoughts, to share opinions, to express emotion, humor, and wisdom, and even to acquire moral and spiritual values. It is learned in the home and in day-to-day experiences. Some of it will, indeed, be learned in school, but teachers cannot be fully responsible for teaching it. In thinking about biliteracy planning, therefore, we suggest that teachers focus on oracy.

Oracy is one part of that oral language umbrella that connects to reading and writing. It is a subset of oral language skills that students need to meet the academic and content objectives. Oracy helps students to demonstrate what they know, think, and can do related to text. It helps students talk about texts. In order to show what they are learning; they need to connect that talk to their writing. Oracy and writing are **expressive language skills**, while listening and reading are **receptive language skills**, and in school too often we do not dedicate enough time to teaching expressive skills. It is the oral language (specifically oracy) skills and writing skills that August & Shanahan found to be missing in components in programs for EB learners in 2006.

It may be helpful to understand the relationship between oral language and oracy by comparing the two to phonological awareness and phonemic awareness. **Phonological awareness** (like oral language) is the umbrella term that involves a continuum of skills that develop over time and that are crucial to reading and spelling success, because they are central to learning to decode and spell printed words. Phonological awareness is the ability to recognize and manipulate the spoken parts of sentences and words. Examples include being able to identify words that rhyme, recognizing alliteration, segmenting a sentence into words, identifying the syllables in a word, and blending and segmenting onset-rimes. Phonological awareness is one of the foundational skills (Kilpatrick, 2015).

Phonemic awareness (like oracy) is a subset of phonological awareness that involves the ability to hear and manipulate the smallest units of sounds (phonemes) in spoken words. This includes blending sounds into words, segmenting words into sounds, and deleting and playing

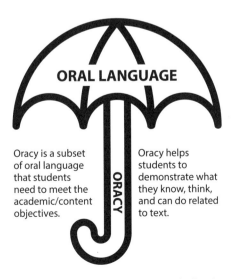

Figure 2.2. The oral language to oracy umbrella. Taken from: Hopewell, S. *Deepen understanding between oral language and oracy.* www.literacysquared.org.

with the sounds in spoken words. Phonemic awareness is also one of the foundational skills (Kilpatrick, 2015).

Teaching oracy requires educators to engage students in discussing ideas, acquiring new vocabulary in context, and developing ever more sophisticated and complex structures for expressing ideas. All students need this, but it is especially important for bilingual learners, who are acquiring knowledge and language through a broader repertoire. These students need us to provide direct and explicit instruction about the language they will need to accomplish their literacy or learning tasks. They need opportunities to rehearse and practice.

Oracy is a research-based and research-tested practice. Research concludes that extensive, explicit oral language instruction facilitates literacy development for emerging bilingual students (August & Shanahan, 2006; Snow & Tabors, 1993). Further, talk is an effective way to build cognition and is essential to literacy instruction (Norman, 1992; Gaunt & Stott, 2018; Britton, 2019). Importantly to biliteracy, authentic instruction in Spanish-speaking countries is primarily rooted in opportunities to connect oracy with writing instruction through which students learn phonemic awareness (Vernon & Ferriero, 1999). Oracy is important for students because it

- Helps them formulate ideas.
- Increases communicative competence.
- Improves accuracy in written work.
- Builds confidence.

Oracy in Literacy Squared

Oracy in Literacy Squared consists of three major components: language structures, vocabulary, and dialogue. Figure 2.3 defines each component and links it to skills that are critical to teaching bilingualism and biliteracy and to relevant foundational skills promoted by the National Reading Panel (NICHD, 2000) and subsequently adopted by the Science of Reading.

The oracy skills defined above are not only important for students in preparation for and in conjunction with learning of writing but are also important in developing the foundational skills of reading in the areas of vocabulary development, reading fluency, and phonemic awareness (in two languages). In Literacy Squared, the teaching of these skills is not done in decontextualized

Oracy Concept	Definition	Connection to Foundational Skills	Connection to Writing
Language Structures	Language students need to express their ideas accurately and in more complex ways (language forms and functions).	Phonemic awareness, hearing sounds in words, learning concept of words	Grammar learned in oral language is used in service to writing. Language forms and functions transfer to written forms.
Vocabulary	Develop and expand students' knowledge of words and concepts, including high utility and technical words	Vocabulary (but taught in context)	Vocabulary learned in oral contexts improves the quality of written products.
Dialogue	Strategically planned questions that elicit communication with others	Fluency	Transfer of oral language to the written word and written expression of complete ideas

Figure 2.3. Oracy concepts, definitions and connections to foundational skills and writing.

ways; rather this teaching is done in the context of learning to read real books. The teaching of oracy connected to reading real texts provides exposure for children to connected discourse, which is particularly critical to teaching English to emerging bilingual learners and to developing bilingualism.

SAMPLE LITERACY UNIT INCORPORATING ORACY: WHAT IS A REFUGEE?

By way of example, we offer the following literacy unit, which was prepared by Dr. Khanh Nguyen-Le, a Literacy Squared colleague. Dr. Nguyen-Le incorporated the three components of oracy that were included in our original conceptualization of the Literacy Squared Framework (dialogue, language structures, and vocabulary development) while also adding a fourth and very important component for **teaching for social justice** that she terms "oracy for empathy" (Nguyen-Le, 2021). The text anchoring this unit is titled *What Is a Refugee?* Dr. Nguyen-Le uses this text to develop concept knowledge and provide opportunities for oracy development. The lesson culminates in writing for real purposes.

Text: Gravel, E. (2019). *What Is a Refugee?* New York: Random House

Grade Level: Second

Summary of Text: *What Is a Refugee?* addresses important contemporary questions including: Who are refugees? Why are they called that word? Why do they need to leave their country? Why are they sometimes not welcome in their new country?

To prepare this lesson, Dr. Nguyen-Le created learning objectives for four different types of oracy. She begins with oracy for comprehension, oracy for dialogue, and oracy for empathy (teaching for social justice). She then used these lessons to move to oracy for writing (see Figure 2.4).

The lesson begins with two readings of the story. The first is simply for children to get the sense of the story. The second is to engage in oracy activities. Oracy engagement is scaffolded through structures that encourage children to interact with the text multiple times in small groups and then to interact across groups to ask and answer questions. Note how the structures change as children are guided through each of the four types of oracy.

Figure 2.4. Four concepts of oracy: comprehension, dialogue, writing and empathy. Taken from: Nguyen-Le, K. (2021). *What is a refugee literacy unit.* Presentation given at the La Cosecha Annual Dual Language Conference, Albuquerque, NM.

An important aspect of teaching language within Literacy Squared is that of *transformations* of linguistic structures. The teaching of transformations is an explicit method of teaching children how to transform one kind of structure into another (e.g., turning a declarative statement into a question) (Gentile, 2004). Teaching children how to transform language is important and is used to teach grammar. It can be used in both Spanish and English. It is particularly important for students learning either language as a second or additional language. Sample transformations are listed in Figure 2.5. The skillful way that Dr. Nguyen-Le incorporated transformations into her unit with the use of a text is presented below.

Oracy for Comprehension Objectives (with writing)

Skill Development

- Listening to understand the story concepts
- Listening to filter out unnecessary information
- Recording information about the text while interacting with peers (writing)
- Transformation—Question/Answer

Language Structures and Question/Answer Transformation From the Text

Language Structure	Question/Answer Transformation
What is a refugee?	A refugee is _____
Why do refugees leave their country?	A refugee may leave their country because _____. One reason a refugee may leave their country is _____.
Are refugees welcomed in their new country?	I think refugees are welcomed in their new country because _____ I do not think refugees are welcomed in their new country because _____

Transformation	Example
Positive → Negative	We have school on Mondays. We do not (don't) have school on Saturdays.
Question → Statement	Chato liked to play with cats. Did Chato like cats?
Switch Person → 1st, 2nd, 3rd	I love recess. Maya loves recess.
Switch Number → Singular to plural	Apple → apples child → children
Change Tense → Present to Past	Want → wanted Go → went
Change Nouns → Pronouns	Frida → she My grandparents → they

Figure 2.5. Gentile's language transformation structures. Taken from: Gentile, L. (2004). *The oracy instructional guide*. Dominic Press.

The graphic shown in Figure 2.6 illustrates how the children will combine oracy and writing in a round-robin share. Students are divided into groups to answer one of the three questions listed in the chart in Figure 2.6. Each group uses information from the text to formulate ideas and to write answers to their question in the appropriate column as shown in the figure. Then, students participate in a round-robin share as illustrated below.

You will note that the students are given multiple readings of the text before engaging in oracy to writing. They are given an authentic oracy structure, which is used to answer questions from the text, and they are engaging in an oracy transformation of question to answers. They are writing to learn how to turn notes into sentences.

Round-Robin Share:

Group 1 students share answers. Other groups write answers in their graphic organizers.

Group 2 students share answers. Other groups write answers in their graphic organizers.

Group 3 students share answers. Other groups write answers in their graphic organizers.

Name: _____

Date: _____

What is a refugee?	Why do refugees need to leave their country?	Are refugees welcomed into new countries?

Figure 2.6. Round robin share and sample graphic organizer.

Oracy for Dialogue Objectives: Engaging Students in Authentic Transformations

Skill Development

- Transforming answers to questions
- Connected discourse through dialogue (beyond sentence stems)
- Authentic conversation

In the next part of the lesson, students are asked to convert responses to questions (a different type of transformation). However, rather than a simple grammar exercise of changing answers to questions, as is often done in second language classes, this lesson chooses a piece of text from the book to engage students in creating questions that were answered in the text. At the same time, students are re-reading text orally in ways that encourage fluency in reading (a foundational skill). The text includes small narratives from several refugee children that can be used to do this transformation. Students are asked to consider the children's written statements from the text and to imagine that they had interviewed one of the children. What questions might they have asked that would result in learning this information? An example of a child named Ayla is included below.

From Nguyen-Le, K. (2021). *What Is a Refugee Literacy Unit*. Presentation given at the La Cosecha Annual Dual Language Conference, Albuquerque, NM. Reprinted with permission.

Language Structure and Transformation: Answer → Question

What questions do you think the author asked to get this answer?

Answer	Question
My name is Ayla.	What is your name?
I had to leave Syria because of the war.	Why did you leave your country?
	Why did you come to the United States?
I love to draw with my sister.	What do you like to do?
	What do you like to do with your sister?
We make funny comic books.	What do you draw?
	What do you like to draw?

From Nguyen-Le, K. (2021). *What Is a Refugee Literacy Unit*. Presentation given at the La Cosecha Annual Dual Language Conference, Albuquerque, NM. Reprinted with permission.

After engaging in this oracy activity as a whole group, the teacher assigns the groups of students a refugee from the book. She directs them to read the refugee's small story and generate questions that would need to be asked to generate these answers. The oracy question in this phase of the lesson is: *"What questions do you think the author asked to get these answers?"* The students are directed to "think backwards" because in most classrooms students seldom are asked to convert answers to questions. Further, question formation in English is difficult for children acquiring English as an additional language. In the above example, children learn the concept of "do" insertion when forming questions in English.

Finally, students are given assignments to assume the character of one of the refugee students in the book and other students are given the assignment to interview the refugee. In this oracy exercise, the interviewer reads the questions, and the child assigned to be the refugee answers the questions. This can be repeated several times in the classroom. Again, note that the text is revisited several times for different purposes to give children opportunities to understand the text, to re-read to develop fluency and comprehension and to develop vocabulary and grammar in context.

Oracy for Writing:
Note Taking, Turning Notes into Paragraphs, Connected Discourse

Skill Development

- Developing questions in context
- Structure for writing beyond oral rehearsal
- Focused listening and writing (interview)
- Oral fluency development with whole-class share

Taking oracy to writing in this lesson involves once again connecting to the text and to the previous oracy lessons. The first step in this process involves asking students what questions a refugee child might ask them. Returning to Ayla's story, we might revisit the language transformation of question to answer with a different focus: refugee → child in classroom.

From Nguyen-Le, K. (2021). *What Is a Refugee Literacy Unit*. Presentation given at the La Cosecha Annual Dual Language Conference, Albuquerque, NM. Reprinted with permission.

These questions that Ayla might ask the interviewer can be used as dialogue practice for writing. In this case, the students are put into pairs to interview each other using the questions they developed in the previous oracy activity. As they interview each other, students write their peer's responses. Each partner gets interviewed and also becomes an interviewer. Notes from partners are used to construct a paragraph about oneself. Figure 2.7 is an example of Dr. Nguyen-Le (Khanh) being interviewed by Ayla, a character in the book.

Notice that Khanh's response demonstrates practice in two types of transformations. The first is additional practice in turning questions to answers, and the second is turning simple

Ayla would ask me:

1. What is your name?
2. How long have you lived in the United States?
3. Do you like to draw?
4. Do you have a sister?
5. What kinds of books do you like to read?

Pair work

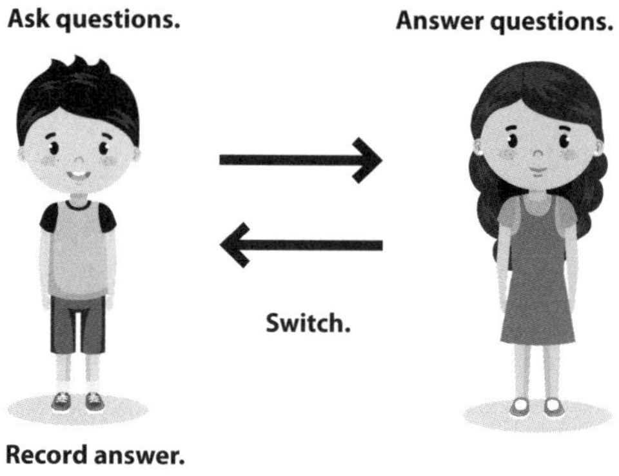

Ask questions. **Answer questions.**

Switch.

Record answer.

From Nguyen-Le, K. (2021). *What Is a Refugee Literacy Unit*. Presentation given at the La Cosecha Annual Dual Language Conference, Albuquerque, NM. Reprinted with permission.

Ayla's Questions
- What is your name?
- How long have you lived in the United States?
- Do you like to draw?
- Do you have a sister?
- What kinds of books do you like to read?

Khanh's Response

My name is Khanh. I had to leave Vietnam because of a war, too. I have lived in the U.S. for 42 years. I love to read, but I'm not good at drawing. I like to read historical fiction. I also have a sister. We like to cook together.

Figure 2.7. Structured dialogue practice for writing and responses.

sentences into connected discourse with appropriate and varied transition words. Further, this type of activity lends itself to direct teaching of paragraph writing with capitalization, punctuation, and spelling, and importantly provides illustrations of connected discourse.

Importantly, once written, this type of activity can lend itself to learning functions of language (in this case how the language of "compare and contrast" works). In the example below, the language function is "compare and contrast" with the transformation of question to answer using the appropriate form for the language function.

Ayla and Khanh

Compare/Contrast Question	Answer	Transformation
How are Ayla and Khanh alike?	Ayla and Khanh are alike because they both have sisters.	They are alike because they have sisters.
	Ayla and Khanh are alike because they are both refugees.	Both Ayla and Khanh are refugees.
How are Ayla and Khanh different?	They are different because Ayla likes to draw, but Khanh does not.	Ayla likes to draw; however Khanh doesn't, and this makes them different.

From Nguyen-Le, K. (2021). *What Is a Refugee Literacy Unit*. Presentation given at the La Cosecha Annual Dual Language Conference, Albuquerque, NM. Reprinted with permission.

Accountability and formative assessment is an important part of all of this oracy work and important in all of Literacy Squared biliteracy units. As a part of the assessment for this part of the unit, Dr. Nguyen-Le asks students to self-assess around two main questions:

- Did the paragraph you wrote answer the questions?
- Did your paragraph connect to that of the refugee from the book (in this case Ayla)? Compare and contrast your pargraph to Ayla's paragraph.

When the paragraphs are finished, the whole class has an opportunity to share. This assessment exercise is not simply a logical way to end the activity. It is also critical for language teaching and learning from a metalinguistic standpoint. In our research, we have found that children sometimes do not get credit for their oral or written answers because they have not totally understood what they are being prompted to do. In this case, they are learning to analyze their own writing around whether they answered the questions and whether they, in fact, engaged in comparing and contrasting two individuals.

In sum, this very short activity is, in fact, a highly effective way of engaging in oracy development via question/answer, turning simple sentences into connected discourse, re-reading what you wrote and reading out loud in front of your peers and engaging in self-analysis to gauge whether you addressed the assignment correctly.

A final and very important addition to our original components for oracy, is Dr. Nguyen-Le's extension to oracy for empathy.

Oracy for Empathy

Skill Development

- Use language that demonstrates empathy for the characters in the book (a first step towards social justice).
- Express and enact ways to make newcomers (whether refugee or not) welcome to the school.
- Good Karma for the future

This section begins with a whole class discussion, once again returning to the text, this time with a focus on why the refugee child, Ayla, had to leave her country. The teacher has children reread her paragraph about why she had to leave her country, followed by a discussion of three questions (see below):

"My name is Ayla. I had to leave Syria because of the war. I love to draw with my sister. We make funny comic books."

What do you think it is like to escape a war?
How do you think Ayla is feeling?
If you were Ayla, what might help you to feel welcome in our school?

From Nguyen-Le, K. (2021). *What Is a Refugee Literacy Unit*. Presentation given at the La Cosecha Annual Dual Language Conference, Albuquerque, NM. Reprinted with permission.

After doing this as a whole class, the teacher once again assigns students to various refugee students discussed in the book. Students are placed in pairs and asked to answer the three questions posed above and write out their answers to these questions. Especially important is the question about how the class might help the new child to feel welcome in the school. Teachers are encouraged to discuss how important empathy is when teaching for social justice. It invites children to respond from their own point of view and lived experiences, and many emerging bilingual children have lived experiences related to immigrating to a new country.

From the oracy standpoint, this is another, albeit more complex. dialogue question that involves question/answer transformations. It involves a rather complex grammar pattern (e.g., "If I were Ayla, I would (might, could, would) _____") and presents an opportunity to teach modals in English. Modals are critical in interpreting the meaning of questions in many grade levels and academic subject areas. For example, in science, children need to know that if you say, "Put these chemicals together and they <u>might</u> explode," means maybe it will happen and maybe it won't. However, if you say, "Put these chemicals together and they <u>will</u> explode," it means that it is a certainty that it will happen. Modals are critical to reading comprehension.

Collectively this wonderful second grade example illustrates how oracy can be developed by engaging children to use real and meaningful texts as the foundation for talking and writing about consequential topics. It shows how oracy can be used to engage children in multiple text readings that can help develop fluency and reading comprehension. Oracy should be a scaffold to writing especially in teaching connected discourse and moving beyond the teaching of decontextualized skills and vocabulary. Language development is much more than vocabulary. Most importantly for Literacy Squared, these types of texts can be paired with Spanish textbooks to develop biliteracy in Spanish and English.

CONSIDERATIONS FOR DEVELOPING BILITERACY

The above lesson illustrates a powerful example of how skills and teaching for social justice can be integrated in ways that address oracy, reading, writing, grammar, and teaching empathy, while concurrently enhancing the teaching of foundational skills. It is important also to consider ways that this type of text might be paired with Spanish language texts to engage in the same kind of teaching using Spanish as a medium of instruction with appropriate oracy to writing activities. Suggested books include:

Areli is a Dreamer/Areli es una Dreamer: Una historia real by Areli Morales

From North to South/Del norte al sur by René Colato Laínez

Waiting for Papá/Esperando Papá by René Colato Laínez

The Upside Down Boy/El niño de cabeza by Juan Felipe Herrera

We All Laugh Alike/Juntos nos reímos by Carmen Beiner-Grand

The theme of these Spanish books provides opportunities for teachers to engage children in cross-language connections between Spanish and English, to learn the difference between immigrants and refugees, and to engage in learning all of the skills spelled out in the lesson above in Spanish.

Utilizing Children's Spanish and English Writing as Formative Assessment in Teaching Oracy and Writing

As discussed in Chapter 1, we have done extensive research on the development of biliteracy in Spanish and English writing. This research has been conducted on thousands of children and analyzed using our Literacy Squared Writing Rubric (see Chapters 1, 4, 5, and 6). Our research has indicated that emerging bilingual learners are quite capable of acquiring oracy, reading, writing and metalinguistic skills in Spanish and English beginning in kindergarten, and that children's writing samples can provide lenses into literacy development that are as powerful as assessments that are solely based on reading. Written products and assessments that employ a biliterate lens enable us to use an assets-based perspective to view writing development in ways that otherwise might be misinterpreted as signs that children are confused or do not have solid knowledge of foundational skills such as phonological awareness or decoding.

At times, bilingual children's writing is seen as evidence that they are underachieving and that two languages may be sources of confusion. We have rejected these observations over the past two decades and provide the following example of a child's writing to illustrate why the deficit and confusion orientations underestimate children's potential and abilities. We also present the example to illustrate the limitations of monolingual interpretations of emerging biliterate behavior.

Esperanza's writing sample in Spanish and English (Figure 2.8) demonstrates the potential of children's writing samples as powerful tools in formative assessments with regard to writing

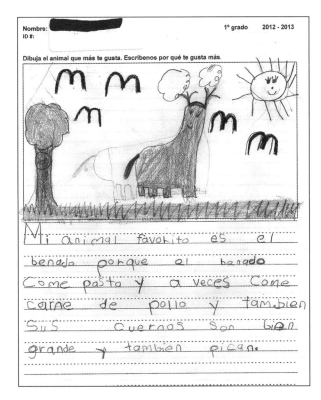 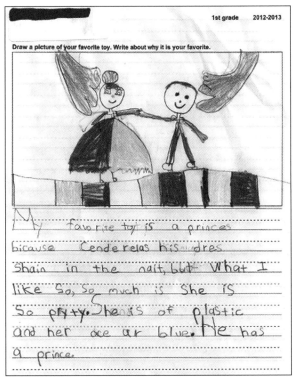

Figure 2.8. Esperanza's writing samples Spanish and English.

and other foundational skills, raises concerns about the current inattention to the teaching of writing, and once again challenges the U.S. education world to emerge from their monolingual myopia.

The writing sample below is from a Literacy Squared partner site. The child, Esperanza, was in first grade at the time of the study and the writing sample was collected in Spanish at the beginning of January and in English in the middle of January. Figure 2.8 includes her writing samples and her own illustrations of her writing. The art products alone are worth viewing!

Each of the texts will be interpreted for the reader so that it is possible to see what the child is trying to communicate. While Literacy Squared has a formal protocol to assess and score these samples, in this chapter we are going to follow a slightly different path and discuss how these samples collectively can inform literacy instruction in ways that monolingual assessment cannot. It is critical that we develop and use protocols that enable us to observe firsthand how children's two languages give us a more holistic picture of language and literacy development including foundational skill development.

Interpretation of Esperanza's Writing

Spanish: Writing Prompt	English: Writing Prompt
Write about your favorite animal.	Write about your favorite toy.
My favorite animal is the deer because the deer eats grass and sometimes he eats chicken and also his horns are very big and also they poke.	My favorite toy is a princess because Cinderella has a dress that shines in the night, but what I like so, so much is that she is so pretty. She is plastic and her eyes are blue. She has a prince.

To begin, we offer overall observations about Esperanza as a writer. First, by placing her writing side by side, we see that she produces about the same amount of text in both languages. She knows the concept of a word, and she can encode and decode words in writing. She has phonological awareness in both languages. She used beginning and ending punctuation in both languages, and used a similar structure in Spanish and English when responding to the prompts. In fact, she responded to each prompt having an introductory sentence that specifically addressed the prompt. She used descriptive language appropriate to each task that included adjectives and adverbs—in Spanish, she even used adverbs for added emphasis to her description (*bien grande*— very big). She linked ideas together to provide details (*porque* and because) and her writing had voice in both languages.

In Spanish, she spelled 70% of the words correctly and correctly spelled all of the words that follow consonant-vowel syllabic rules including multisyllabic words. Clearly, she can decode words in Spanish, she has graphophonemic awareness, and she has the vocabulary necessary to write the description. From her writing we see an emerging biliterate learner who has learned foundational skills in the context of learning to write.

Her writing sample in English is, perhaps, more interesting in that it would be difficult to read and understand if a teacher were monolingual in English. When we have done this in Literacy Squared, we have had teachers score samples such as this one as "unreadable." We disagree. The writing is unreadable from a monolingual lens because of the reader's limitations, *not the child's*. When we read the child's sample using a bilingual lens (Spanish and English) which is what the child is using to write, we see a different picture. We also see a picture of an emerging bilingual learner who needs explicit oral ELD to help accelerate her already impressive progress in English.

In English, she spelled 60% of the words correctly, indicating a good command of the high-frequency words encountered in first-grade English texts (which aids in reading fluency). She follows the structure of the work she produced in Spanish, indicating a cross-language connection that has helped her self-expression, and she is using her nascent knowledge of English vowel combinations—albeit incorrectly in English, but with Spanish logic; she is not guessing. She is also using her knowledge of the phonological system of Spanish to write in English and her knowledge of the syntax of Spanish to write. Examples include:

- shain in the nait –shine in the night
- pryty–pretty
- ace–eyes
- He has a prince–she has a prince
- ar–are

To the monolingual reader, the sample may seem unreadable, but with our bilingual lens, we see a child who is using her entire linguistic repertoire in two languages to express herself in writing. Rather than viewing the writing as unreadable, the bilingual lens enables us to assess what the child *can do* and use the information as a formative assessment in our teaching. From the viewpoint of foundational skills, this child can decode words and she has graphophonemic awareness. Her writing helps us to understand how to help her with her English language development. For example, pronoun agreement (princess = she), syntax (she is of plastic = she is plastic) and common spelling issues that also perplex native English speakers (e.g., bicause = because). Importantly, words like nait (for night) and shain (shine) are words that she already knows the meaning of and therefore teaching her the standard ways they are spelled will be easier because she is not learning to decode a word that has no meaning to her.

We want to emphasize that we fully understand that this child needs to learn the standard code for writing in English; however, we see in her writing her potential, and through a bilingual lens she is credited with what she knows and not labeled as "unreadable" and in need of more phonics or unnecessary literacy interventions.

Finally, in Literacy Squared we have argued that children who are fortunate enough to be in bilingual settings do not need to learn the foundational skills (especially phonics) twice. In most of our classrooms, children learn foundational skills in Spanish first and then we begin to teach English phonics by explicitly teaching what is different between English and Spanish (see the Approach to Phonics Webinar Series at www.literacysquared.org/resources). There is precious little time in a school day to adequately include all required content areas and subjects. This is exacerbated when a teacher is charged with teaching in two languages. We would advise teachers *not to waste time by teaching things twice.*

SUMMARY: LITERACY, ORACY, AND WRITING

To return to where we began with the chapter, we once again express grave concerns about the lack of attention being given to the teaching and learning of both oracy and writing in the age of the greater emphasis on teaching foundational skills and the subsequent narrowing of the curriculum. When we wrote our first book (Escamilla, et. al., 2014), we argued that the teaching of writing, particularly in Spanish, was critical to the teaching of reading and we expressed concern that literacy teaching in the United States, at that time, had been too focused on reading. All these years later, we are even more concerned and believe writing instruction has been nearly eliminated from the literacy curriculum in many states, particularly in states that are aspiring to implement quality dual language biliteracy programs.

We end this chapter with an appeal to teachers and schools, particularly those in bilingual/dual language contexts to give the teaching of writing and oracy equal weight to reading, and to enhance and expand the literacy curriculum by including a wide range of writing activities into the daily classroom activities. As a reminder, August and Shanahan (2006) found that children learning English as an additional language acquired decoding skills as ably as their English-speaking peers; however, they lagged behind in comprehension and writing. We stress that oracy and writing are foundational skills, which can amplify the teaching of other foundational skills, which are especially critical to comprehension in learning to read in Spanish and English. The development of biliteracy requires the development of a biliterate pedagogy that is built on a comprehensive approach to biliteracy, and explicit attention to teaching for social justice.

In this chapter, we have provided a research base and rationale for our concerns about the narrowing of the curriculum. We then provided a rationale for giving oracy and writing equal attention to reading and writing in the bilingual reading block, and we provided one example of a literacy unit that connects oracy and writing with a specific focus on teaching for social justice. Our children deserve more, not less.

Questions for Reflection and Action

- How do you integrate writing and oracy into your daily literacy instruction?
- What resources are you using to teach empathy and focus on social justice?
- List all of the PD opportunities you have had in the past 2–3 years related to literacy.
- What was the nature of the PD?
    - To what extent was it focused on the needs of emerging bilingual learners?
    - Did the PD include writing and/or oracy training?
    - What kind of PD would you like to see in your school?

3 TheDictado Method for Writing Instruction

"With one dictado, I hit seven standards in twenty minutes."

—Chicago Area Public School Teacher

Key Terms

Cross-language strategy

Metalinguistic awareness
- Within-language metalinguistic awareness
- Cross-language metalinguistic awareness

Self-extending linguistic system

Talk-through

Teaching points

theDictado

Guiding Questions

- What is the difference between **within-language metalinguistic awareness** and **cross-language metalinguistic awareness**?
- What is the role of the **talk-through** in **theDictado** procedure?
- How will you use student writing samples to determine **teaching points** for theDictado?

Let's face it. Writing is hard. Teaching writing is harder. We understand how difficult it is to teach multiple genres, to balance developing a love for thoughtful imaginative writing with the need to teach students to write a grammatically complex sentence, and to help students understand that they have opinions and ideas that are valuable and worthy of being recorded. Should you start with grammar, phonics, punctuation and spelling, or is it more important to emphasize that writing must effectively communicate a message? Are these, indeed, actually separable? We believe that teachers should plan lessons to emphasize that brilliant ideas and interesting information are best conveyed through well-structured, accurately punctuated, and grammatically sound sentences. When strung together, the sentences should vary, flow, and include precise and appropriate word selection. Complicating this is the role of genre, motif, conflict, argument, figurative expression, analogy, syllogism, moral, character, setting, plot, and so forth. This list is far from complete, but as teachers you can appreciate the challenge. There are many elements to consider when helping students to become proficient writers. It is not enough simply to expose students to exquisitely written books and to give them time to play with putting words and ideas on paper. Students need explicit guidance on how to communicate effectively in writing, and they need a reason or motivation for writing.

As we emphasize throughout this book, children's writing in both Spanish and English should be evaluated based on the product they generate rather than the process they use to get there. We argue that educators should consider the content, structural elements, and spelling of these products both separately and together, and that no single piece of writing should be used to summarize a bilingual learner's writing abilities. At a minimum, an educator should have one piece of writing in Spanish and one piece of writing in English, and these should be examined side-by-side to create a more holistic understanding of the writer. Further, the evaluation system can be both formative and summative; however, a formative evaluation is more useful in its ability to inform instruction. Bilingual writing requires bilingual interpretation. We hope that the evaluator of bilingual learners' writing will be bilingual, but we understand that this is not always the case. When a monolingual educator is faced with the writing of an emerging bilingual learner, it is imperative that that person seek out the assistance of someone with more linguistic and cultural knowledge to help interpret the work.

It is our contention that students need to understand all of this beginning at a very young age. Their teachers need to design and implement purposeful and deliberate instruction that connects languages while expanding students' opportunities to learn. We are also well aware that the time a teacher can dedicate to literacy instruction is limited. Language arts instruction must include attention to reading, writing, speaking, listening, processing, critiquing, creating, and analyzing. Further, in bilingual classrooms, students must learn how to accomplish these in two languages with the added need to attend to metalinguistic analysis within and across languages. By any standard, this is a monumental task for both teachers and students. One strategy that we advocate teachers incorporate into their repertoires to help attend to all of this is *theDictado*.

In this chapter, we will define and extend the purpose of theDictado while providing guidance to teachers about how to implement it with fidelity while ensuring students are held accountable for the learning. We will place particular emphasis on the value and importance of the talk-through and its usefulness in raising students' metalinguistic awareness. Differently than our previous writing about theDictado, we will use student samples to help teachers understand how to analyze students' writing to inform the creation of complex and sophisticated dictados designed to stretch students linguistically. Additionally, we provide ideas for differentiating theDictado as needed and for extending it into online or virtual learning environments.

TheDICTADO: DEFINITION, PURPOSE, AND IMPLEMENTATION BASICS

With our colleagues, we introduced theDictado in *Biliteracy from the Start: Literacy Squared in Action* (Escamilla et al., 2014). In a nutshell:

> TheDictado is a writing method intended for use in both Spanish literacy and literacy-based ELD. Literacy Squared uses an adaptation of the Mexican approach; however, the strategy is common throughout Central and South America and is therefore culturally familiar to many of the families who enroll their children in bilingual schools. The method is used to refine language arts skills in both Spanish and English, as well as to teach content, spelling, conventions, and grammar in an integrated way. More importantly, it can be used to develop students' self-correction and metalanguage skills.
>
> TheDictado involves having the teacher dictate a series of phrases or sentences to the students. The students and teacher then collaborate to create a corrected model of the focus text. Students amend their sentences using a two-color system to draw attention to errors. The same phrases or sentences are repeated throughout the week, giving students multiple opportunities to practice and learn the targeted content, conventions, grammar, and spelling (p. 57).

Purpose: Developing Metalinguistic Awareness

TheDictado is a **cross-language strategy** that provides students repeated opportunities to read, write, speak, and listen in service to developing metalinguistic awareness and advanced understandings about how languages work. **Metalinguistic awareness** is the ability to see and understand language as a process and as an artifact. It is the understanding of how languages work. It involves the ability to monitor speech production, analyze language as a decontextualized object, evaluate competing hypotheses about effective communication, and articulate and justify linguistic alternatives. A person with well-developed metalinguistic awareness not only regulates and uses language effectively but also is able to consider consciously the extent to which alternative uses would impact interpretation. These reflections include all of the various building blocks of language systems, including phonology, phonics, vocabulary, morphology, syntax, pragmatics, discourse varieties, registers, and writing conventions. Metalinguistic awareness, or the ability to reflect upon and manipulate language, develops separately from the ability to name these building blocks.

Effective bilingual communicators understand these elements within a particular language as well as by comparison to other languages. Within-language metalinguistic awareness is the ability to look at a single language and understand how it functions in both its oral and written forms. In oral English, for example, a student with metalinguistic awareness will understand how varying the placement of the word *only* in a sentence can change its meaning. Consider the following two statements as evidence: 1) *Only* the teacher wrote on the blackboard (she was the sole person to write there); and 2) The teacher *only* wrote on the blackboard (she did not write elsewhere). It is not just word order that affects meaning. Consider the role of punctuation in writing in the following examples in Spanish and English. First, in Spanish: 1) *Te deseo buenas noches* (I bid you good night) or 2) *Te deseo. Buenas noches* (I desire you. Good night). Similarly, in English, we offer an oldie, but goodie: 1) A woman without her man is nothing; or 2) A woman: without her, man is nothing. The word order is identical; yet, the placement and inclusion of particular punctuation marks completely alters the meaning.

Rudimentary elements that can be developed by raising students' within-language metalinguistic awareness include language rules related to spelling and phonics. Effective written communication requires explicit attention to how words are encoded. In Spanish, for example, we need to teach students about the "la h muda" (the silent *h*) or that before the letters *p* or *b* one uses the letter *m* (*imposible, campo, temprano, cambio, ambos*) but before the letter *v* one uses the letter *n* (*invierno, envidia, convertir, bienvenida*). Other such rules include the difference in when to use *y* (*Tráeme pan y carne*) versus *e* (*Tráeme aguja e hilo*) or when and how to apply accents. Every language has spelling, grammar, punctuation, vocabulary, and word order/choice nuances. These need to be taught and discussed explicitly.

Cross-language metalinguistic awareness is the capacity to analyze the similarities and differences one encounters when examining two or more languages concurrently. When bilingual learners engage in contrastive analysis exercises that elucidate these characteristics, they cultivate a deeper understanding of each of their languages individually while simultaneously developing a **self-extending linguistic system** designed to increase their ability to recognize patterns, form analogies, and refine connections across languages (Hopewell, 2017; Hopewell & Abril-González, 2019). Nurturing these capacities through direct and explicit language comparisons prepares students to use and apply the totality of their language repertoire in service to learning. We hypothesize that by explicitly raising students' awareness of how languages are mutually supportive, we can advance students' entire linguistic repertoires as well as their understanding of how languages work.

We refer to the unique bilingual ability to use cross-language metalinguistic analysis as a building block to formulate and test hypotheses as a "self-extending system" with a deliberate hat tip to Marie Clay and her work with *Reading Recovery* (Clay, 1991). Clay stressed the reciprocal relationship between reading and writing, in which attention to one contributes to the development of the other. We extend this notion into the development of a multilingual repertoire by recognizing that not only are reading and writing reciprocally related, so too are the languages that students acquire. If we endeavor to raise students' metalinguistic awareness and teach them explicitly to connect their languages, they will become better consumers, producers, and analyzers of language in its oral and written forms. The ability to scrutinize and systematically evaluate the similarities, differences, and patterns across languages provides a framework for developing hypotheses that encourage students to establish the ability to continue to learn without direct instruction. In essence, it is the enactment of a self-extending language learning system.

Let us return to the monolingual example we discussed above of the need to teach students about "la *h* muda" (the silent *h*). Once students understand the concept that words are sometimes encoded with letters that are not pronounced aloud, they can consider whether this is true only in Spanish, or if it holds true in other languages. Obviously, if the language of comparison is English, they will quickly see that there are many words containing silent letters. Certainly, we regularly teach the silent *e* and its function, but how much more powerful is it to have the students become language detectives who discover that many letters in English can be silent? Consider the following words: *debt, muscle, Wednesday, bake, fifth, **sign**, **ghost**, knife, salmon, autumn, people, coup, island, castle, guide, two*. This list is not exhaustive of every letter that may be silent. Knowing this, students will understand why they sometimes need to develop mnemonics or simply memorize particular spelling patterns.

This is a very basic example of an overly simplified cross-language comparison. Let us, therefore, look at a more powerful one that is based in morphology, or the study of the formation of words. When a student is taught that words ending in *-dad* in Spanish function similarly to those ending in *-ty* in English, an entire class of words is newly available. A student can know that the English equivalent to *actividad* is *activity* or that *electricidad* is *electricity* but may not yet have been taught the equivalent for *capacidad* or *atrocidad*. Armed with the knowledge that patterns across languages are somewhat stable, the student could hypothesize that the English equivalents are *capacity* and *atrocity*, even if she had never previously been introduced to these words, and she would be right! This is a powerful self-extending linguistic system. It creates the conditions under which a student can apply what was learned about cross-linguistic language similarities when confronted with an unknown word in one of their languages.

Implementing theDictado: An Introduction

TheDictado invites a focused examination of the linguistic similarities and differences within and across languages, and it affords children extended opportunities to expand their knowledge of writing in both Spanish and English. In Literacy Squared schools, theDictado spans grade levels K-5, though we have known of schools that have chosen to implement it all the way to high school.

Elsewhere, we have described in detail the procedure for implementing theDictado in grades K–5 (Escamilla et al., 2014) and have worked with Sobrato Early Academic Language (SEAL) to produce a video titled *theDictado, Bilingual 2nd Grade Classroom* to demonstrate the strategy in action (https://www.youtube.com/watch?v=EV278nEX_UM); therefore, the following description will be brief.

TheDictado begins when the teacher creates a meaningful and instructionally appropriate passage to work on with her students over the course of a single week. The passage should reflect grade-level language arts expectations and should alternately be presented in Spanish one week followed by English the next week. The length and complexity should be such that the passage is challenging for the majority of the students but can be dictated and discussed in no more than 20 minutes. Half of the 15 to 20 minutes should be the teacher reading the passage aloud while the students record it in writing. The other half should be the talk-through in which the teacher recreates the passage in front of the student while providing direct and explicit discussion elucidating the teaching points. Children identify and correct their approximations every time theDictado is given (3 to 5 times per week). We recommend that teachers strive to complete a minimum of 24 Dictados in a school year with half being in Spanish and half being in English. For a more detailed and precise discussion of the procedure, including resources for self-evaluation and standard correction codes, please see *Biliteracy from the Start: Literacy Squared in Action* (Escamilla et al., 2014).

In the more than 19 years that we have been working with teachers to develop and refine theDictado procedure and technique, we have determined that it has enormous potential to serve as a powerful method for developing writing, as well as metalinguistic development in Spanish and English; however, we also believe there are important steps that must be included if theDictado is to be effective. In particular, we see the need to move beyond teaching only basic skills (i.e., standard spelling and punctuation) to ensuring increasingly complex sentences and thoughtfully connected discourse. Further, we cannot emphasize enough that quantity does not equal quality. We would rather see brief, but precise and complex, passages than those that are verbose and lengthy but do not challenge the students and take too much time to record leaving little time for discussion. As mentioned previously, there is limited time in a school day, and much to be accomplished. We will never gain more teaching time; therefore, we need to be efficient, precise, and focused with the time that we have.

TheDICTADO IN PRACTICE

The remaining sections of this chapter present a step-by-step guide for how to create and implement theDictado, with examples.

Where to Begin: Creating theDictado

One of the beautiful things about theDictado is that it is a meaning-based practice that is adaptable to a variety of contexts, languages, curricula, learning goals, and proficiency levels. Unlike prepackaged programs that profess to know and teach the precise grammar, editing, and vocabulary students will need to become better writers, theDictado centers the student and the current context and content for learning. While better achievement on high-stakes tests may be a welcome side-effect of a faithful engagement with theDictado, the strategy was developed and promoted to ensure that bilingual students become adept independent writers in two languages.

Because it is not a pre-packaged program, however, it places a burden on the teacher to create and plan grade-appropriate dictados that will stretch students' abilities while teaching explicitly how language works. While this sounds difficult and time-consuming, it need not be. The substance of theDictado will stem from your curriculum, grade-level standards, and an analysis of your students' writing.

The Content of theDictado   Let us begin with the content. First and foremost, the substance of theDictado must be meaningful, and this should be highlighted for students. After all, one goal of theDictado is to move away from decontextualized spelling lists or rote grammar worksheets. If students are going to grasp your teaching points, they need to understand the passage well enough to notice the component parts. If all of a student's brain capacity is occupied trying to make sense of the content, her ability to grasp and master the teaching points is diminished. A successful dictado avoids silly phrases that emphasize a spelling pattern (i.e., *The fat cat sat on the mat*) or obscure words that detract from the learning context (i.e., *The constable's speech was delivered with a lamprophony she found reassuring*). In a holistic biliteracy framework, teachers strive to make meaningful connections across the day and across learning environments. TheDictado is situated in this framework. Therefore, the content should be linked to a text that students are reading, a writing genre they are learning, or a subject matter they are studying. It's that simple.

Creating appropriate passages from student evidence takes practice, but with a trained eye, teachers begin to notice patterns across students' writing as a matter of course. Importantly, a teacher need not analyze every student's writing to understand the needs of the group. A small sample of students' writing in Spanish and English will quickly reveal patterns that can be addressed in theDictado.

Analytic Framework for Planning theDictado   To help nurture teachers' ability to prepare dictados, we have created a helpful analytic framework to aid teachers to deconstruct student writing. The template gives teachers a concrete way to understand better how to analyze student writing with the goal of identifying students' writing needs. The analytic framework is included here in two parts as shown in Figures 3.1 and 3.2. Note that Part 1 asks teachers to examine and list very specific elements of a student's writing: Phrase/sentence-level considerations, use of transition words, vocabulary choice, punctuation issues, cross-language potential, and spelling.

Genre	Student Behaviors	Transformations
Phrase/sentence level		
Transitions		
Word level		
Punctuation		
Cross-language Connections		
Spelling		

Figure 3.1. Analytic framework for planning a dictado, Part 1: Working from a student's writing sample.

In many ways, this is reminiscent of the qualitative side of the Literacy Squared Writing Rubric (see the Chapter 1 Appendix). Not only does the template ask teachers to look at students' writing and list their specific behaviors; it takes it a step further. The analytic framework provides a column for teachers to transform the students' approximations into more complex, sophisticated, and mature language. Transformations should echo how an adult might express the same thought that the child is approximating. It is from these transformations that the teacher creates theDictado. After all, the goal we share for our students is for them to obtain the mature language that the teacher possesses and uses, with all of its nuance and access to a variety of registers.

Then, in Part 2, the framework provides a space to indicate theDictado that was created with a checklist to name the teaching points that will be addressed. All genres will not be addressed in

Final Dictado

Teaching Points	Date: Grade: Genre:
Phrase/sentence level __ **Transitions** **Word level__** **Punctuation__** **Cross-language Connections__** **Spelling __**	Title: _____

Figure 3.2. Analytic framework for planning a dictado, Part 2: Working from a student's writing sample.

every dictado; however, over time, one should be able to point to where each has taken precedent. As a self-reflection exercise, we encourage you to look at your dictados at the end of each month to be sure that you have included teaching points that move beyond spelling and punctuation.

Using the Analytic Framework to Create Dictados To create appropriate dictados that have the potential to advance a class's language and literacy proficiencies, you should begin by choosing 2 to 3 students' writing samples to analyze using the analytic framework. As you read and analyze, note not only what individual students are accomplishing and approximating with language, but also the patterns that are consistent across students. For each writing sample, complete a single analytic framework template. Upon completion, note what elements are evident across different students' writing. You may choose to incorporate a particular word or teaching point in your dictados in response to the needs of a single student; however, it is much more likely that you will focus on the patterns you are noticing across a number of students. If, for example, most of the students in your classes are writing compositions comprised of simple sentences, your dictados will focus on how to write an effective complex or compound sentence. If your students are effectively including complex sentences, but are omitting the comma after the dependent clause, then punctuation may be a higher priority.

Over time, there will be less and less need to record your observations directly on the analytic framework, but as you are developing your skills of observation, it is constructive to practice the full process using the template. Note, though, that when students begin writing longer pieces, and are taking more risks in their writing, there may not be space on the template to record everything. In these cases, we suggest that you make copies of the students' writing and that you use different colored highlighters to demarcate approximations that may need to be addressed (i.e., one color for discourse, one color for phrases, one color for spelling, etcetera). While using the template is a valuable way to establish evidence for the choices you make with regard to the teaching points in your dictados, highlighting and annotating a text can serve a similar purpose. We have known teachers who have felt empowered when being observed or questioned by administrators when they can produce students' writing samples and the analytic framework to defend particular teaching points within their dictados. Remember, as you are creating dictados in each language, you want to look for opportunities to make cross-language connections. These may happen at the discourse level as you focus on genre, at the sentence level where you examine syntax, at the word level in terms of transition words and lexicon, or at the very basic level of spelling and punctuation.

How to Analyze a Student's Writing Systematically

By way of illustration, we will use a single student to illustrate the process of systematically analyzing a student's writing. To begin, as always, we implore you to analyze students' writing samples side-by-side, including a sample from each language, if possible. It is helpful to have a photocopy of the work, so that you can highlight and annotate directly on the text.

The student we have selected is a fourth-grade student who was developing biliteracy in Spanish and English in a Literacy Squared research site. The samples included here are representative of the writing of her peers, and therefore serve as exemplars from which the needs of many students can be extrapolated.

Writing Samples: Spanish and English Figure 3.3 is an example of the first page of a fourth-grade student's Spanish and English writing samples with the evaluator's highlights and annotations. (Note that the educator used multiple colors of highlighters to call attention to different features and to make brief annotations directly on the samples.)

Figures 3.4 shows the original Spanish and an English writing sample from the same fourth-grade student. In Spanish, the student responds to the prompt "Who is your best friend in the whole world? Write why this person is your best friend." In English, the student responds to the prompt "If you could be someone else for the day, who would you be? Why would you want to be that person?"

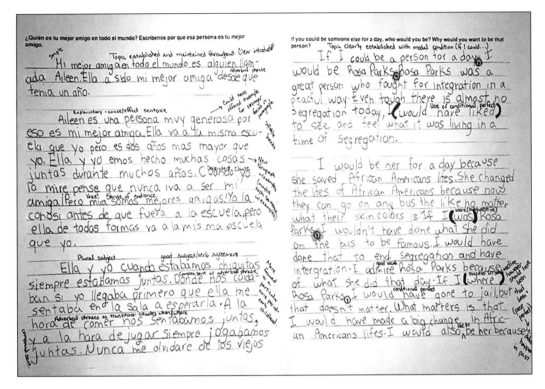

Figure 3.3. An example of the first page of a fourth-grade student's Spanish and English writing samples with the evaluator's highlights and annotations.

Identifying Strengths and Areas for Development When completing the analytic framework for this student's writing in Spanish and English, we first noted her strengths. In both pieces of writing, she uses an effective topic sentence. She is relatively successful at organizing her sentences so that they transition smoothly, often inserting adverbial phrases to denote when and where events did, or could have, taken place. We noted that her English vocabulary is more sophisticated, though this is likely because she has chosen a topic that is related to curriculum. She uses simple and repetitive vocabulary in Spanish and she squeezes multiple topics into single paragraphs. Although she uses complex and compound sentences in both languages, she demonstrates that she has not yet learned that a dependent clause must be followed by a comma. As we note both what she is doing and what she is approximating, we begin imagining a dictado that would allow us to highlight some of the linguistic features that she still needs to develop. There is both a science and an art to finding the right balance of teaching points within any given dictado. As classroom teachers, we would look at the writing of multiple students, conferring with the standards and any grade level scope and sequence we were expected to follow, and consider any content connections or texts we were reading. No individual dictado can ever address everything a student needs, so we must carefully craft our sentences while being selective about our foci.

Two Dictados Addressing Areas the Student Needs to Develop The following are two dictados we might use in response to the writing we have just analyzed. The teaching points are shown in bold type. They include comma placement, the role of prefixes, and advanced vocabulary and spelling.

<u>**Separate** Is Never Equal</u>

Although it was once legal to require students of different races to attend **separate** schools**,** it no longer is. Thanks to the efforts of **courageous** and **admirable** people**,** this practice is now **il**legal. **Un**fortunately**, in**equality still exists.

The Dictado Method for Writing Instruction

EXAMPLE 1: SPANISH

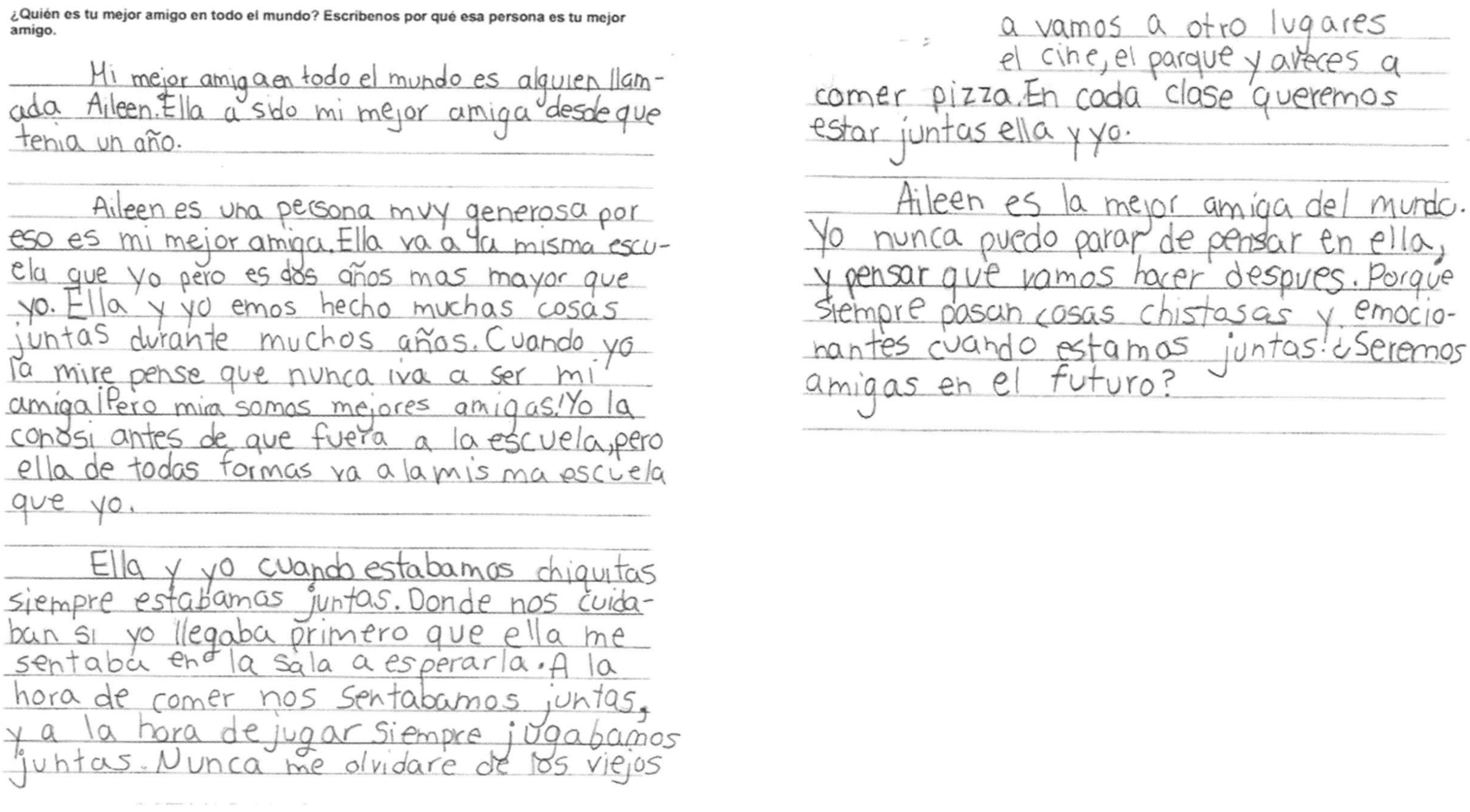

¿Quién es tu mejor amigo en todo el mundo? Escribenos por qué esa persona es tu mejor amigo.

Mi mejor amiga en todo el mundo es alguien llamada Aileen. Ella a sido mi mejor amiga desde que tenía un año.

Aileen es una persona muy generosa por eso es mi mejor amiga. Ella va a la misma escuela que yo pero es dos años más mayor que yo. Ella y yo emos hecho muchas cosas juntas durante muchos años. Cuando yo la mire pense que nunca iva a ser mi amiga. ¡Pero mira somos mejores amigas! Yo la conosi antes de que fuera a la escuela, pero ella de todas formas va a la mis ma escuela que yo.

Ella y yo cuando estabamos chiquitas siempre estabamos juntas. Donde nos cuidaban si yo llegaba primero que ella me sentaba en la sala a esperarla. A la hora de comer nos sentabamos juntas, y a la hora de jugar siempre juagabamos juntas. Nunca me olvidare de los viejos

a vamos a otro lugares el cine, el parque y alveres a comer pizza. En cada close queremos estar juntas ella y yo.

Aileen es la mejor amiga del mundo. Yo nunca puedo parar de pensar en ella, y pensar que vamos hacer despues. Porque siempre pasan cosas chistosas y emocionantes cuando estamos juntas. ¿Seremos amigas en el futuro?

TRANSLATION TO ENGLISH FROM SPANISH:

My best friend in the whole world is a person named Aileen. She has been my best friend since I was one year old.

Aileen is a very generous person and because of this, she is my best friend. She goes to the same school as I, but she is two years older than I am. She and I have done a lot together over the years. When I first saw her, I didn't think she'd be my friend. But, look, we are best friends! I knew her before I went to school, but, in any case, she goes to the same school as I.

Figure 3.4. The original Spanish and an English writing sample from the same fourth-grade student whose writing appears in Figure 3.3.

(continued)

Figure 3.4. *(continued)*

She and I, when we were little, we were always together. At our babysitters, if I got there before her, I would sit in the living room waiting for her. When it was time to eat, we always sat together and when it was play time, we always played together. I will never forget those times.

We do other things together. We go to the movies, the park, and sometimes to eat pizza. In every class, she and I want to be together.

Aileen is the best friend in the world. I am always thinking about her and what we will do later. Because we always have fun and do exciting things when we are together. Will we be friends in the future?

EXAMPLE 2: ENGLISH

If you could be someone else for a day, who would you be? Why would you want to be that person?

If I could be a person for a day I would be Rosa Parks. Rosa Parks was a great person who fought for integration in a peaceful way. Even tough there is almost no segregation today, I would have liked to see and feel what it was living in a time of segregation.

I would be her for a day because she saved African Americans lifes. She changed the lifes of African Americans because now they can go on any bus the like no matter what their skin colors is. If I was Rosa Parks I wouldn't have done what she did on the bus to be famous. I would have done that to end segregation and have integration. I admire Rosa Parks because of what she did that day. If I where Rosa Parks, I would have gone to jail, but that doesn't matter. What matters is that I would have made a big change in African Americans lifes. I would also be her because

I would have the oppetuntie to make a big change.

Rosa Parks wasn't the only one to end segragation. That's why I would like to be her, because she joined the people who where against segregating. I would have also felt what it was to go to work a place where they wouldn't pay you that much, where they don't care about you, and worst that they don't even know you exist or work there. Her story is sad and if I was here I would have gone through all that but at least by just saying a little word I would have made a big diffrence in the world.

When the day would be over I would have seen and felt how had segregation was. It would still be worth it because I would have been a person who fought and went to jail, but changed the whole world.

<u>El poder de uno</u>

Aunque puede ser difícil de imaginar, una sola persona ordinaria es capaz de hacer el mundo un lugar mejor. No es necesario ser **extra**ordinario o particular**mente ingenioso**. No importa qui**é**n eres, d**ó**nde est**á**s o en qu**é** etapa est**á**s. Todos pueden ayudar a alguien.

These dictados are meaningful connected texts that are linked by a theme of social justice, though they come at it from quite different places. Each contains elevated vocabulary and looks at prefixes and suffixes. Grammatically, they are similar, allowing for a cross-language connection about beginning sentences with subordinating conjunctions (*aunque* and although) and the accompanying need for a comma. While there is some overlap in teaching points, they are not identical.

Determining the Teaching Points

Teaching points are the grammar, vocabulary, spelling, and structural elements that are intentionally included in theDictado because students have demonstrated that they do not yet control them or because they are required according to the standards or a district-level scope and sequence. Each dictado should have 3 to 6 teaching points. By using the analytic framework outlined above (Figures 3.1 and 3.2), the teacher can work from the broader sentence and phrase complexity level to the more finite details of spelling and punctuation. TheDictado is the perfect place to teach explicitly how the component features of language work together as an integrated system. These features include phonology, phonics, morphology, syntax, semantics, pragmatics, and register. A dictado's teaching points should always include spelling and punctuation. The remaining teaching points should include elevated vocabulary, sentence complexity, and similarities and differences across languages with explicit attention to what transfers across languages and what does not. Often, because dictados are regularly linked to the genres being read and written in class, the teaching points will be genre specific. The teaching points in Spanish and English will differ, but when possible, will have overlap, especially when demonstrating a cross-language feature. Teaching points are the focus of the talk-through.

Conducting the Talk-Through

The most crucial step in theDictado procedure is the talk-through. This is the point at which the teacher uses direct and explicit instruction to teach about language, conventions, grammar, and spelling. It is here that she models and generates metalinguistic awareness and helps students to make cross-language connections. During the talk-through, the teacher reconstructs a correct model of the passage on the board or using a document camera. The reconstruction of the message happens every time theDictado is given. There are no shortcuts here. It may be tempting to have the passage prewritten and posted for the students to consult for self-correction purposes. This divergence from the established procedure does not allow the teacher to emphasize orally the teaching points, and often leads to sloppy, inaccurate, and meaningless corrections by students. Students' focus is increased when they are watching the message be recreated and discussed. The guidance from the teacher helps students to discriminate and solidify the lessons. Repeated text reconstruction allows the teacher to emphasize any issues she noted while circulating and observing students' attempts to encode theDictado. There is an expectation that students will participate in the talk-through. The teacher should elicit student input and should notice that the students have more to say on days two through five as they internalize the teachings from the previous days.

As theDictado is reconstructed, the students are expected to follow along and make corrections to their work. Through self-correction, students gain awareness of the aspects of writing that continue to require their attention. All students should have access to a standard marking code to indicate their approximations and corrections. As a reminder, it is not easy to follow along while double-checking and correcting one's work. Go slowly and work in phrases rather than word-by-word. Remember, the talk-through comprises about half of the entire time dedicated to theDictado strategy. Better to work through it at a reasonable pace with lots of explicit attention to language development than to rush through it leaving students behind or to skip it all together. This is the time when students become metacognitively focused on their individual learning goals and across days begin to see their advancement. Again, the power of theDictado is the repeated experience with the talk-through.

Differentiation TheDictado is a whole class strategy and is meant to be at a level that is beyond what the majority of students could successfully produce independently. It should include teaching points that students are expected to master and to begin to apply to their independent writing. Sometimes, however, we have a student or two whose needs vary significantly from those of the whole group. While we still encourage these students with additional needs be included in the whole group practice of doing theDictado, we offer the following suggestions:

1. Copy theDictado onto a sentence strip. Cut the strip into phrases or words, and have the student arrange them appropriately as you read the message.

2. Use a cloze structure in which some words are already written for the student, and blank lines are offered in the places the student will insert individual words.

3. Draw lines on the student's page, such that each line indicates a word in theDictado.

4. Encourage the student to attempt the entire dictado, but only require that the student complete the first sentence and be sure that the teaching points in that sentence are appropriate for that student.

5. Use the 3-day plan with the whole group, but pull together a small group for two additional days of practice (5-day plan).

Importantly, take care not to predetermine what a child will or will not be able to handle in a dictado. Scaffolds, accommodations, and modifications have a place, but they are meant to be temporary and we have seen many students successfully and proudly participate in theDictado despite predictions that it will be too challenging. The predictability and structured routine helps. Students know what to expect, how to participate, and typically show rapid improvement.

Online Accommodations

We recognize that interactive strategies are challenging to implement virtually, but we also understand that online and distance learning is not likely to disappear any time soon. While we have some suggestions, we are grateful to teachers who continually innovate and share their successes with us. There is no single right way to do this, so we encourage you to play with different techniques and to take advantage of all the features you have available in the applications and platforms available to you.

To begin, let us acknowledge that completing the process in fifteen to twenty minutes may not be possible. Students face multiple distractions and technological challenges while at home that may add an element that is not typical in a face-to-face teaching environment. Make whatever time adjustments you need, keeping in mind that theDictado is only a small part of your language arts instruction. Some ideas that you might employ to help keep the length reasonable include: 1) adjust the length of theDictado, 2) give fewer total dictados across time, 3) involve families and care-givers in administering theDictado as homework so students get additional practice, 4) give theDictado during your small group instructional time rather than to the whole group, and 5) create a balance between synchronous and asynchronous opportunities to engage with the material.

Administering theDictado Synchronously When giving theDictado virtually and in real time, there are a few things you should take into consideration. First, remember, not everyone has the same bandwidth, so having students repeat aloud together may feel chaotic. Rather than eliminating the oral repetition of the message, we recommend that you have students mute themselves. You can then monitor the video to be sure all students are participating. Additionally, you may ask one or two students to unmute and lead the repetitive part. This will allow you to hear individuals without the distraction of the cacophony of too many voices.

Also, it will be important that you have a means of recreating theDictado and conducting the talk-through. Teachers have shared with us that they employ a variety of applications for this such as Pear Deck (peardeck.com) or Kami (Kamiapp.com) amongst others. If you are using Google Classroom or Zoom, however, we recommend you employ the White Board feature while sharing your screen. With the White Board, you are able to draw lines to indicate where you want students to write or how many words they will write. You can also use the stamps feature to remind students to skip lines. Finally, of course, it is the space you will use to conduct the recreation and talk-through. If you prefer not to use an online application for the recreation and talk-through, we suggest using the camera feature of your iPhone to recreate the experience of using a document camera or Elmo. Through the Zoom screen-sharing feature, one can project what the iPhone camera is detecting. By attaching the phone to an inexpensive flexible iPhone holder, a teacher can use paper and pencil to reconstruct and talk through the dictado message.

An important consideration will be to have a system in place for students to share their work with you. Within an application like Kami are features students can use to save and share their work. Alternatively, students can take photos of their writing to upload and send. We know of teachers who simply ask their students to hold their work up to their video cameras. Teachers then take screenshots. In addition, there is the matter of motivating students to be willing to share their work. We know of one teacher who motivates her students by connecting the students' completed dictados to collecting points (such as Dojo points on ClassDojo.com).

To the extent possible, we want younger students to continue to encode their dictados by hand. Not only does this help them to develop automaticity and fluency in writing, it also makes it less likely that they will enable and rely upon spell-check. If, however, you feel that having students use a keyboard will facilitate the process, we understand. In times of virtual learning, we trust teachers to make the best pedagogical decisions for their particular group or learning context.

Finally, and this will help us to segue to the next section, remember that your live sessions can always be recorded for later viewing. These recordings can be made available for students who were unable to attend, for families for use with homework, or as material for students to review independently (i.e., asynchronous applications).

Asynchronous Accommodations There are many platforms educators can use to coordinate asynchronous teaching and learning (e.g., Canvas Studio or Google Classroom), but one commonly used application is SeeSaw (web.seesaw.me). For the purposes of this chapter, we will discuss its possible use in accommodating asynchronous learning with theDictado. As mentioned above, synchronous experiences can be recorded. Alternatively, recordings can be made without students using applications like Screencastify (screencastify.com) or Screenpal (screenpal.com). Recordings can then be uploaded into SeeSaw using the multimedia link option. When designing dictado work with SeeSaw, begin by creating a new activity and giving it a title. Instructions can be typed in Spanish and/or English, and there is a voice recording option to give students an alternative way to understand what they are to do. Students then follow along and write/self-correct their dictados. SeeSaw integrates with technology so that students can photograph their work and video record themselves reading back the dictados. A benefit of SeeSaw is that once students have entered the virtual classroom, all of their documents and work are stored in their own personal account or file and teachers receive alerts when they have contributed something new.

While uploading videos to SeeSaw can facilitate the process of administering the entire dictado, some teachers take a hybrid approach. They administer theDictado synchronously, but record themselves doing the recreation and the talk-through for students to view and complete asynchronously. Others record themselves giving theDictado and ask the students to complete this part asynchronously, and to come prepared to do the talk-through during their live teaching time. Either option has the advantages of saving time in the virtual face-to-face time and allowing students to proceed at an individual pace with the self-correction.

There are a plethora of platforms. We are not advocating for any particular one, and while we highlighted SeeSaw, we only do so because it integrates features we think will be helpful. We encourage teachers to explore the applications that are supported by their districts and to take advantage of the many features that allow multimedia sharing of photographs and video recordings.

Accountability

A well-constructed dictado has 3 to 6 explicit teaching points that anchor the work across the week. As theDictado is given during the week, the focus is on listening carefully, encoding thoughtfully, recreating interactively, and self-correcting accurately. With repeated opportunities to practice, students develop the metacognitive skills to evaluate their attempts and to commit to memory the places they can improve. By the end of the week, most students will demonstrate marked improvement. Should you desire to grade a student's dictado, we recommend collecting the final version and grading only the teaching points. Did the student master the points that you carefully selected as important? Some teachers create a rubric in which they check off the individual teaching points for each dictado, but this is not necessary. Others recreate theDictado a final time and have student self-grade based on whether or not the teaching points were successfully included. At the end of the day, the point is not who does the grading or even what the final grade is. Improvement across time indicates learning, and if a student has demonstrated over the course of the week that he or she is more successful, then there are celebrations to be had. And, finally, once most of the students have mastered a particular teaching point, the true accountability comes in their independent writing. You should expect and demand that students apply what they have learned through theDictado to their writing throughout the school day.

SUMMARY: TheDICTADO

Over the years, we have examined hundreds, perhaps thousands, of students' dictado notebooks and have observed the implementation of theDictado in dozens of classrooms to better understand the role and the impact of theDictado on students' biliteracy development. Our evidence suggests that theDictado is most effective when it is implemented schoolwide, and students experience it across the years. We recommend, therefore, that administrators, policy makers, and educators support emergent bilingual learners with a minimum of 3 to 4 years of consistent explicit instruction in writing strategies through the employment of theDictado. We also have evidence to suggest that the number and type of structural elements as well as the selection of vocabulary used is more important than the number of sentences produced. As stated earlier, quality is more important than quantity.

The strength of the methodology of theDictado is that it provides a platform to engage bilingual learners in a metalinguistic discussion about language. Students come to understand the internal workings of a particular language (e.g., Spanish or English), and they come to understand how those languages are similar to or different from one another. This results in a self-extending linguistic system that gives students the tools and the knowledge to reflect upon and use language in ways that are unique to bilingual learners and proffers them a long-term linguistic advantage. We cannot emphasize strongly enough that consistency of implementation and complexity of passages matter. While we recommend alternating weeks by language and that theDictado be implemented three times per week, we also want to remind the reader that theDictado is not the entirety of the writing program. It should take no longer than 20 minutes a day and should comprise a small, but specific part of the biliteracy instruction. Ultimately, the lessons learned through theDictado should be acquired such that students can employ them in their independent writing. After all, the goal is not to get good at doing dictados; it is to nurture and develop competent bilingual writers.

Questions for Reflection and Action

- Select writings samples from three of your students. Be sure you have samples in both languages. Using the analytic framework, analyze the students' use of sentence structures, transition words and phrases, vocabulary words, punctuation, and spelling. What do you notice that is similar across students? Write one dictado in Spanish and one dictado in English that will elevate students' writing and meet the needs of all three students.
- Discuss with a colleague why theDictado must be encoded by the teacher each day during the talk-through.

4 Nurturing Biliteracy in Emerging Writers in Kindergarten

"Los niños son seres que ignoran que deben pedir permiso para empezar a aprender."
—Emilia Ferreiro, 1991

Key Terms

Collaborative writing	Early biliterate writing development
Concept of word	Modeled writing
Cuaderno	Shared writing

Guiding Questions

- What is the potential in kindergartners' biliterate writing in paired literacy contexts?
- How can different pedagogical approaches be used to embark kindergarteners on their biliterate writing trajectory?
- In what ways can we honor young EB children's cultural, linguistic, and experiential knowledge as they enter school, oftentimes for the first time, through paired literacy instruction?

When should we begin to teach young EB children to write in both Spanish and English? Won't they be confused if they learn literacy in two languages? What if they don't know how to hold a pencil? Can we use the Literacy Squared Writing Rubric to assess our kindergartners' writing? Should we even teach writing in kindergarten at all? These are some of the many questions we have been asked across the years and that we will address in this chapter.

Young EB learners come into kindergarten with varying understandings and abilities in literacy in both languages, oftentimes without formal schooling or explicit instruction. Young bilingual children learn about literacy from their daily experiences with others in their homes and communities. They also recognize and make determinations about language use when interpreting and reading environmental print. For example, when we asked preschool Spanish-English bilinguals to read labels and signs (e.g., Walmart bags, tortilla wrappers, and tubes of toothpaste), they did so by using the language associated with the function of the item. These literacy skills and abilities are important to consider when understanding young children as they come into our classrooms.

Research in alphabetic languages has demonstrated young children progress in a typical sequence in writing (e.g., Clay, 1975; Ferreiro & Teberosky, 1982); however, each child progresses through this sequence with great variability. For children learning two or more languages and literacy systems, it is important to consider the whole child and the totality of knowledge they bring from their experiences with language, print, and interactions with others. In fact, without much direct instruction, young simultaneous bilingual children demonstrate the ability to write in two languages (Snow et al., 2015; Soltero-González & Butvilofsky, 2015).

We encourage biliteracy instruction in kindergarten to be founded upon asset-based views of what young bilingual children know about literacy, as well as an understanding of how their social and cultural experiences outside of school inform their overall knowledge. We believe that sound biliteracy instruction will support teachers and schools in meeting state and district standards. Through careful observation and assessment, teachers can create developmentally, culturally, and linguistically appropriate methods to build children's confidence in the process of becoming bilingual and biliterate. Further, when children have authentic opportunities to engage in semiotic representations with purpose, they become active contributors to the teaching and learning process.

RESEARCH SUPPORTING BILITERATE WRITING INSTRUCTION IN KINDERGARTEN

In 2009, Literacy Squared began working in kindergarten classrooms in the states of Colorado and Oregon. Although not surprised, we were thrilled with young bilingual children's abilities to learn and develop writing in both languages. We also documented children's positive biliteracy trajectory results when paired literacy instruction was introduced in kindergarten (Butvilofsky et al., 2017; Hopewell et al., 2016). In a longitudinal study by Butvilofsky and colleagues (2016), the cohort of children who started all components of the Holistic Biliteracy Framework in kindergarten demonstrated, on average, higher overall writing results in Spanish and English in first and second grade when compared to cohort groups that started paired literacy in first or second grade.

When we first started Literacy Squared in kindergarten, we only collected Spanish writing samples and did not collect English samples from kindergarten classrooms for research purposes. We recommended modeled, shared, collaborative and independent instructional writing practices in Spanish, and primarily modeled and shared writing practices in English; additional guidance for these instructional practices is provided later in this chapter. Motivated by findings from a replication of Ferreiro and Teberosky's (1979) work (Soltero-González & Butvilofsky, 2015), we later began collecting writing samples from kindergarten classrooms in both languages for research purposes from an urban school district in Colorado. At this site, we also decided to collect writing samples at the beginning, middle, and end of the year. This data collection procedure provided greater insight into learning how kindergarten children took up biliterate writing at various points in the school year, instead of viewing kindergarten writing from only one point in time and just in Spanish.

Utilizing the Literacy Squared Biliterate Writing Rubric, we were able to document kindergartners' progression of writing development from entrance to the end of kindergarten in both Spanish and English, as indicated in Table 4.1 (Butvilofsky et al., 2016). At the beginning of the year, almost all kindergartners produced a drawing in both languages in response to the language of the prompt given, with an average content score of 1.2 (out of a possible 10). Some children attempted to write some sounds or syllables in words scoring at levels 0 to 2 in spelling, and there was minimal use of structural elements, or SE (scoring 0). By January of their kindergarten year, the children were expressing at least one complete thought (content level 3),

Table 4.1. Kindergarten students' biliterate writing outcomes, 2015–2016

	n	Spanish					English				
		Content	SE	Spell	Overall	SD	Content	SE	Spell	Overall	SD
Aggregate	75										
Fall		1.2	0.1	0.5	1.9	1.9	1.1	0.3	0.2	1.4	1.4
Winter		2.8	1.1	2.8	6.7	3.3	2.9	1.3	2.7	6.9	3.2
Spring		3.7	1.3	2.7	7.7	3.9	3.6	1.4	2.2	7.2	3.4

using a subject and verb when writing in both languages. They also included, at least one form of punctuation, usually periods (scoring a 1 for structural elements), and they incorporated their phonetic knowledge to represent most sounds in words. By the end of the year, most kindergartners were able to express two ideas (content level 4) in both Spanish and English, they continued to use at least one punctuation mark (SE level 1 or 2), and they encoded words using invented spellings (level 3 or 4).

PROFILES IN BILITERACY: A NUANCED ANALYSIS OF EARLY BILITERATE WRITING

In this section, we provide student samples that illustrate the variability and progression of **early biliterate writing development** as demonstrated by EB kindergarteners participating in Literacy Squared classrooms. Early biliterate writing development means that EB children progress, in both of their languages, through typical stages of writing development in alphabetic languages—drawing, writing letter strings that do not represent sounds, beginning to write letters that do represent some salient sounds in words, and finally, alphabetic writing in which there is nearly a one-to-one correspondence between sounds and letters. From the earliest stages of their writing, these children are becoming biliterate.

As found in biliterate writing research conducted by others (Durán, 2017; Gort, 2006; Soltero-González & Butvilofsky, 2015) the children in Literacy Squared classrooms developed their writing abilities similarly across languages as will be described below. For each of the paired samples, we present the quantitative scores from the Literacy Squared Writing Rubric, to illustrate the rubric's utility in that it can be applied as early as kindergarten and to capture growth and inform instruction (see Escamilla et al., 2014, Chapter 7 for detailed explanation of the rubric; see also Chapter 1 Appendix). As you read and interpret these quantitative scores, keep in mind that students can score up to 10 in content development, up to 5 in structural elements, and up to 6 in spelling; for detailed explanation of what different scores mean, see the rubric in the Chapter 1 Appendix.

Stage 1: Drawing Represents Writing

Since beginning our research with kindergarten children and collecting their writing samples via writing prompts, we have observed children demonstrate variability in their ability to represent meaning via the semiotic system of symbolism through drawing, scribbles, and the alphabetic principle.

The earliest representations of writing presented by children in the Literacy Squared project have been through the form of drawing, as illustrated in the biliterate writing samples of Lizeth shown in Figure 4.1. At this stage of writing development, drawing stands for writing. Upon closer analysis, Lizeth's Spanish sample has both a drawing that represents the members of her family, and a character/letter above each of the persons drawn, which most likely represents their names. The Spanish sample demonstrates Lizeth's initial emerging knowledge of letters representing sounds. In her English sample, it is clear Lizeth understands the prompt, as her drawing contains a house and other details that surround the house, a sun, tree, a small animal creature, and possibly herself. While we were not present for this production, we might expect that Lizeth would read her drawing as if it has a written message.

Stage 2: Child Produces a String of Letters

As children's understanding of print increases, so does their capacity to produce letters and letter-like forms. At this stage of writing development, writing and drawing may be the same, in that the child will draw and produce strings of characters or letters; however, there is no connection between the letters written and the sounds the letters represent. In other words, the reader cannot interpret the message as written.

While the child may not have letter–sound correspondence, the child knows print carries the message. This understanding is represented in Carolina's samples in Figure 4.2, where her

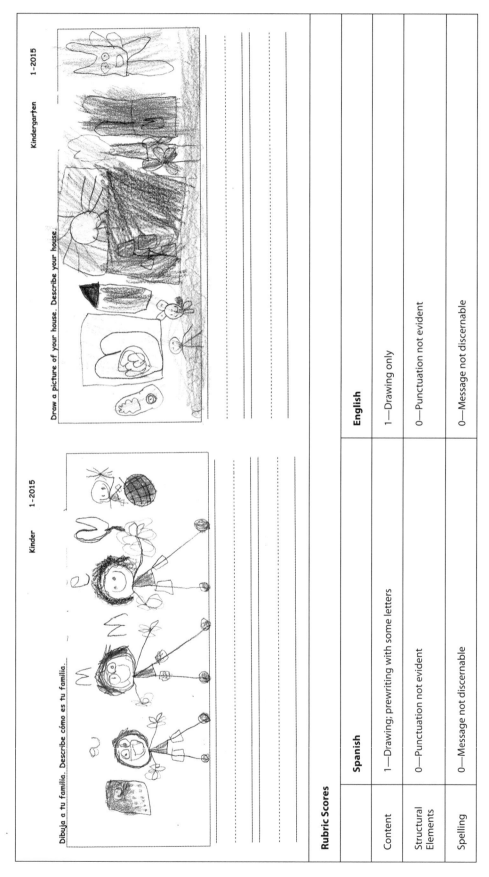

Figure 4.1. Drawing represents writing. Samples produced by Lizeth.

Nurturing Biliteracy in Emerging Writers in Kindergarten

Figure 4.2. Strings of letters. Samples produced by Carolina.

illustrations provide a response to the prompt, and she writes a string of letters in each language. Although we do not require students to narrate or interpret their writing for the actual prompts, Carolina's teacher recorded her dictated message. In Spanish, the child said her favorite place is, "*La pool porque está soleado*" (The pool because it is sunny). In English, the teacher recorded the following in response to the prompt asking about the child's favorite game at recess: "I like to play marbles at recess with my friends because it is fun."

At this and the previous level of writing development, it is important that teachers closely observe children as they draw and encode to understand which behaviors they may be exhibiting. It could be that Carolina is at a more advanced level of conceptualizing writing if she is breaking words into syllables or phonemes, and thus each character/letter represents a syllable or sound. This level of development is higher than just interpreting a string of letters. Thus, it is important to remember that the numeric score cannot provide the whole story of the child's writing knowledge. Both Lizeth and Carolina scored a 1 in content in each language, but that should not be interpreted to mean that they possess the same understanding of writing.

Stage 3: Child Writes Salient and Beginning Sounds or Represents Syllables

As soon as children understand letters represent sounds, they may begin representing salient sounds they hear in spoken language through writing. This level of encoding signals children's beginning understanding of alphabetic knowledge, although the **concept of word** may not be developed. In some cases, they may represent initial sounds for each word or for each syllable. They often use invented spelling based on phonological knowledge.

In the initial stages of writing development in Spanish, children typically identify and represent vowel sounds in their writing; while in English, children usually begin representing consonants. This stage in writing is especially evident in David's English sample in Figure 4.3, where the nine letters he had written express the message, "I like to play basketball," which the teacher had encoded from the child's dictation. In analyzing this writing, we observe that David identified the salient consonant sounds in the words <u>t</u>o <u>p</u>lay <u>b</u>asket<u>b</u>all, and approximated the spelling of the word *like* with "lec." Similarly, in Spanish, David represented a few graphemes for his message which he later dictated to his teacher, "<u>E</u>n <u>un</u> la<u>go</u> <u>p</u>or<u>que</u> puedes <u>n</u>adar" (In a lake because you can swim.). As illustrated in the previous samples presented (Figure 4.2), David's writing abilities are comparable across languages. However, if the teacher had not written his message, it would be difficult to infer the meaning from the letters written. Hence, it is necessary to *be observant and talk with the child* as they write, for it is hard to interpret what they know at these early stages of writing development if they do not tell us orally. David also demonstrates an understanding that a sentence begins with a capital letter in both samples, and in the English sample, he placed a period at the end of his writing. Because this child was in a Literacy Squared classroom, where writing samples were collected in both languages, we can appreciate the totality of his abilities and ensure instruction is based on his potential.

Stage 4: Child Learns Alphabetic Writing

When children enter the alphabetic stage of writing (see Figure 4.4), they have established a nearly one-to-one correspondence between sounds and letters, although spelling may be unconventional. At this stage of writing, the concept of word is still developing and thus children may be joining words together *(jaydensic/*hide and seek*)* or they may be taking words apart at the syllable level *(con migo/conmigo* [with me]*)*. EB learners will also draw upon knowledge from one phonetic system, such as Spanish, and apply that knowledge to encode words in English. In examining Salome's English sample in Figure 4.4, she writes the /j/ in Spanish to represent the /h/ in the word *hide*, because the /h/ in Spanish is silent. Further, the child used the /ay/ from Spanish to represent the long /i/ in English, as it phonetically and orthographically makes sense. This transfer of knowledge, while not standard, demonstrates EB children's expansive phonemic and phonological knowledge. What the child needs, then, is to learn the appropriate phonetic/orthographic representation in English. This necessitates explicit instruction, which can occur

Nurturing Biliteracy in Emerging Writers in Kindergarten

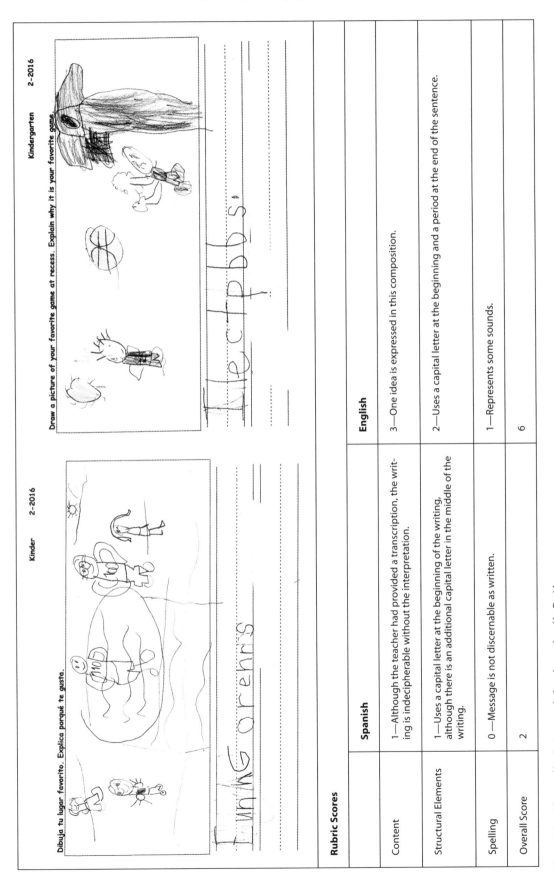

Figure 4.3. Salient and beginning sounds. Samples produced by David.

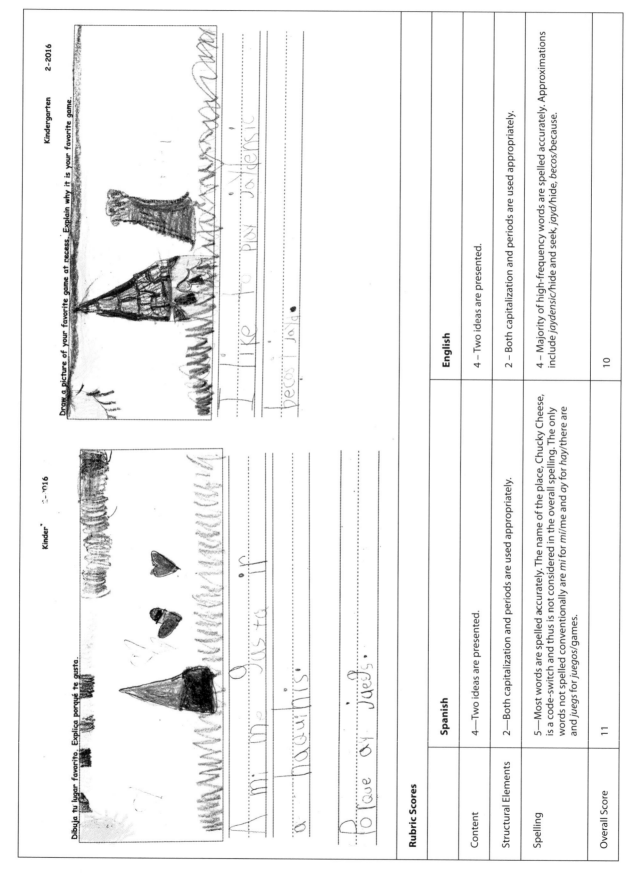

Figure 4.4. Alphabetic stage. Samples produced by Salome.

through theDictado (see Escamilla et al., 2014; and Chapter 3 of this book for specific directions on how to implement this strategy), as well as many opportunities to write and read in both languages.

As illustrated in the several writing samples presented here by EB children in kindergarten, we can observe the range of writing skills and knowledge the children display. What is remarkable, though, is how their abilities are quite comparable across languages. It is also important to remember to consider the totality of what the children can do across languages, especially for the majority of children entering U.S. schools who have been exposed to both Spanish and English. While they may not have had many formal literacy opportunities, they have had ample opportunities and exposure to various forms of literacy that we need to account for when we seek to understand all they know.

The Biliterate Writing Trajectory: Kindergarten

The writing samples from Lizeth, Carolina, David, and Salome, all EB learners, illustrate a range of writing development achieved in Spanish and English as they engage in biliteracy instruction. Children's earliest writing attempts do not always result in a discernable written message; however drawing and scribbling in their earliest form represent meaning and should be considered as such. Later, they begin using letter strings, first randomly and then representing specific sounds/syllables; drawing and writing convey ideas with increasing clarity; and children begin to use one or more structural elements with greater control. Writing samples for all four of these emerging writers illustrate how they are emerging as *biliterate writers* with comparable skill development in both Spanish and English. Young emergent biliterate writers use their full linguistic, cultural, and experiential knowledge to communicate messages, and they are not confused when expressing themselves through their biliterate writing. Using a holistic bilingual lens, it is essential to understand how young EB children demonstrate their knowledge of writing across languages through asset-based perceptions. This is the starting point of their trajectory toward biliteracy.

INSTRUCTIONAL IMPLICATIONS

In what follows, we propose authentic, meaningful, and integrated instructional approaches to build upon the literacy knowledge young EB learners bring to school, as well as opportunities to develop this knowledge in both Spanish and English via paired literacy instruction. We also want to emphasize the important role writing plays in literacy development as writing should be given equal importance to reading in the primary grades (Graham, 2020; Jiménez et al., 2003). Thus, we promote purposeful writing via modeled and shared approaches that are intricately connected to reading. In addition, we emphasize the importance of engaging children in shared reading experiences, interactive story reading and telling, and the use of *rimas/canciones* (poems/songs) during biliteracy instruction. These writing and reading approaches are natural and authentic means to engage children in developing early literacy skills such as concepts about print, oral language and oracy development (see Chapters 1 and 2 for more on oracy), and phonemic and phonological awareness; and they serve as springboards for developing reading and writing.

DAILY WRITING INSTRUCTION IN BOTH SPANISH LITERACY AND LITERACY-BASED ELD

Using our analyses of kindergarteners' biliterate writing samples, we have several recommendations for providing biliterate writing instruction in kindergarten. As was evident in the previous samples, all children produced a drawing and/or writing in *both* languages, meaning it is appropriate to provide writing instruction and opportunities to write in Spanish literacy *and* literacy-based ELD. Thus, we maintain that teachers should have high expectations of kindergartners because they can and should write every day in both languages. To begin, we recommend committing to, at a minimum, 30 minutes of daily writing instruction, with at least 15 to 30 minutes in Spanish literacy and 10 to 20 minutes in literacy-based ELD. In addition, we encourage opportunities for writing in the other content areas.

This daily writing instruction in both languages should include certain important elements, discussed below: a meaningful real-world purpose and foundational writing skills.

Meaningful and Authentic Purpose for Writing

Regardless of children's previous learning opportunities and emerging abilities upon entry into kindergarten, we firmly maintain that all writing opportunities be meaningful and serve a purpose. Identifying the *purpose* and *audience* for writing provides the young writer context and connection to the reader for using the productive domain of writing. As we observed in the above writing samples, when children entered kindergarten, the majority had the foundational understanding that, through the semiotic representation of drawing, they were communicating their ideas. Working from this foundation then, all writing activities are grounded in demonstrating how writing serves a communicative function in both languages. When writing has a real-world purpose, all the foundational aspects of writing can be integrated and are not treated as prerequisites for biliterate writing instruction. To further promote meaningful writing instruction, we encourage the use of culturally responsive pedagogies (Paris & Alim, 2014, 2017), texts, and purposes for writing. Culturally responsive practices emphasize the inclusion of students' culture *and* language to promote social justice and equitable learning opportunities. When children see themselves in the materials used in school and they can draw on their full linguistic repertoire, it encourages learning. Creating meaningful purposes and functions for writing also motivates the communicative function of writing (see Chapter 6 for more ideas).

Foundational Writing Skills

Foundational aspects of writing that should be addressed and taught in kindergarten within paired writing instruction include learning to hold a writing instrument; efficient letter formation to facilitate fluency and readability; phonemic and phonological awareness, spelling/phonics instruction; idea development/sentence construction; and beginning and ending punctuation. Additionally, when available, young learners should be provided opportunities to use technology such as tablets, laptops, and desktop computers for multiple purposes in producing writing and visual information (e.g., drawing, graphics, etc.).

Kindergartners should be exposed to writing instruction from the beginning of their entry to school, despite not being able to recognize or produce letter sounds or names. As explained previously, the foundation for producing and interpreting print is based upon the child's ability to interpret symbols, such as those found in environmental print, and produce meaning, through drawing and print-like symbols or letters. What is essential is that the focus for writing is on meaning. Thus, one of the first words young children often produce is their name, followed by names of family members (e.g., *mamá*, mom, etc.). Through this knowledge, foundational aspects of print can be taught and learned. Considering this, we emphasize teaching from the whole to part. These skills can be taught holistically via our recommended approaches: modeled, shared, collaborative, and independent writing; theDictado; and time set aside for word work that is meaningfully connected to other spoken or written texts.

Phonological Awareness in Biliteracy Instruction
Across time, we have been asked, in what ways should phonological awareness be taught within paired literacy instruction? Based upon research, young EB learners are able to transfer their phonological awareness from one language to the other. In kindergarten, we recommend teaching phonological awareness skills in Spanish literacy in ways that are authentic to Spanish. In developing phonological awareness in Spanish, emphasis is placed upon the ability to manipulate syllables. To reiterate, though, this work is done from the whole to part and returning again to the whole (e.g., word, syllable, phoneme,

word). As an example, we would work on identifying the syllables in the word *mariposa, ma-ri-po-sa*, (butterfly) and *not start* from the syllable to the word. Other meaningful ways to teach phonological awareness are through the use of songs and rhymes, and of course in daily writing instruction via modeled and shared writing. As these concepts and skills are developing in Spanish, attention can be given to applying them in English, signaling similarities and differences. (For authentic Spanish materials, visit LiteracySquared.org and find the *Ficheros* (files) under the Resources tab.)

Pedagogical Approaches in Writing for Kindergarten

In *Biliteracy from the Start: Literacy Squared in Action*, we propose a pedagogical model and teaching approaches for the development of biliteracy (Escamilla et al., 2014, p. 11), wherein we provide suggestions for teaching modeled, shared, collaborative, and independent writing in both Spanish and English across grades (Escamilla et al., pp. 53–57). These steps are listed in brief below and explained further throughout the chapter.

Steps for Implementing the Teaching Approaches to Develop Biliterate Writing

- Activate background knowledge by engaging children in a dialogue about their personal experiences related to the topic.

- Negotiate the text by setting the purpose for writing and identifying the audience. Explain what will be written and the structure.

- Compose the text while explicitly explaining the writing skills/process being taught and emphasize the language being used. Draw attention to metalanguage within and across languages. Provide students opportunities to discuss what they observe in the modeled writing.

- Revise and edit the writing. Take time to reread the text with the students to make sure it is comprehensible. Revise to include more precise language and to expand the complexity of sentences. Edit the text in order to maintain the structure of the genre, as well as for general conventions, spelling, and mechanics.

- Extend the learning by providing opportunities for students to view the text and analyze the purpose, structure, message, and audience.

In kindergarten, the different approaches provide varying levels of support depending upon the children's knowledge of print awareness, language abilities, and of course, writing abilities across languages. Instructional decisions are based upon children's experience and abilities viewed holistically across languages. Table 4.2 provides a summary of the different levels of writing development demonstrated in the previous student samples, along with goals and instructional scaffolds that can be integrated during writing instruction in both language environments. An important reminder: while we encourage the use of all approaches, including all of them in a unit or lesson is not required. Rather, the approaches are used to ensure students are successful with the anticipated outcome.

Modeled Writing   **Modeled writing** in both Spanish literacy and literacy-based ELD involves the teacher planning and demonstrating the process and purpose for writing; the teacher can also use modeling to demonstrate the multiple uses of writing as a communicative and learning tool, as will be discussed in later chapters. In modeled writing, the teacher encodes the message and students watch as they participate orally in the composition of the written piece. The text produced by the teacher is at a higher level than what the students could independently compose.

Table 4.2. Early writing development, goals, and instructional scaffolds

Level of development	Goals for children	Scaffold—Supports within writing instruction
Drawing represents writing	• Distinguish between drawing and writing • Write name • Begin using letters (especially from name) and letter-like symbols to represent language	• Emphasize that words can be encoded in writing differentiating between drawing and print • Within shared writing, share the pen when a known sound/letter needs to be written • Provide opportunities for child to dictate stories to an adult and encode their words
Strings of letters	• Begin identifying salient sounds in words, such as vowels in Spanish and consonants in English • Develop ability to distinguish the concept of word in spoken language • Learn meaningful words	• Help child identify known sounds and letters in reading and writing • Encourage writing known sounds/letters to represent words • Count the number of words when encoding messages • Reinforce writing of known words, especially name
Salient sounds/ Syllabic stage	• Identify more phonemes within syllables and match to graphemes (use invented spelling) to write complete words • Understand concept of word in print with spaces between words	• Use horizontal lines to represent the number of words being written • Enunciate words syllabically and help identify known sounds in modeled/shared writing
Alphabetic	• Learn high-frequency words in both Spanish and English • Begin learning English spelling patterns • Solidify concept of word	• Reinforce similar letter-sound correspondence in Spanish and English to make cross-linguistic connections • Begin introducing different letter-sound correspondence across languages

From Cabell, S. Q., Tortorelli, L. S., & Gerde, H. K. (2013). How do I write . . . ? Scaffolding preschoolers' early writing skills. *The Reading Teacher, 66*(8), 650–659; adapted by permission.

Within the kindergarten classroom, modeled writing serves as a means to demonstrate how language is encoded in print. That is, modeled writing establishes the knowledge that what is said can be encoded or written down using graphemes to represent the oral sounds of language. Further, we want to establish that everything that is written can also be read. While the main purpose of writing is to communicate ideas and messages, other foundational skills can be taught in an integrated manner. It is important to note that modeled writing is planned ahead of time by the teacher with specific instructional moves. These might include attention to teaching beginning and ending punctuation, teaching concepts about print (see Table 4.3), or developing metalinguistic awareness (e.g., identifying cognates, commonalities of grapheme–phoneme relationships between languages). Within a modeled writing lesson, the teacher is voicing their thought process and explicitly telling and showing children. The students are listening, following along, and asking questions. The writing produced by the teacher is usually above what the average child in the class can do independently and serves as a model for the students to reference.

Shared Writing   In **shared writing**, the teacher and students take turns constructing a written text together; all students in the class participate in the writing of the text. Shared writing in kindergarten reinforces the notion that speech can be recorded in print, and the product is an

Table 4.3. Teaching Concepts About Print During Writing

- Distinguish between pictures and words
- Directionality
  - Read and write from left to right
  - Return sweep
- Concept of word, spaces between words
- Letters/syllables make up words
- First/last letter
- First/last word
- Capital and lowercase letters
- Concept of sentence with ending period

Figure 4.5. Collaborative writing: Text feature of labeling in literacy-based ELD.

exemplar for the children's reference for writing and reading. Within kindergarten classrooms, we encourage daily shared writing opportunities. Shared writing is highly interactive in that the children and the teacher negotiate writing a text based upon a shared experience. Shared writing experiences are also fast-paced and include many opportunities for oracy development.

To make the writing experience shared, the teacher either shares the pen or has children write alongside her on small white boards or in their notebooks/*cuadernos*. The *cuaderno* is a place where children can record their ideas with teacher support and that also serves as a resource to be referenced again and again. If the teacher uses the strategy of sharing the pen to have children encode on the larger writing space (e.g., butcher paper, sentence strips, board), it is essential to know each child's abilities, so their contributions are productive. For example, if the message being written is, "*Mañana vamos al zoológico*" ("Tomorrow we are going to the zoo"), children who have knowledge of the letter *m* would be invited to write the letter *M* in *Mañana*.

Collaborative Writing In **collaborative writing**, children write with their peers and the teacher monitors their work, providing further assistance as needed. This approach encourages greater student involvement in the actual encoding, revising, editing, and publishing processes. It is also an opportunity for students to talk about what they intend to write.

In kindergarten, the purpose for collaborative writing is for children to have the opportunity to talk with one another, after having explicit instruction in oracy and writing, and the inclusion of realia, images, drawings, and other items to serve as mediating tools to guide their work. During this time, children are encouraged to produce writing jointly, which includes the use of drawing, labeling, dictating, and writing (see Figure 4.5). To promote active engagement, it is essential to group children heterogeneously, considering children's writing development as well as language abilities. Doing so, serves to ensure the collective product is scaffolded by peers. The teacher, paraeducator, or family volunteers can support as needed.

PAIRED LITERACY LESSON

To illustrate how to support biliterate writing development at the kindergarten level, we explain the various writing approaches suggested for kindergarten through a larger biliteracy unit, *Así soy yo*/All about me, that incorporates the comprehensive biliteracy framework (see Figure 1.1 in Chapter 1) and connections to children's lived experiences. In this biliteracy unit, we paired several texts in Spanish and English to create a cohesive unit that provides instruction in writing, reading, oracy and metalanguage (see Figure 4.6). However, we will only describe the writing portions of the lessons related to *Mi familia calaca*/My Skeleton Family in Spanish literacy and *Sundays on Fourth Street* in literacy-based ELD.

Pedagogical approaches	Spanish literacy	Literacy-based ELD
Interactive read aloud	*Mi Familia/My Family* by George Ancona. Children's Press, 2005.	*Sundays on Fourth Street / Los domingos en la calle Cuatro* by Amy Costales (author) and Elain Jerome (illustrator). Arte Publico Press, 2009.
Shared reading	*Mi Familia Calaca / My Skeleton Family* by Cynthia Weill (author) and Jesus Zarate (illustrator). Cinco Puntos Press, 2013.	*Things I Like* by Anthony Browne. Dragonfly Books, 1989. *My Family and I / My Familia Y Yo*, fourth edition, by Gladys Rosa-Mendoza (author), Carolina Cifuentes (editor), and Jackie Snider (illustrator). Me+mi Publishing, 2001.
Modeled, shared, collaborative, and independent writing	Informative text about family and descriptive text about family	Descriptive text of places visited on Sundays

Figure 4.6. Texts and pedagogical approaches used in *Así soy yo* biliteracy unit.

Lesson Overview

To frame the biliteracy unit, we worked from the Common Core State Standards (CCSS) for kindergarten as identified in Table 4.4. Unlike monoliteracy environments, within paired literacy instruction, the same or different standards can be addressed in each of the literacy environments. When addressing the same standard in both environments, we recommend doing the heavy lifting in Spanish and reinforcing the skill in the other language. In other words, it is not necessary to have to reteach a skill or standard in each language; rather, we remind children that we are reinforcing what is being used across languages, thus making cross-language connections. We would also like to note the importance of providing time and space to teach foundational skills that are authentic to each language. In this particular unit, we utilized songs and poems to reinforce phonological awareness and alphabetic knowledge in both environments. Again, we draw on the full linguistic and conceptual knowledge children have and build upon their resources instead of being duplicitous and redundant. We also distinguish similarities and differences across languages, thus developing young children's metalinguistic skills.

Spanish Literacy   The objective for Spanish writing in this lesson is for children to create a book similar to *Mi familia calaca*/My Skeleton Family by Cynthia Weill (Cinco Puntos Press, 2016), in which family members are identified and described with at least one adjective, similar to the way Anita, the main character in the book, describes the members of her family.

Table 4.4. Overview of Common Core Writing Standards and pedagogical approaches addressed in the kindergarten biliteracy unit, *Así soy yo*

	Spanish literacy	Literacy-based ELD
Standard	**CCSS.ELA-LITERACY.W.K.2**: Use a combination of drawing, dictating, and writing to compose informative/explanatory texts in which they name what they are writing about and supply some information about the topic.	**CCSS.ELA-LITERACY.W.K.3**: Use a combination of drawing, dictating, and writing to narrate a single event or several loosely linked events, tell about the events in the order in which they occurred, and provide a reaction to what happened.
Approaches	*Modeled, collaborative, and independent writing, based on a mentor text Preparing for theDictado via shared writing	*Modeled, shared and collaborative writing Preparing for theDictado via shared writing

© Copyright 2010 National Governors Association Center for Best Practices and Council of Chief State School Officers. All rights reserved.

For example, when Anita is describing her grandfather, she says, *"Mi abuelito. Él es tan tierno"* ("My grandfather. He is so sweet."). The children's books will be shared with the class so that they can learn about each other's families.

Shared Writing   To begin the lesson, the teacher introduces the book and conducts a shared reading of the text with the children, guiding them to focus on how Anita describes each person. After the reading, the children are asked to identify Anita's family members, *¿Quiénes son los familiares de Anita?* (Who are Anita's family members?) Once children have an opportunity to discuss this with their peers, the teacher engages in a shared writing. First, she asks children to name the characters as she places a picture of some of the characters on the chart (comparable to how children *write* ideas by drawing or choosing a picture). After identifying some of the characters, the teacher conducts a shared writing to encode the family members' names on the chart (see Figure 4.7). As the teacher begins, her focus is on having children identify

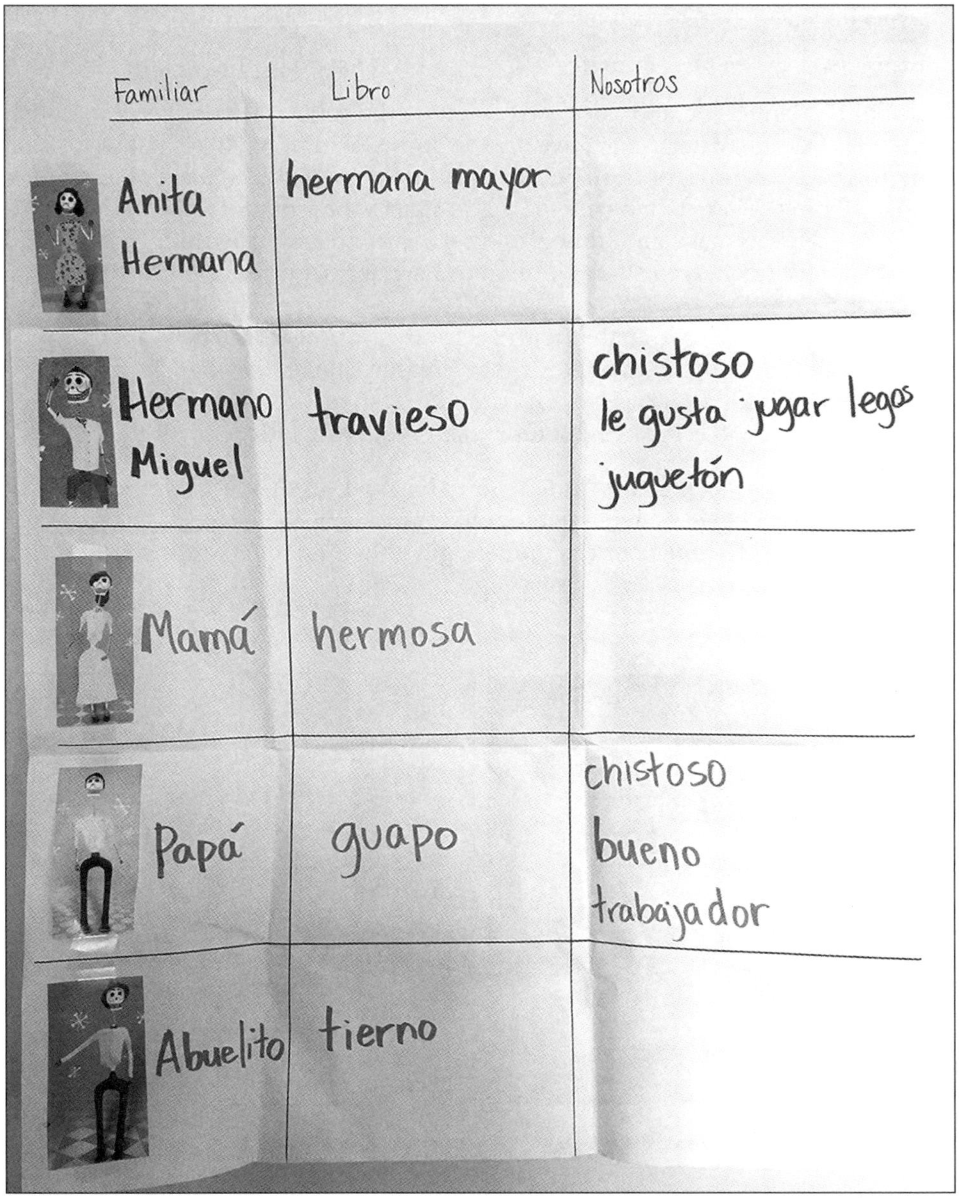

Familiar	Libro	Nosotros
Anita Hermana	hermana mayor	
Hermano Miguel	travieso	chistoso le gusta jugar legos juguetón
Mamá	hermosa	
Papá	guapo	chistoso bueno trabajador
Abuelito	tierno	

Figure 4.7. Chart with family members and descriptive words from the text, *Mi familia calaca*, and children's elicitations.

the syllables for each name, "*Vamos a escribir Anita. A ver, ¿cuántas sílabas tiene la palabra Anita? Díganlo conmigo. Todos, A-ni-ta.*" (We are going to write Anita. How many syllables does the word Anita have? Say it with me. Everyone, A-ni-ta.) The children say, "*tres*" (three) The teacher carries on, "*Muy bien, A-ni-ta. ¿Quién quiere ayudarme a escribir la primera parte, A?*" (Very well, A-ni-ta. Who wants to help me write the first part, A?) This continues until all of the names of the characters are identified.

To continue, the teacher then guides students to think about how Anita described the characters on the chart and has them interact with one another. "*¿Cómo es el hermano de Anita? Quiero que digan el nombre del personaje y cómo es, por ejemplo, El hermano es travieso.*" (What is Anita's brother like? I want you to say the name of the character and describe what they are like, for example, The brother is mischievous.) Once students have had time to talk, they come back and carry on with encoding the adjectives in their corresponding spot on the chart. To prepare students to think about their own family members, an additional oracy activity is conducted with the following questions and language structures.

- *¿Tienes un/una ____?* (Do you have a ____?)

- *Sí tengo un/a ____. O No, no tengo un/a ____.* (Yes, I have a ____. No, I do not have a ____.)

Pictures of the family members are used to guide the conversation between children (See Figure 4.8). It is extremely helpful to have various forms of manipulatives to assist young children. In this instance, the images of the characters in the book allow for children to clearly identify what/whom they are talking about. It also makes the workflow of children efficient, allowing time to focus on oracy and not on finding someone and something else to talk about. We would encourage teachers to allow children to have at least three opportunities to interact with classmates.

After the children have shared with each other, the teacher elicits their descriptions and writes the adjectives on the chart under the column labeled *nosotros*. To close the lesson, the teacher reminds children that they will write a book about their own family, and the words generated on the chart will serve as a resource when they write independently.

Modeled Writing   To prepare students for the creation of their family books, the teacher models the process of writing her own book. Once again, the book *Mi familia calaca* is read to situate the writing. The focus of the modeling will be in demonstrating how to use the chart created previously (Figure 4.7) as a reference for writing, as well as developing the concept of

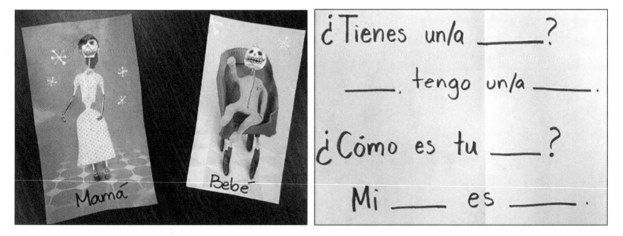

Figure 4.8.   Materials used for oracy activity related to describing the family members in children's families.

word for all levels of writing development. The modeling begins with the teacher identifying herself for the first page of the book. This empowers the students who are in the beginning stages of writing to use what they know, their name, in their writing. *"Para la primera página voy a escribir de mí, y decir, Hola, soy Sandra. Soy la hermana menor."* (For the first page of the book, I am going to write about myself. Hello, I am Sandra. I am the youngest sister.). The teacher carries on by having students restate the sentence and count the number of words. As the teacher begins to write, a horizontal line captures the number of words to be written. The second page, modeled for children, is for another family member, but this time reference is made to the chart to help describe that person. *Este es mi* ____. *Él es* ____. (This is my ____. He is ____.) (See Figure 4.9 for the teacher's final product). The structures used will be posted and can be copied, or a prewritten cloze can be created so all students at all levels of writing development can participate.

Independent Writing We cannot emphasize enough the need for children to have multiple purposeful opportunities to engage in writing every day within paired literacy. As illustrated in the previous description, through modeled and shared writing experiences, children would have acquired skills to apply to their own writing and literacy. For this unit, children would create a multiple-page text with related visual representations of themselves and at least two other family members for a book. As modeled by the selected text, *Mi familia calaca*, and the teacher's writing, children will create the text through the process of drafting, revising, and editing with adult support. Through the scaffolded writing and oracy opportunities, children have the support needed to reach the objective (see Figure 4.10).

Figure 4.9. Modeled writing of book about family members.

Figure 4.10. Scaffolded student sample of final product for book on family.

Literacy-Based ELD

To ensure children become biliterate, we recommend *daily* opportunities for writing in English as well as Spanish. It is not uncommon for educators to ask, how is it possible for children to write in English when they are also writing in Spanish? While not wanting to disregard such concerns, our response involves creating cohesive and coordinated ways in which to provide daily writing instruction and writing opportunities in both languages through paired literacy instruction. As teachers and students become accustomed to how the language environments within a biliteracy unit are organized, it becomes apparent how knowledge developed in both environments is mutually beneficial, as knowledge is shared and built to serve learning in both languages. Within the *Así soy yo* biliteracy unit for kindergarten, children will be exposed to a variety of writing opportunities alongside oracy.

In this unit, several books were read with different purposes; however, in this chapter we will provide details about the instruction emphasized with the text *Sundays on Fourth Street* by Amy Costales (Arte Público Press, 2009) to highlight the different pedagogical approaches for writing instruction. *Sundays on Fourth Street* is about a Mexican American girl who goes on an excursion to several places on Fourth Street with her family. The foci of the lesson with the text are for children to ask and answer questions about the text and to retell, both orally and in writing, several events from the story in chronological order.

Shared Writing   To begin this lesson, the teacher places a chart up with different images of places in the community, shown in Figure 4.11. Through an open dialogue, the teacher activates

Figure 4.11.   Map of the community to label with the children through shared writing.

the students' background knowledge of places within the community they may go to with their families on Sundays, as the book to be read is about a girl who goes to several places on Fourth Street with her family. The teacher provides the following question and language structures to lead dialogue between students:

- Where do you go with your family on Sundays? Who do you go with?

    Language structures (varied based on language proficiency):

- I go to ____. And you?
- I go to ____ with ____. How about you?
- On Sundays, I go to ____ with ____. How about you?

After children have opportunities to share their experiences with one another, they return to the whole group. Then, through shared writing, the teacher records the names of places the children mention on chart paper or on the community map, as they will return to this resource again for their own writing. (As a reminder, creating print-rich environments does not mean simply posting things on the wall, but rather it also includes providing resources that students help create, which they can use as they grow and develop in their literacy skills.)

The teacher then conducts an interactive read-aloud of the text, stopping to engage the students to reflect and respond to questions. After the reading, the children are assigned to small groups to retell the story using printed pictures from the text and temporal language: First/In the beginning, Second, Then, After, Last/At the end (of the day). The teacher provides the following questions and language structures to encourage talk:

- Where did the family go first?
    - First, they went to ____.
- Where did they go next?
    - ____, they went to ____.

Community, Cultural, and Social Connections: Kindergarten

Biliteracy instruction involves not only providing writing, reading, oracy and metalanguage instruction, but also opportunities for young EB children to develop their bilingual, biliterate, and bicultural identities. At this young age, we aim towards engendering wider community, cultural, and social connections. In this paired biliteracy unit, the reading and writing learning opportunities foster children's sense of themselves as part of a broader community beyond their family. In Spanish literacy, children learn and share more about themselves and their family; and in literacy-based ELD, they read and write about how they and their family are part of a community with whom they interact.

Modeled Writing   Images of the main events from the book are copied and distributed to facilitate the sequencing of events and to provide added support. Students are encouraged to work collaboratively and to use their full linguistic repertoires to retell the story using the images from the book. That is, while we encourage students to work in English, this is an opportunity for them to demonstrate their comprehension of the text; therefore, *we do not prohibit them from using Spanish while discussing with their peers.* Furthermore, grouping the children heterogeneously by language ability allows for children to scaffold one another. Once students have retold the main events chronologically, the groups come together, and the teacher conducts a modeled writing of two of the main events (see Figure 4.12) and creates a word bank of the places visited.

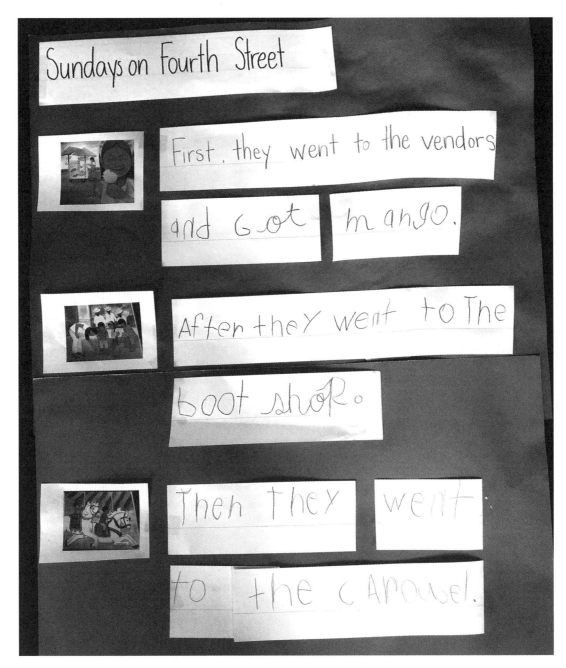

Figure 4.12. Modeled and collaborative writing with retell of main events from the book, *Sundays on Fourth Street*.

Collaborative Writing Once the model is created, students are sent back to their collaborative groups to write the other events on sentence strips using temporal words, the word bank, and language structures. One strategy to ensure all children are contributing during collaborative writing tasks is to assign a different colored pencil to each member of the group. This provides a visual reminder that everyone contributes to the task. The benefit of encouraging collaborative work with children is that they engage in talk, learn and support one another (see Figure 4.12).

Independent Writing While we do not recommend independent writing in literacy-based ELD in kindergarten, we had one of the project teachers in a research school have her students

Figure 4.13. Cristal's independent writing, *Sundays with My Family*.

create small books detailing what they do on Sundays. As can be seen in Figure 4.13, the student wrote independently because she had several scaffolds to work from to create her text, through oracy practice and through modeled, shared, and collaborative writing. Some children only drew pictures and dictated their stories for their teacher to encode; others encoded salient sounds; while others wrote full sentences independently. The value of providing supported independent practice is that the child's potential becomes visible, and appropriate instruction can be provided.

SUMMARY: BILITERATE WRITING IN KINDERGARTEN

In this chapter we provided an overview of the different profiles of early biliterate writing development in EB kindergarteners using the Literacy Squared Writing Rubric. We emphasize the importance of providing meaningful and integrated writing instruction daily in both Spanish and literacy-based ELD that are connected to culturally relevant texts. Shared writing in both environments is an efficient way to teach many concepts about print and other foundational biliteracy skills. We also emphasize that skills taught do not need to be taught twice, thereby making efficient use of the limited instructional time teachers have.

Questions for Reflection and Action

- In what ways can you collect writing samples from your kindergarten students and analyze them in a holistic manner using the Literacy Squared Writing Rubric?
- How can you use the information gleaned from the writing rubric and other observational data to inform biliterate writing instruction?
- How are the writing approaches described in this chapter different from the ways you provide writing instruction? How might you identify ways in which to incorporate some of the instructional approaches such as shared or collaborative writing in your paired literacy units/instruction?
- Given the diverse nature of your EB learners, how are you honoring their cultural funds of knowledge and developing a sense of community?

5 Cultivating Biliterate Writing in Grades 1 and 2

"Since childhoods vary in terms of communicative practices, there is no simple or singular pathway into literacy."

—Dyson, 2015

Key Term

Lotta Lara

Guiding Questions

▶ Why should increased emphasis be placed on writing in the teaching of EB learners?

▶ Why should direct and explicit approaches to teaching writing be emphasized over process approaches?

▶ How can an integrated approach to biliteracy be beneficial to teaching EB learners?

Within Literacy Squared, we honor the varied communicative practices of young EB learners, especially as they draw on their full linguistic repertoire to engage in biliteracy learning. As first graders learn to share their knowledge and their thoughts through biliterate writing, it is of importance to take an asset-based lens to understand the strategic ways in which they apply everything they know across languages.

In this chapter we present writing samples from EB children in first grade. As in the previous chapter, all of the children's samples are presented side-by-side as our focus is to examine biliteracy development. Our emphasis as always is on starting with the big picture, which in our view is what children are trying to communicate; then we provide a more detailed analysis. Most importantly, we always examine children's writing from an asset-based orientation. The student samples that follow illustrate these perspectives.

DIEGO'S STORY: BILITERACY IN GRADE 1

Diego was in the middle of first grade when the writing samples were collected in a Literacy Squared school in Colorado. He had been in a transitional bilingual program since kindergarten. Diego's Spanish and English writing samples are shown in Figure 5.1. The translation of Diego's Spanish sample is, "My favorite animal is the anaconda because it is super long and it has things on its head but they are its colors and they live in Africa."

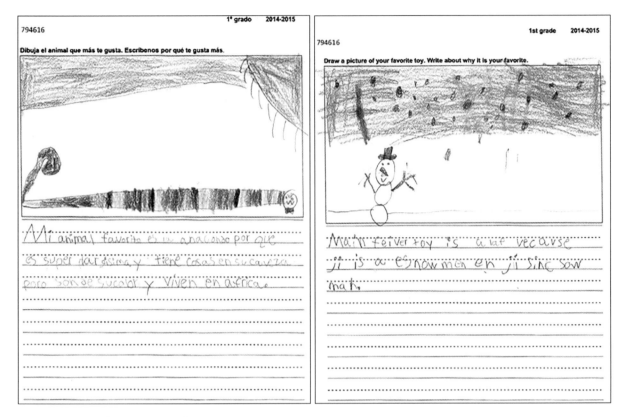

Figure 5.1. Diego's biliterate writing samples.

Diego's Developing Biliteracy

Our work with teachers has taught us that there are multiple viewpoints of Diego's biliteracy. One viewpoint would focus on misspelled words and errors in conventions in both languages. However, we would suggest that the reader start with what the child is trying to communicate. In Spanish, it is clear that he responded to the prompt asking about his favorite animal and provides a rationale for why the anaconda is his favorite animal. To begin, we note that Diego has the ability to communicate in writing with specificity. Rather than just write about a snake, he wrote about a specific type of snake, the anaconda, indicating a more precise way to identify his favorite animal. Additionally, he knows that the anaconda is indigenous to Africa. Further, in his description of the anaconda, he doesn't just use the language of *grande* (big) or *largo* (long), but he used the word *super larguisima* (very long) and he knows that this emphasizes his knowledge to the reader. A more conventional analysis of this writing might say that he wrote only one run-on sentence, he is missing accent marks, and he lacks knowledge of subject/verb agreement. Our position is not that this is unimportant; however our first point of entry is to view what the child can do and can communicate.

Because we are examining biliteracy, we also need to analyze the child's English writing, which will provide a more holistic understanding of the totality of writing abilities. Similar to the Spanish sample, Diego responds to the prompt in English by identifying his favorite toy and he includes a rationale. It is important to note that a bilingual lens is necessary to interpret Diego's English writing sample. Without such a lens, one could easily think the child is confused by two languages or very limited in English. Utilizing a bilingual lens, we can see how strategic Diego is in applying the totality of his writing knowledge to convey his message. Interestingly, his favorite toy is Olaf that comes from the movie "Frozen," which is a very popular children's movie. Important in this sample is Diego's ability to appropriately describe and name Olaf in that he knows he can "sing so much." Clearly, Diego can write to the prompts in both languages and provide a rationale for his favorite animal and toy. As with Spanish, however, a more conventional analysis might judge parts of his writing as unreadable (*main, ji, en, sinc, mah* for my, he, and, sings, and much). To reiterate, we support the idea that across time Diego needs to develop more conventional ways of spelling in English. However, his spelling approximations should not lead in concluding that he is a poor writer in English. He clearly can communicate a message if only we adults are skillful enough to read it and we read with a bilingual lens.

The Need to Examine the Child's Full Repertoire

Throughout this chapter we will emphasize and illustrate our belief that biliteracy in writing can only be understood by looking at the totality of the child's repertoire in Spanish and English. This is why we developed a side-by-side writing assessment tool (see the Chapter 1 Appendix for the Literacy Squared Writing Rubric and Escamilla et al., 2014) for a detailed description of the tool). Further, biliteracy in writing is absolutely dependent on children having frequent and varied opportunities to learn and write in both languages. Opportunities to learn include both direct instruction and teaching that is informed through continued observations of children's developing abilities across two languages. Our perspectives have been informed by years of observing and teaching in biliterate contexts. The remainder of the chapter will first provide a short summary of our research on biliterate writing from first grade, as well as representative student writing samples, followed by instructional suggestions for teaching writing in biliterate contexts.

GENERAL TRENDS IN BILITERATE WRITING IN GRADES 1 AND 2

The sections below discuss how biliterate children's writing evolves during first and second grade. We present quantitative data about how children's writing develops in the three major areas included on the Literacy Squared Writing Rubric: content, structural elements, and spelling. We also describe what a biliterate writing trajectory might look like across grades K–5.

Trends from Quantitative Results in Grades 1 and 2

Quantitative data across time have indicated that children's writing grows and develops between first and second grades in the areas of content, structural elements, and spelling. It is important to note that this occurs when children are in programs that value and teach in both Spanish and English. Table 5.1 below presents the mean score on the Literacy Squared Writing Rubric for first and second grades. The reader will note that the content score in Spanish increases from 4.2 to 5.1 over the course of two years, demonstrating that the mean score has improved from children writing two basic ideas around a prompt, to writing a main idea and several supporting details. During the same period of time, in English, children increased their content score from writing one idea, score of 3.4, to writing a main idea with supporting

Table 5.1. Snapshot Analysis of Writing Results from Aggregate Literacy Squared: Projects for Grades 1 to 2, 2009 to 2015.

Grade	n	Spanish					English				
		Content	SE	Spell	Overall	SD	Content	SE	Spell	Overall	SD
1	2,622	4.2	1.6	3.5	9.2	3.4	3.4	1.5	2.4	7.2	3.4
2	2,412	5.1	2	4.2	11.3	2.5	4.7	1.9	3.4	10	2.7

details, a score of 4.7. In content, children grew more in English than in Spanish, but what is most important is that across the years, children's abilities in writing are very similar, indicating developing biliteracy. The same trend is noted in structural elements and spelling for both languages. Children move from using one or more structural elements incorrectly to using one or more structural elements correctly. In spelling, they move from only representing some sounds in words to being able to represent sounds in most words by spelling the majority of high frequency words correctly. Composite /overall scores also increase from first to second grade, with children starting lower in English than Spanish but narrowing their scores between Spanish and English across time. Composite scores in Spanish grew from 9.2 to 11.3 and in English from 7.2 to 10.

Biliterate Writing Trajectories

We believe that if EB learners have opportunities to learn in biliterate contexts with attention to writing instruction in both Spanish and English they have the potential to expand their abilities across time. Unlike our work in biliterate reading, we have not established a formal writing trajectory. We have, though, hypothesized what a biliterate writing trajectory could look like based on our rubric, and many children's writing samples produced in the past. As illustrated in Figure 5.2, we can anticipate that children in general would perform with higher abilities in Spanish, and their English writing would only be slightly behind. The trajectory below represents a composite/overall score that includes content, structural elements and spelling and spans a range between 0 and 21.

In first grade we could expect children to score comparably in both content and structural elements, as we have seen the ability to express ideas and use punctuation is similar across languages. Thus, first graders should be writing an introduction or main idea with several ideas to support, which would be a level 5. We would also expect them to use beginning and ending punctuation and at least another form of punctuation in both Spanish and English, which would be at least a level 2 or 3 in structural elements. The greatest difference in the writing of first graders across languages would be spelling. We would expect children to have greater orthographic knowledge in Spanish than English.

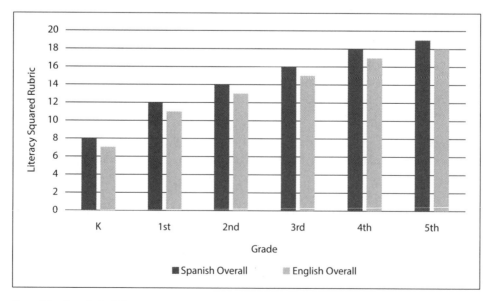

Figure 5.2. Hypothetical biliterate writing trajectory.

ABEL'S STORY: BILITERATE WRITING POTENTIAL IN GRADE 1

Abel attended first grade at a bilingual school on the Arizona/Mexico border. His Spanish and English writing samples are shown in Figure 5.3. The translation of Abel's Spanish sample is, "The animal that I like best is the mouse. I like the mouse because you can have one in your house. The mouse is small and cute. He eats cheese. He has two long front teeth. Mice are grey, black and white. If I had a mouse, his name would be 'sol.' Mice live in the jungle."

Rubric Analysis Using a Bilingual/Biliterate Lens

When viewed through a bilingual/biliterate lens, Abel's writing development can be evaluated as follows using the Literacy Squared Writing Rubric.

Content   When his Spanish writing was scored with the Literacy Squared Writing Rubric, he scored a 6 in content because he includes a main idea, and his writing includes many descriptive details related to his favorite animal: *tiene dos dientes largos enfrente; son de color gris, negros y blanco*. Similar to Abel's Spanish sample, in English, Abel responded to the prompt and wrote a lot of text. Abel scored a 6 in content in English because he identified a main idea—his favorite toy is a car. He provides many sentences describing the car.

Structural Elements   In reviewing both samples, it is clear Abel controls beginning and ending punctuation. However, in Spanish, he includes a comma to separate ideas in a list; thus he scores a 3 because he controls beginning and ending punctuation in ways that make sense, and he used an additional punctuation mark. In English he earned a 2 because he does not include additional punctuation beyond capital letters at the beginning of, and periods at the end of, sentences.

Spelling   For Spanish spelling, he earned a 5, because the majority of words are spelled accurately. Most approximations are developmental to Spanish, meaning a child in a Spanish-speaking country would have similar approximations. These approximations include the omission of accents on the word *ratón*/mouse and *sería*/would be; and the use of *b* for *v* as written in the words *biben/viven*/live and *selba/selva*/jungle. In English, Abel's spelling is approaching standardization and most high-frequency words are spelled correctly; thus he earned 4 points.

Trends from Qualitative Analysis Using a Bilingual/Biliterate Lens

Using the Qualitative Analysis section of the Literacy Squared Writing Rubric (see Chapter 1 Appendix), we examine the linguistic elements exhibited in Abel's writing across languages. The qualitative analysis also provides insight into the biliterate strategies EB children employ as they bring their full linguistic repertoire to the writing task. We can also understand how some abilities are present in one language and not the other, and how abilities may transfer.

Discourse   Looking across languages, we can observe Abel understands the genre of explanatory texts in both languages. In both samples, he provides the main idea that addresses the prompt and provides many details in support. He also writes about the same amount of text in both languages, but in English his supporting details are written in a list-like fashion, while in Spanish the sentences seem to be more cohesive, in that the ideas are related to one another. For example, the second sentence expresses that the mouse can be a pet, and the following sentence in a way expands the idea of a house pet because it explains they are small. In English, Abel includes a title to his composition, but he does not have one in the Spanish sample.

Sentence/Phrase Level   When examining Abel's writing at the sentence level, we see differences across languages. In Spanish, the sentences are more varied, in that a combination of

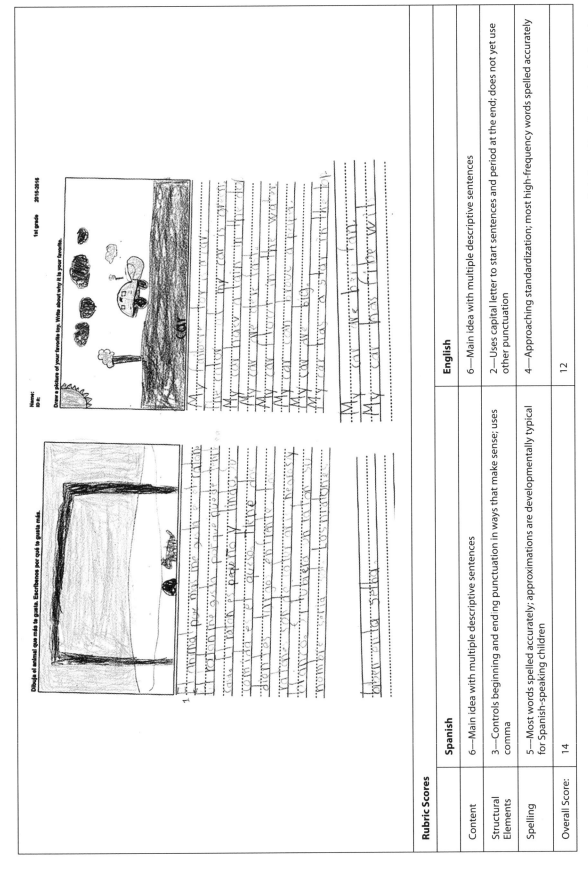

Figure 5.3. Abel's biliterate writing samples. Spanish Sample: *El animal que mas me gusta es el raton. El raton me gusta porque puedes tenrlo en casa. El raton es pequeño y lindo. Su comida es el queso. tiene dos dientes largos enfrente. Los ratones son de color gris, negros y blanco. Si tubiera un raton su nombre seria sol. Los ratones biben en la selba.*

simple, compound, and complex constructions are included. He also includes more complex syntax by using the conditional tense in the sentence, "*Si tubiera un raton su nombre seria sol.*" (If I had a mouse his name would be 'sol'.) In English though, the majority of Abel's sentences have a consistent structure that begins with "My car" and is followed with a description. In English, we also note the utilization of Spanish syntax when demonstrating possession: "the color of my car is green" instead of "My car is the color green." We note other syntactical approximations related to singular and plural noun/verb agreement, such as "My car are very fast" and "My car are big."

Phonics Level Abel has appropriate knowledge of the phonetic systems from both languages to encode words. There are a few instances in which he uses Spanish phonetics to encode words in English: the *ai* to represent /ī/ in *lain/line*; *ei* for /ā/ ; and the Spanish vowel *i* for *y* in *beri/very* and *ee* in *wheels*.

The Biliterate Writing Trajectory: Grade 1

The writing samples from Diego and Abel illustrate what the biliterate writing trajectory might look like for EB children in first grade through second grade. By this age, children have gained more control over the physical act of forming letters, along with a solid understanding of letter-sound relationships. This allows them to express ideas with greater nuance and in greater detail—as seen in both Diego's and Abel's writing samples. Their language becomes more precise and descriptive. They can begin to use a larger repertoire of sentence structures (syntax) and other structural elements with increasing control in both languages.

Remember, across grades, it is important to view children's writing through a lens that is biliterate and asset based. What are they *already doing*, or *attempting*, in one language that might help you better understand their writing in the other language?

INSTRUCTIONAL IMPLICATIONS

Within Literacy Squared we have always espoused an integrated approach to teaching reading, writing, oracy, and metalinguistic development. For that reason, we will discuss our implications for instruction based on larger units of paired literacy instruction. We also understand the need for teachers to teach to the standards defined in most of the country by the Common Core State Standards (CCSS). For this reason, we are presenting our implications for writing instruction as we would propose it being taught via a paired biliteracy unit.

To illustrate how we might support Abel and others to become better writers, we explain our writing strategies that would be taught as part of a larger paired biliteracy unit titled *Abuelita llena de vida*/Abuelita Full of Life. The children's bilingual book, *Abuelita llena de vida*, by Amy Costales (Cooper Square Publishing LLC, 2007), provides an excellent example of descriptive writing that illustrates concretely how main characters can be compared. In the paired biliteracy unit, the entire book was used as a mentor text in Spanish literacy, while in literacy-based ELD, we adapted the text for a shared/repeated Literacy Squared reading strategy, **Lotta Lara**. This strategy focuses on developing oracy through explicit planning and increasing reading fluency through repeated reading. The teacher uses the same book or text three times over a one-week period, in sessions of 20–40 minutes, with students reading the book a total of nine times. The teacher selects a text that is personally and culturally relevant, prereads the book and plans oracy objectives and instruction, and then does the multiple readings of the text, starting with one completed read-aloud and then using echo reading, choral reading, and partner reading, with explicit oracy and comprehension instruction throughout. (For more about Lotta Lara, see Escamilla et al., 2014, pp. 25–26.)

In the following lessons we illustrate how the texts were used as a tool to promote biliterate writing.

Modeled, Shared, and Independent Writing Approaches

In *Biliteracy from the Start: Literacy Squared in Action* (Escamilla et al., 2014), we propose a pedagogical model and teaching approaches for the development of biliteracy (p. 11) wherein we provide suggestions for teaching modeled, shared, collaborative, and independent writing in both Spanish and English across grades (pp. 53–57.). The different approaches provide varying levels of support depending upon the children's knowledge of genres, as well as their writing and language abilities. Not all approaches need to be included in each unit; however, some approaches may be repeated, with the end goal of ensuring children will be successful at meeting the literacy standards and objectives. Such instructional decisions are based upon children's experience and abilities viewed holistically across languages. Alongside teaching to the standards, we maintain that writing needs to be authentic and purposeful for children to tap into their potential. Thus, the use of culturally responsive texts and purposes for writing assist in this development, as do the approaches utilized.

In Table 5.2, we provide the CCSS literacy standards and the approaches utilized to teach to the standards presented in the biliteracy unit, *Abuelita llena de vida*. Because we believe that reading and writing are intricately connected, the main text that will be read in Spanish literacy will support teaching the standards, most importantly the writing standards. In the book *Abuelita llena de vida*, Amy Costales utilizes the literary element of simile and contrasting ideas to describe Abuelita. This element becomes central for developing children's conceptual knowledge of how to describe characters, but it is also used for writing their explanatory text, which will be related to writing about their own grandparent or important family member in Spanish. Thus, the book serves as the mentor text, and as the character is explored, the text is deconstructed and metalanguage is taught so that the children can write their own texts.

Spanish Modeled Writing   To begin the unit, we drew from the *Ficheros* from the *Secretaría de Educación Pública (SEP) de México* (1995) to teach antonyms (see Figure 5.4). In doing so, children can begin developing an understanding of the element of contrasting used in the book to describe Abuelita. With the teacher's guidance a list of descriptive words for people can be generated alongside an antonym, so that children can then draw from this list when they write their descriptive compositions about their own grandparents (see Table 5.3).

After the teacher has conducted an interactive reading of the book, children are asked questions to elicit descriptions of the main character and to begin to make some connections to their own grandparents. Language structures are purposefully taught so that children can begin utilizing the structures from the text as descriptive words that are contrasted:

Table 5.2. Overview of Grade 1 Biliteracy Unit, *Abuelita llena de vida*

	Spanish literacy (30 minutes)	Literacy-based ELD (30 minutes)
CCSS Standards	**CCSS.ELA-LITERACY.RL.1.3** Describe characters in a story using key details. Use illustrations and details in a story to describe its characters, setting, or events.	**CCSS.ELA-LITERACY.RL.1.9** Compare and contrast the experiences of characters in stories.
	CCSS.ELA-LITERACY.W.1.2 Write explanatory text in which you name a topic, supply some facts about the topic, and provide some sense of closure. **CCSS.ELA-LITERACY.W.1.5** With guidance and support from adults, focus on a topic, respond to questions, and add details to strengthen writing as needed.	**CCSS.ELA-LITERACY.W.1.1** Write opinion pieces in which you introduce the topic or name the book you are writing about, state an opinion, and supply supporting details.
Approaches	• Whole group interactive read aloud • Modeled, collaborative, and independent writing based on a mentor text • TheDictado	• Whole group shared reading and *Lotta Lara* (repeated reading) • Shared and collaborative writing • TheDictado

© Copyright 2010 National Governors Association Center for Best Practices and Council of Chief State School Officers. All rights reserved.

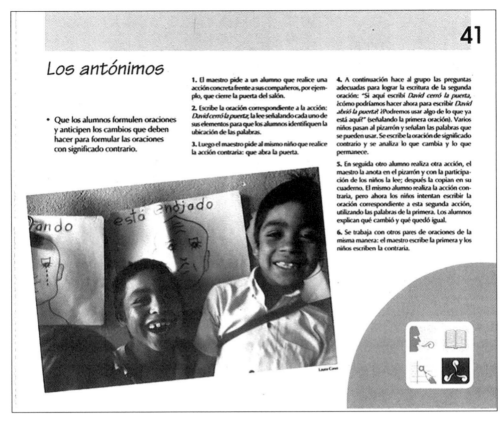

Figure 5.4. Fichero on antonyms. (Adapted from Fichero: Actividades Didáacticas Español primer grado. Pubished by Secretaría de Educación Pública, 1995.)

*Es **viejita**, pero es **vivaz**. Su piel está **arrugada**, pero es **suave** para besar. Ella es **frágil**, pero sus brazos son **fuertes**.* (She is old, but she is lively. Her skin is wrinkled, but soft to kiss. She is frail, but her hugs are strong.)

The teacher introduces a graphic organizer to deconstruct the ways in which the author describes the main character. This list includes how the character looks, what she does, and what she does with her grandson, José, who is instrumental in describing her. Through a modeled writing, the graphic organizer is filled out with the children's ideas recorded as they engage in dialogue (see Figure 5.5). The graphic organizer is used in the process of writing in that it will help children plan what it is they will write about.

From the graphic organizer, the teacher models how to write a description/explanatory text of Abuelita with children's input. Emphasis is given to utilizing the structure repeated in

Table 5.3. *Descripciones de los abuelos con antónimos* (Grandparent descriptions with antonyms)

Chistosa/o	Serio/a
Trabajador/a	Flojo/perezoso
Feliz/contenta/o	Enojón
Fuerte	Débil
Cocina rico	No sabe cocinar
Cariñosa/o	Reservada/o
Joven	Viejo, anciano, mayor de edad
Bajita/o	Alta/o
Gordita/o	Flaca/o

| Abuelita llena de vida |||
¿Cómo se ve?	¿Qué hace?	¿Qué hace con José?
• tiene trenzas largas • el pelo es color gris • tiene surcos alrededor de su boca • es viejita • tiene la piel arrugada	• cocina chiles • hace chocolate para José • siembra una huerta con chiles y tomates • le hace trenzas a la hermanita • cuenta frijoles con la hermanita • le escucha a José leer • persigue al paletero	• va al parque y compra helado y camina • baila • lee y cuenta cuentos a José • colorea • duerme en el mismo cuarto • canta

Figure 5.5. Graphic organizer of Abuelita.

the book, *Abuelita es _____, pero es _____*. Then, the teacher models how to include at least one description from each column, and how to combine ideas to make sentences more complex (see Figure 5.6). Through modeled writing, the teacher can elicit ideas from the children, but provides explicit instruction in how to extend writing and teach beyond children's current ability. This also includes teaching the process of writing, such as rereading to ensure cohesiveness, using appropriate spelling and extending children's use of punctuation. Expanding children's linguistic skills can and should be done during modeled and shared writing. For example, suppose the teacher asks the children to think of a sentence to describe Abuelita, and a child says, *"Ella es viejita"* (She is old). The teacher can elicit more language by asking, *"¿Puedes decir más? ¿Quién puede agregar más descripción?"* (Can you say more? Who can add more detail to this?) and another child responds, *"Tiene pelo gris"* ([She] has gray hair). The teacher could then demonstrate how to combine those ideas to create a compound sentence incorporating metalanguage, *"Ahora piensen en cómo podríamos unir esas dos ideas para crear una oración más compleja"* (Now let's think about how we could join those ideas to create a more complex sentence). A child remarks, *"Abuelita es viejita porque tiene pelo gris"* (Abuelita is old

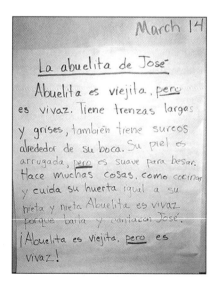

Figure 5.6. Modeled writing: La abuelita de José.

because she has gray hair). The teacher responds by pointing out that the word *porque* provides an explanation and reminds children that they need to do this in their own writing. Modeled/shared writing are opportunities for explicit instruction to expand students' languages and writing abilities.

The English translation of the writing shown in Figure 5.6 is as follows:

> José's Abuelita. Abuelita is old, but she is lively. She has long gray braids, she also has wrinkles around her mouth. Her skin is wrinkled but is soft to kiss. She does many things, like cook and care for her garden just like her grandchildren. Abuelita is lively because she dances and sings with José. Abuelita is old, but she is lively!

Spanish Collaborative Writing

To assist children in gaining the skills to write their independent descriptive/explanatory composition, the teacher gives them the opportunity to collaborate with another classmate or classmates to write a description of José, the other main character of the book *Abuelita llena de vida*. Although José is a main character, the author does not describe him in as great detail as Abuelita, so the children must infer some of his qualities from the book by using the illustrations. This skill is one of the CCSS standards and is addressed purposefully in this lesson. Children can be organized in pairs or triads to complete the graphic organizer on José (see Figures 5.7 and 5.8), and then given the opportunity to write a composition about him collaboratively or independently. As evident in the sample provided, the children were able to identify aspects of José in their writing and categorize them adequately. Looking at the child's independent composition in Figure 5.8, it is evident that he was able to incorporate the language structure of "*Aunque ____ es ____ es ____*", demonstrating his ability to select contrasting ideas and coordinate them.

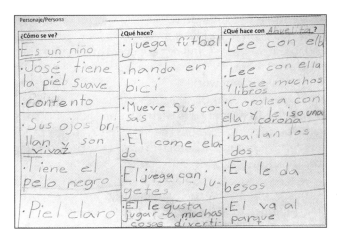

Figure 5.7. Student's graphic organizer of José from *Abuelita llena de vida*.

The child's composition shown in Figure 5.8 reads as follows in Spanish:

> José. Aunque José es jugueton es tierno. Tiene el pelo negro y la piel clara. Es un niño felis sus ojos brillan. José juega futbol y come chiles con su aduelita. Su aduelita es vibas pero Jose debe que moder sus cosas aun lado para que su aduela pueda cader y dormir. Aunque Jose es jugeton es tierno.

The English translation of this composition is as follows: José.

> Although José is playful he is kind. He has black hair and light skin. He a happy child and his eyes twinkle. José plays soccer and eats chiles with Abuelita. His Abuelita is lively but José has to move his things to the side so that his Abuelita can fit and sleep. Although José is playful he is kind.

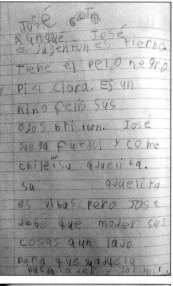

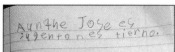

Figure 5.8. Student's collaborative writing.

Spanish Independent Writing Ultimately, the goal was for the first graders to be able to write a composition with the inclusion of a topic, some details, and some sense of closure. It is the modeled/shared and collaborative lessons and experiences that serve to improve children's independent writing. It is the explicit instruction, and clear guidance to connect what they were shown to implement in their independent work.

In Literacy Squared, we maintain the importance of ensuring instruction is culturally responsive. By having children interview their parents or grandparents to write about them, we deliberately connect home to school. The children were given the graphic organizer and interview questions to take home for homework, so that they could gather appropriate information for their composition. They were also asked to bring a photo of the person they were writing about.

As seen in Figures 5.9 and 5.10, the two children met the writing standard because they introduced the topic, provided details, and included a conclusion.

The English translation of the composition shown in Figure 5.9 is as follows:

My grandpa is nice. My grandpa Popis plays Mario videos and I win. My grandpa does not like his new clothes, but I like his clothes. He takes care of his donkey, his cow and his goat. My grandfather pinches my cheeks. He plays hide-n-seek with me. He looks handsome with his white hair. He is old but he plays with me.

The English translation of the composition shown in Figure 5.10 is as follows:

All About My Grandfather. My grandfather is old, but he takes care of his ranch. He liked to ride horses. My grandfather has a moustache and beard. My mom would stay with them and their grandparents. My grandfather is old, but he takes care of his ranch.

Through the use of a mentor text, modeled/shared, and collaborative writing, children have multiple opportunities to practice their writing skills.

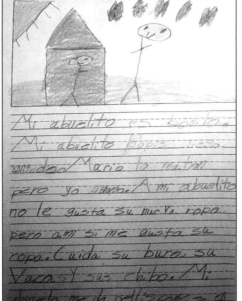
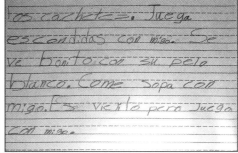

Escritura independiente

Figure 5.9. *Mi abuelito es bonito.*

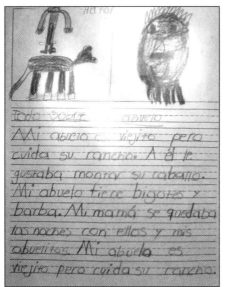

Escritura independiente

Figure 5.10. *Todo sobre mi abuelo.*

Community, Cultural, and Social Connections: Grade 1

When working with EB learners, we constantly need to remember to see them through a holistic lens: linguistically, culturally, and socially. In this unit, we asked first graders to learn more about their elders and brought that knowledge into the classroom community. In doing so, we are bridging home to school, thus valuing children's home community and their cultural and linguistic funds of knowledge. We also ensure children have meaningful opportunities within the classroom to learn with one another, through shared and collaborative writing approaches. As a result, social connections are amplified, and children have an opportunity to continue to develop their identities in the broader community. We encourage thoughtful choices around text selection, as well writing assignments, and pedagogical approaches as part of developing a bilingual, biliterate, and bicultural pedagogy.

Literacy-Based ELD

Developing biliteracy requires thoughtful attention to how instruction in both languages needs to be intentional to build upon the totality of children's literacy and linguistic strengths. Over the course of time, we have oftentimes observed teachers' hesitancy to provide writing instruction and/or opportunities to write in English. However, as we illustrated through the children's writing samples presented throughout this book, EB children transfer their skills across languages, and through explicit instruction are quite capable of producing writing in both languages. Through a holistic bilingual lens, teachers can draw upon the knowledge children exhibit across language to inform instruction. Reflecting upon Abel's samples presented at the beginning of the chapter, we see many abilities across languages. In English, though, instruction needs to focus upon the expansion of ideas and building complexity of sentences. Knowing he has those skills in Spanish, and the ability to encode and use other elements in English, the teacher can plan instruction to build upon this knowledge in English.

In Literacy-based ELD, the text from *Abuelita Full of Life* was adapted to avoid duplicity, to account for linguistic complexity, and to shorten the text (see adapted text in Figure 5.11). The adapted text would be read using the Lotta Lara reading strategy (see Escamilla et al, 2014, pp. 25–26). The English writing focus for this biliteracy unit includes a modeled retell and an opinion piece. Through shared and collaborative writing, children will identify their favorite character in the book, provide some details justifying their choice, and include an ending or conclusion indicating they understand the need for closure.

Because children understand the detailed text from the Spanish literacy environment, they bring that knowledge to the English environment. The modified English text provides the language structures in English to enable children to work on English grade-level standards, and the modified text in English to support this work. Most importantly, we believe that oracy instruction is essential to biliteracy instruction in writing, especially in literacy-based ELD. Thus, as the teacher leads the children through the lesson, oracy instruction supports the writing. The following example details how a teacher can use oracy to support the writing instruction.

Adapted text of Abuelita Full of Life

Abuelita is old, but she is lively.

Abuelita sleeps in Jose's bedroom. José has to move his things, but he doesn't mind one bit.

Abuelita plants a garden. José has to play soccer at the park, but he doesn't mind one bit.

Abuelita and José color together.

Abuelita and José read together.

Abuelita says she is too old to ride a bike, but she can chase the ice cream man.

Abuelita says she is too old to learn English, but she can talk to the bus driver.

Abuelita says she is too old for José's music, but she dances *reggaetón*.

Abuelita is old, but she is lively.

Figure 5.11. Adapted from Costales, A. (2007) Abuelita, Full of Life., (Martha Avilés, Illus.). Luna Rising.

Oracy to Prepare for Writing Activate prior knowledge about *Abuelita* by using what the children knew in Spanish and providing sentence stems to help them express what they know in Spanish in English. For example, the teacher could elicit information orally from children using the following sentence stem and keeping a writing list of children's responses. By keeping a list of the children's responses in English and Spanish the teacher can assess vocabulary related to description. (For the sake of linguistic and cultural authenticity, we chose not to change the word *abuelita* to *grandmother*.) Also, to build oracy for Literacy-based ELD we taught the song, "Grandma is Coming" to help build vocabulary and reading fluency, and we asked children to choose and describe their favorite character to build up their descriptive vocabulary and explicitly teach transformation from a question to a declarative sentence.

Language Structure:

- ▸ Abuelita is _____ (old, nice, busy, smart....) because_____.

Dialogue:

- ▸ Who is your favorite character and why?
- ▸ My favorite character is_____ because_____. How about you?
- ▸ Just like you, my favorite character is ____ because _____. Or
- ▸ Unlike you, my favorite character is _____ because _____.

Modeled Writing Utilizing the modeled writing approach in literacy-based ELD is important, as EB children need multiple opportunities to use language and see it encoded in meaningful ways. Modeled writing provides an opportunity for the teacher to guide children into purposeful writing while they co-construct the message. While children are providing input into what is written, the teacher has control of inserting specific teaching points.

After children read the adapted text through the Lotta Lara strategy multiple times, it is beneficial to dedicate attention to providing opportunities for children to retell the story orally and in writing. It is important to note that the children have the capacity to comprehend text, but need explicit and planned opportunities to learn how to retell in English. Thus, the inclusion of oracy and scaffolded dialogue related to retelling precedes the shared writing (see Figure 5.12 for scaffolded dialogue prompts).

Questions	Language Structures
Who are the main characters in *Abuelita Full of Life*?	The main characters in *Abuelita Full of Life* are ___ and ___.
What is Abuelita like?	Abuelita is ___ and ___. Can you tell me more about her?
• Provide bank of words: lively, old, strong, fun, silly, talkative	• Sure! Abuelita is ___.
What does Abuelita like to do?	Abuelita likes to ___ and ___. What else does she like to do?
• Provide pictures/bank of words: cook, garden, dance	• She **also** likes to ___.
What is José like?	José is ___ and ___. Can you tell me more about him?
• Provide bank of words: generous, kind, fun, bilingual, silly	• Yes! He is also ____.
What does José like to do?	José likes to ___ and ___. What else does he like to do?
• Provide bank of words: ride bikes, play soccer, dance, eat	• He also likes to ____.
What do Abuelita and José do together?	Abuelita and José like to ____ and ____. Or Together/both like to ___. Can you tell me more about them?
• Color, play, read	• Yes, they both like to _____
Do you know anyone like Abuelita or José? How are they similar?	Yes! I know ____. This person is like ___ because___. Do you know anyone like Abuelita or José?

Figure 5.12. Scaffolded dialogue for retell of *Abuelita Full of Life*.

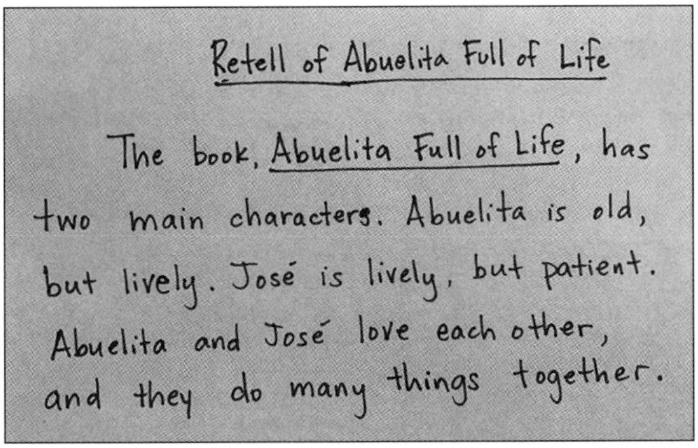

> Retell of Abuelita Full of Life
>
> The book, Abuelita Full of Life, has two main characters. Abuelita is old, but lively. José is lively, but patient. Abuelita and José love each other, and they do many things together.

Figure 5.13. Modeled writing of a retell.

After children have the opportunity to discuss the story with one another, the schema/organization of a retell is given and the teacher guides the students through a modeled writing. The retell needs to include the name of the text, which is the introduction, and some details relating what happened in the story. The teacher engages the children in a discussion of ways to organize the text and on what aspects they want to include (see Figure 5.13).

Shared Writing   The Literacy Squared version of shared writing uses and expands on monolingual English versions of shared writing but always begins with oracy and includes keeping a writing notebook (that we call the *cuaderno*). The oracy structures for this book include the language structures to note differences (contrasts) and similarities (comparison). For oracy we might provide the following language structures:

Abuelita is_____, but José is not.

Abuelita _____, but José does not.

After rehearsing the sentence stems we would ask students to write the following in their *cuadernos* using a color coding system that differentiates differences and similarities. (Below, the emphasized words are shown in bold.

Differences—to provide a contrast.

Example: Abuelita is **old**, but José is not.

Example: Abuelita **gardens**, but José does not.

The above provides a shared writing model that students can then be asked to write from. For example, the teacher might say, write a sentence to show a contrast between friends.

My example: Xochitl is **short**, but Carlos is **tall**.

This type of shared writing, kept in a student's *cuaderno*, is important, for several reasons. First, it provides additional practice of the sentence stem. Second, it is a record to refer back to after the chart and oral structures are removed from the walls of the classroom, and third, it gives students practice in writing their own examples.

Shared writing can also give us the opportunity to teach English grammar in context, differentiate questions and answers, and focus on words that connect discourse.

1. Ask/Answer Questions (rehearsed in oracy, written in *cuaderno*; with red pencil used to mark questions and dark pencil used for the answer sentences):

How are Abuelita and José the same?

Abuelita and José are the same because they both like to dance.

Table 5.4. Dictados for Abuelita Paired Biliteracy Unit

Spanish Dictado	English Dictado
Abuelito	*Abuelito Sings*
El abuelo de Marta es mayor de edad. Abuelito dice que es demasiado viejo para jugar fútbol, aunque zapatea con mucha fuerza cuando baila.	Marta and grandpa dance together. Abuelito likes to sing, but Marta does not. He sings "Las mañanitas" to her.
Enfoque de instrucción: *estructuras lingüísticas (comparaciones usando aunque); palabras de alta frecuencia (para, con, dice); vocabulario (demasiado, mayor de edad); puntuación (coma y puntos)*	**Teaching Points:** Language to compare and contrast (*together, but*); high-frequency words (*but, does, not*); vocabulary (*enjoys, together*); cross-language connection (code-switches: proper name, song in Spanish); pronouns (*he, her*)

2. Pronoun usage (rehearsed in oracy, written in *cuaderno* with pronouns marked in color):

   Abuelita is old, but José is not. **He** is young.

   José plays soccer, but Abuelita does not. **She** gardens.

   They walk in the park together.

TheDictado

TheDictado, an innovative writing strategy from Literacy Squared (see Escamilla et al., 2014, pp. 57–64 and Chapter 3 of this book) supports children's biliterate writing and is incorporated into every paired biliteracy unit. We suggest theDictado be created based upon children's strengths and needs and that they address some aspects of the overall writing objectives of the unit. All dictado lessons incorporate language, spelling and punctuation teaching points. In this particular unit, the Spanish dictado is a description of a grandparent that includes descriptive language and the same language structure from the text. Similarly, the English dictado is a descriptive text of Abuelito, and attention is given to the language of comparing and contrasting (Table 5.4).

SUMMARY: BILITERATE WRITING IN GRADE 1

In this chapter we provided profiles of two first-grade EB learners. Through writing samples a teacher could get the gist for how each student's writing is the same and different across languages. We then provided examples of how this writing can be analyzed using two different frameworks. Most importantly, we provided a detailed example of how this formative writing assessment can be used to create paired biliteracy writing opportunities in ways that integrate with other language arts and literacy skills and with attention on ways in which literacy-based ELD is different from monolingual instructional methods. We stress the importance of writing as we frequently observe that writing is not given the emphasis that it merits as children progress in their biliterate development. Finally, from this assessment we can see the important role that writing plays in early literacy development and stress that it is a foundational skill and an important vehicle for teaching other foundational skills such as vocabulary and fluency.

Questions for Reflection and Action

▶ With other teachers at your school, generate a list of potential culturally and linguistically diverse books for developing paired biliteracy lessons with a focus on writing.

▶ How can you honor children's cultural and linguistic funds of knowledge to develop their sense of themselves as members of a social community?

▶ We noted in this chapter that retelling is a skill that is particularly challenging in English for EB learners. What other first-grade challenging literacy skills might be the focus of paired biliteracy units?

▶ How are the writing approaches discussed in this chapter similar to ones used in your school and how are they different? Identify some changes you can start to implement in upcoming lessons/biliteracy units.

6 Developing Biliteracy via Genre Studies in Grades 3 to 5

Biography

"Children's resources for learning are rooted in their everyday experiences and in their stories of those experiences."

—Celia Genishi & Anne Haas Dyson, 2015

"I have seen many good things and many bad things in my life, but what I loved most was when I was a little girl and started going to school."

—Luz Jiménez as cited in Amescua (2021). From Amescua, G. (2021). *Child of the flower-song people: Luz Jiménez, daughter of the Nahua.*

Key Terms

Genre studies

Linguistic, cultural, experiential knowledge

Guiding Questions

▶ How can **genre studies** support biliterate writing development in the upper elementary grades?

▶ How can we ensure students learn about writing in both language environments while we avoid being duplicative and also widen their understanding of different genres?

▶ How can we promote and preserve students' linguistic and cultural wealth in sustaining ways through writing?

As students progress on their biliteracy trajectories in the intermediate grades, it is of utmost importance to honor, sustain, and build upon emerging bilingual learners' linguistic and cultural knowledge. Over nearly two decades, Literacy Squared has impacted thousands of children and hundreds of educators, and we have always promoted the inclusion of culturally and linguistically responsive materials for paired literacy instruction. As we aim toward ensuring equitable educational opportunities for minoritized emerging bilingual learners, we take this opportunity to make explicit how integrating children's linguistic, cultural, and familial wealth into these learning environments can be accomplished through well-thought-out genre units of study. In doing so, children can cultivate their biliterate writing abilities by drawing upon their vast funds of knowledge.

Although we all work toward ensuring emerging bilingual learners have the right to bilingual education, we also need to continue to disrupt the status quo concerning whose knowledge counts within the classroom by using writing to draw on students' and communities' funds of knowledge (Moll et al., 1992). As stated in Chapter 1, we will no longer tolerate beliefs that minoritized, linguistically diverse students do not have the cultural or linguistic knowledge to access the curricula. Rather, we argue for widening students' understanding of the three text types/genres promoted in the CCSS to ensure children understand the functions of, and purposes for, using writing as a meaningful, communicative, biliterate act.

The three writing genres addressed in the CCSS beginning in kindergarten are opinion/persuasive writing, informative/explanatory writing, and narrative writing. As children progress on their writing journeys through elementary school, the level of complexity and sophistication of skills increase in the language standards, including standards for grammar and vocabulary. So do expectations around the student's organization of ideas and idea development as well as the integration of content knowledge and ability to research. Opinion/persuasive writing involves stating an opinion in kindergarten, and next, providing reasons in first and second grade, and evolves to students writing opinions on topics supporting a point of view with logically ordered reasons and organization in fifth grade. Informative/explanatory writing includes the ability to identify a topic and provide details about the topic in the primary grades. In the fourth and fifth grades, students must examine a topic, group related ideas into paragraphs and incorporate facts, definitions, examples; use "precise and domain specific language"; and provide a conclusion. Narrative writing begins in kindergarten with students recounting loosely related events, and by second grade, students will recount events in sequence with details that describe actions. In the third and fourth grades, students must include effective techniques, such as dialogue and pacing, and include sensory details in their narrative writing (Common Core State Standards, 2010).

In this chapter we aim to answer the following questions educators of EB learners ask: Are we establishing a purpose for biliterate writing beyond completing graphic organizers or solely responding to text? What communicative function and purpose does writing serve, and to whom are we writing? Are we capitalizing on opportunities to widen students' understanding of the different kinds of texts that can be grouped under the three main genres of the CCSS? Are we harnessing all the linguistic, cultural, experiential, and familial knowledge EB learners possess to nurture their biliterate potential?

We have organized this chapter to include a framework to expand upon the CCSS genres for biliteracy instruction. Our framework includes connections to students' linguistic, cultural, and experiential wealth as a means for EB learners to increase their agency as they learn to write the world from the vast knowledge and wealth they possess. We then provide an example of how to incorporate students' lived experiences in meeting the CCSS, through a fourth-grade biliterate writing unit on biographies.

EXPANDING UPON THE MAIN WRITING GENRES TO DEVELOP BILITERACY

Over the years as we have engaged teachers in the side-by-side analysis of students' biliterate writing using our recommended prompts and the Literacy Squared Writing Rubric, we are taken aback in hearing teachers' astonishment when they are asked to capture their students' writing abilities across languages. For many teachers, it may be the first time they analyze students' biliterate writing side-by-side. They are often surprised at how much their students can write in both languages and how the prompts themselves elicit many more written ideas than some of the writing directed by the curriculum and standards. This newfound awareness of students' biliterate writing potential affirms the importance of providing students opportunities to bring their **linguistic, cultural, and experiential knowledge** when learning about and engaging in biliterate writing. It is not uncommon for writing instruction, due to limits in time and the narrowing of the curricula, to focus solely on using writing as a means to demonstrate reading comprehension.

Thus, within Literacy Squared, we not only promote writing instruction in both language environments drawing upon students' strengths and needs, but we explicitly teach children the sociocultural/social nature of writing beyond writing for the teacher, classmates, and/or the test maker. To do this successfully, we must expand upon the CCSS and provide explicit instruction on how different types of writing are used for different purposes, functions, and audiences. Effective biliterate writing instruction necessitates establishing authentic, communicative purposes for engaging in writing. Our emerging bilingual learners need to understand how a diversity of written text types serves to prepare them beyond college and career readiness.

Drawing from the work of Kaufman and Rodriguez (2003), we identify several texts that align with the three CCSS genres (opinion pieces, informative/explanatory texts, and narratives) to expose students to the wide range of texts and engage them in genre studies (see Table 6.1).

Table 6.1. Variety of Texts Aligned to the CCSS

CCSS Genres	Purpose/Function/ Language analysis	Diversity in text types	Questions/prompts to pose to connect to students' funds of knowledge
Opinion	To persuade; modify behavior; draw attention *What language is being used to convince you to change your mind, buy something, vote for someone, etc.? What images are associated?*	Editorials	What is a concern you have about your community? To whom and in what way can you express your concern?
		Advertisements	What advertisements do you see around your community (print, media, and on-line)? What are they trying to sell and how?
		Brochures	
		Letters, emails, texts	How do you and/or your family use letters, emails, and texts to communicate with family. How do each serve a different purpose?
		Public announcements, billboards	What announcements/symbols do you see in your neighborhood? What announcement could you write to persuade your community in some manner?
Informative/ Explanatory	Inform, define, describe, explain, build knowledge *What language is being used to explain, give information? Procedural, definitions, sequential, chronological*	Scientific texts/ reports, experiments	How is climate change affecting your community or your extended family's community/well-being?
		Historical texts	Explain your family tree/lineage. Describe your family's origin. How has your community changed over the last 30 years?
		Biographies, timelines	Create a timeline of your life. What are the important events you want to share? Create a timeline of important events from your family.
		Instructions, directions, maps, recipes	Write directions to get to school. Write a family recipe. Provide directions on how to carry out a family tradition.
		News reports/ articles, daily news	What news have you heard recently? Where did you read or hear the news? What information did you learn? Have you been able to get the news in different languages? How do you think authors with diverse cultural/national/linguistic backgrounds provide a different perspective?
		Interviews	What do you want to learn from the interviewee? What stories do you want to know/remember from the interviewee?
		Invitations, lists	Help create a shopping list. Create a birthday wish list. Create an invitation for a family/community/school event.
		Letters, emails, texts	Write a letter/email to a friend/family member that lives far from you and tell them about a recent event.
		Announcements, signs	What signs do you see in your community? How do they serve the community?
Narrative	To entertain; relate a series of events imagined or real; aesthetics	Narratives	What family stories/customs would you like to capture in writing?
		Poetry, songs	Write the lyrics to a favorite song. What does this song mean to you?
		Diary writing	Keep a journal or diary to record important events, thinking, or to record dreams.
		Retells	Ask a family member to retell the story of your birth and write it. What is a family favorite movie/show/book? Retell it in writing.
		Myths, legends, folktales	What is a legend/folktale that is told/read/watched in your family?
		Dichos, jokes, *trabalenguas, adivinanzas*	What are some of the *dichos*, jokes, *adivinanzas* told in your family? What do they mean?

In designing such genre studies, consideration must be given to the structure of the text type, an audience for whom the writing is being done, the purpose and function for the text which requires establishing the language function, and most importantly, consideration of accessing the knowledge students already possess.

While we may recognize the purpose for each genre type, we often limit exposure to a genre by only focusing on a single text type. For example, when teaching about the genre of opinions, children may only be asked to write a composition sharing their opinion about a certain topic using text evidence to substantiate their thinking (e.g., "What is your favorite ____? Explain why"; or "Which perspective do you agree with? Explain why with evidence.") To differentiate the opinion across languages, students may be asked to provide opinions about different topics.

While it is an important skill for students to express their opinion in writing, we do not have the time to be duplicative across environments. Rather, we can think more strategically and creatively to teach different text types within the genre that serve a similar function and purpose but are written for different *audiences*. We might be more effective in teaching the purpose and function of opinion/persuasive writing if we also include other text types within the selected genre of opinions, such as public announcements and editorials. Public announcements/ billboards surround us, and they serve to persuade their audience about topics relevant to our students' lived experiences. As such, teachers might engage students in creating posters related to convincing their community to be more inclusive. In the poster project illustrated in Figure 6.1, students had an established audience, understood the structure for the text, and could use their full linguistic repertoire to engage the reader. The posters were part of an art project for the Boulder History Museum in Colorado to promote inclusive practices. Students could choose the languages to express themselves. To expand upon the genre of opinion, students can conduct research about their selected topic and write an editorial to the appropriate audience using the structure of a letter and linguistic elements to serve the purpose and function of persuading the community to be inclusive. In that way, students learn the discourse structure of explaining their perspectives and requests through letter writing. More importantly, by addressing current community events/concerns, we center on social justice teaching and learning.

When designing genre studies, keep in mind that students need to understand the text structure as well as the language that is used to accomplish the writing's function and purpose. This type of analysis necessitates a strong connection between reading and writing, just as is emphasized in the early grades. By reading a variety of texts within each genre, we can teach text structure, which can serve as schema for writing and comprehension.

Instruction should also attend to the ways in which language use, discourse style, and syntax can be different for each text type and across languages. For example, when writing/reading directions for a scientific experiment, the imperative mood is used to make demands in simple sentences, whereas a scientific report is written primarily in the past tense and provides extensive elaboration of the scientific process including hypotheses, results, and interpretations. The use of code-switching or translanguaging in narrative writing gives voice to writing. Research (Montaño-Harman, 1991; Saéz, 2003) has established differences in how cohesive structures differ between Spanish and English, such as the use of cohesive markers (e.g., *en el mismo sentido*/in the same way, *por casualidad*/by chance) that are used more frequently in Spanish than in English. Identifying and being explicit about these differences will increase students' biliterate writing abilities.

By attending to the different text types within the three genres, we can capture the knowledge emerging bilingual learners already have, create authentic purposes for learning about the various genres, and provide meaningful opportunities for students to bring their knowledge and what is important to them to their writing. By widening students' awareness of genres, we are teaching in culturally and linguistically responsive ways.

The last column in Table 6.1 contains suggested prompts/questions to connect students' funds of knowledge to different text types within the main genres. The suggested questions/prompts are

Developing Biliteracy via Genre Studies in Grades 3 to 5: Biography

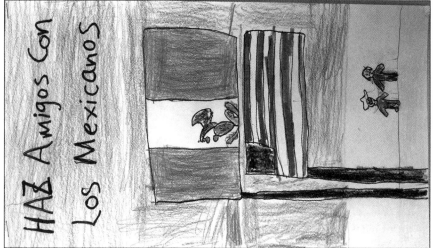

Figure 6.1. Posters to promote inclusivity. (Provided by Ms. Cohen at Columbine Elementary.)

not expansive but provide ideas for how to elicit students' experiential knowledge, develop oracy, and honor and incorporate connections between school and home.

In the sections that follow, we provide an overview of a genre study incorporating the aspects discussed (purpose/function, text structure, audience, language instruction). While we could have selected from any of the genres listed in Table 6.1, we chose to elaborate on the fourth grade biliteracy unit designed with the Comprehensive Biliteracy Framework (see Figure 1.1) connected to biographies, as this is a commonly explored genre in third through fifth grades.

BACKWARD PLANNING FOR BILITERATE WRITING

Creating this fourth-grade biliteracy unit studying genre involved a backward planning process. The first step is to analyze students' writing in both Spanish and English to identify strengths and skills that are less developed. The next step is to determine the instructional implications that will inform unit planning.

Understanding Students' Biliterate Abilities: Mateo

Before embarking on the backward planning for the biliteracy genre unit, keep in mind what your students can do in their biliterate writing. We provide a brief analysis of a fourth-grade student's biliterate writing prompts to determine strengths as well as teaching points for the biography unit. Mateo has been in biliteracy instruction since kindergarten and produced the two samples in Figure 6.2 within a few weeks of each other. Mateo's school has a transitional bilingual model. The Spanish sample is a response to the fourth grade Literacy Squared Spanish writing prompt ("Who is your best friend in all the world? Explain why that person is your best friend"); and the English sample is a response to a prompt that served as a formative writing assessment before beginning a unit on biographies ("Who is an adult in your family that is very special to you? Why are they special to you? What do they say and do that makes them special?"). The prompts were collected under similar conditions.

The English translation of Mateo's Spanish composition is as follows:

> Enrique is my best friend because he always wants to play with me when no one else does. He is someone very special in my life, he is someone that will defend me when other kids bother me. He is someone that will never stop believing in me, he also shares everything with me. He and I play at his house and the park. He always helps when I need it and when there is no one to play with, I can count on him to play. He helps me with everything, and he is not bothered by it. Another thing he does with me is when I feel nervous or scared, he helps me get those thoughts out of my head. Also, he walked with me to the bus stop. Enrique is a very special friend, and I don't know what I would do without him.

We scored each sample with the Literacy Squared Writing Rubric and provided a brief explanation of scores earned in Figure 6.2. Below, we elaborate on a qualitative analysis.

Based on the side-by-side analysis of the samples in Figure 6.2, Mateo scored higher overall in English because he included a clear introduction, while he did not do so in Spanish. He also had nearly accurate spelling in English, whereas in Spanish most approximations did not include accents, particularly for the preterite past tense (*quería*/wanted, *compartía*/shared; *había*/there was); indicative preterite (*ayudó*/helped, *paró*/stopped); high-frequency words (*también*/also, *alguién*/someone); and the diacritic accent to differentiate a pronoun from an article (*él*/he, *el*/the). The sentence structures and use of punctuation are similar across languages where he controls beginning and ending punctuation and uses commas to separate independent clauses. It is worth noting that Mateo is in a transitional bilingual program model and as students enter third grade, they receive only two hours of Spanish literacy instruction, and the rest of the day is in English.

Taking into consideration what we learned from the quantitative rubric, we can then analyze Mateo's bilingual linguistic abilities using the qualitative side of the Literacy Squared Writing Rubric (see Chapter 1 Appendix). At the discourse level we analyze how students organize their writing, which also includes punctuation to guide the reader. In English, Mateo writes a

Nombre: _____ 4° grado 2021-2022
Fecha: 2/11/22

¿Quién es tu mejor amigo en todo el mundo? Escríbenos por qué esa persona es tu mejor amigo.

Enrique es mi mejor amigo porque el siempre quería jugar conmigo cuando nadien mas quería. El es alguien muy especial en mi vida. El es alguien que me defendia cuando otros niños me molestaban. El es alguien que nunca para de creer en mí tambien comparte todos sus cosas conmigo. Yo y el jugabamos en su casa y en el parque. El siempre me ayudaba cuando yo le nesesitaba y cuando no habia gente para jugar yo podia count on el. Para jugar. El me ayudo con todo y a el no le molestaba ayudarme. Otra cosa que el hacia conmigo fue que cuando yo me sentía nerviosó o mareado el dice cupula sacala ese pensamiento de mi cabeza tambien el caminaba conmigo a la parada del bus. Enrique es un amigo muy especial yo no se que haría yo sin el.

Name: _____ Date: 1/7/22

Think about an adult in your family that is very special to you and then respond to the following questions.

1. Who is an adult in your family that is very special to you? What do they do and say that makes them special? Why are they special to you?

My grandpa is someone very special to me he makes me feel very loved and cared for. He makes me laugh and loves me with all of his heart. he makes me feel like I ame a king. He always comes to my birthday and always gives me what I ask for and gives me so much love and efection. He is so nice and always finds a way to make me happy. Whenever I ame sad he always cheers me up. My grandpa is someone very special to me, and I would not trade him for the world.

Rubric Scores

	Spanish	English
Content	6 – Main idea with descriptive language and some complex sentences.	7 – Includes a clear introduction and conclusion. Has a variety of sentences and includes descriptive language.
Structural Elements	3 – Controls beginning and ending punctuation and uses commas to separate independent clauses within a sentence.	3 – Controls beginning and ending punctuation and uses commas to separate independent clauses within a sentence.
Spelling	4 – Most approximations omit accents.	5 – Mostly accurate spelling with only two approximations: *ame/am, efection/affection*.
Total Points	13	15

Figure 6.2. Mateo's fourth-grade biliterate writing samples. (Provided by Ms. Hilary Barthel from Columbine Elementary.)

complete introduction: "My grandpa is someone very special to me, he makes me feel very loved and cared for." He then provides supporting ideas to back-up the main topic. Mateo did not provide a clear introduction in Spanish; however, all the ideas written relate to reasons Enrique is his best friend. Conclusions are included in both samples, and they are constructed similarly. In relation to punctuation, as noted in the quantitative analysis, Mateo incorporates commas to separate independent clauses within a sentence.

When looking at the sentence/phrase level in both Spanish and English, Mateo relies on beginning almost every sentence with the subject's name or related pronoun. There are a few instances where he uses a transitional phrase, as he did in Spanish: *"Otra cosa que el hacia conmigo fue que cuando yo me siento nervioso o miedoso el me ayuda a sacar ese pensamiento de mi cabeza"* ("Another thing he did for me was when I feel nervous or scared, he helps me get rid of that thought from my head."). Examining syntax, Mateo does not apply the rules of accentuation when conjugating verbs. At the word level, Mateo used the English word "count" in the phrase: *"Yo podia* count *en el"* (I could count on him.).

Determining Instructional Implications for Unit Planning

After analyzing Mateo's writing holistically, it is important to think of instructional implications that will inform the genre unit along with planning dictados across language:

- Reinforce the importance of always introducing the topic with a title and providing a clear introduction, since the skill was apparent in English. This is the efficiency of analyzing students' writing holistically.

- Despite having a limited amount of time to compose when given the prompts, fourth-grade students need to group related information/ideas in paragraphs or sections.

- Attention will be given to metalanguage instruction on learning rules for accentuation for the preterite and imperfect tenses as well as the diacritic accent to differentiate homophones: *él* (he); *sé* (to know).

As will be detailed in the next section, many of the instructional implications from Mateo's analysis address the writing standards selected for the biography unit. Taking the time to become familiar with the Literacy Squared Writing Rubric and analyzing students' Spanish and English writing will facilitate purposeful and efficient biliterate writing instruction.

SAMPLE FOURTH-GRADE BILITERACY UNIT: BIOGRAPHY

Working from analyses like Mateo's, the teacher can plan a unit based on grade-level writing standards, with learning objectives focused on the biography genre. Working from these standards and objectives, the teacher selects the texts from the genre, creates related exemplar texts, and plans the literacy foci and writing instruction as described below.

Overview

In general, biographies are meant to honor someone for their extraordinary spirit. In some way we all know someone like that and can share/memorialize them. For this fourth-grade biliteracy unit, students will focus on biographies and autobiographies as text types within the larger genre of informative texts. Students will be exposed to a variety of biographies and autobiographies in each language environment. For writing in Spanish literacy, students will identify a family member, elder, or other person of interest to interview and write the person's biography for the purpose of understanding the world from a family/community perspective and to keep it as a *recuerdo*/record (Lopez et al., 2020). In literacy-based ELD, students will select a person of interest (recommended: from a minoritized community) to research and write an autobiography for a living wax museum event where they will share what they have learned with classmates and others in and outside of school.

The Writing Standards: What Will Students Know and Be Able to Do?

- CCSS.ELA-LITERACY.W.4.2. Write informative/explanatory texts to examine a topic and convey ideas and information clearly.
- CCSS.ELA-LITERACY.W.4.2.A. Introduce a topic clearly and group related information in paragraphs and sections; include formatting, illustration, and multimedia when useful to aid comprehension.

Using the Holistic Biliteracy Framework, Figure 6.3 provides an overview of the unit's objectives for both language environments. As the objectives are identified, it is of great importance to explore how students will be held accountable for the skills across languages by engaging in backward planning. Backward planning involves gathering texts and creating written exemplars.

Text Selection and Exemplar Creation

In Literacy Squared, we recommend exploring a variety of texts from the chosen genre and always suggest that the teacher create a written exemplar or completion of the tasks being asked of the students to anticipate how to plan instruction. When reading the texts and composing the exemplars, attention should be given to the following:

1. The structure of the texts (discourse style, rhetorical style);
2. All aspects of oracy, including transitions/phrases, precise language/vocabulary, language structures;
3. Metalanguage (syntax, verb tense, morphology); and
4. Cross-language connections (similarities and differences between languages).

Always create exemplars that demonstrate the biliteracy potential and grade-level expectations/standards, and note areas that may require differentiated instruction, particularly to language.

Before writing an exemplar, it is important to identify texts for biliteracy instruction in both languages. Text selection requires teachers to assess the materials available not only by content, but by the languages to determine what can be accomplished in Spanish and what can be accomplished in English. While we want to expose students to a variety of texts, it is important to choose texts that are related to the content students know and understand. Texts should connect to the content being studied in other parts of the school day (i.e., science and social studies). As intermediate-grade students are exposed to texts with increased complexity, we often

LECTO-ESCRITURA (30-45 minutos)	**LITERACY-BASED ELD (30-45 minutes)**
Lectura: Aprender sobre la estructura del género y cómo leer biografías sacando ideas importantes. Diferenciar entre biografías y autobiografías (punto de vista). *Escritura*: Tomar apuntes de una entrevista; escribir una biografía organizada por párrafos con ilustraciones de un familiar/conocido para compartir con tu familia y la clase. Establecer punto de vista. *Oralidad*: Desarrollar una entrevista creando preguntas; transformar declaraciones a preguntas; revisar preguntas; usar palabras de sucesión.	**Reading**: Read a variety of biographies/autobiographies to gather information on a single topic. Consider point of view (first person versus third person). **Writing**: Take notes and write a multiparagraph first person narrative. Present information to the audience in the form of a "living wax museum." **Oracy**: Transformations from first person to third person and appropriate pronoun choice and verb tense. Present information learned in first person to a small audience. Ask and answer questions.

Figure 6.3. Biography genre study objectives.

find the foci of a literacy lesson to be on the concepts in the text rather than on the skills needed to understand the structure of the genre. For example, if students are reading a biography on Nelson Mandela, the literacy teaching focus might be to explain the concept of apartheid, rather than on noticing how a biography is organized chronologically. As mentioned above, we recommend attending to conceptual knowledge needed for the texts; this should happen explicitly to build schema prior to reading text.

If the texts/curriculum in your school do not reflect the diversity of the school and community, make sure to critically address the perspectives being presented and those not being presented. Make every attempt to find more culturally and linguistically relevant texts and multimedia resources. Seek out the help of your school and local librarian to find relevant texts in a variety of reading levels. For this unit we selected an assortment of biographies paired across languages (see Figure 6.4) to represent students' backgrounds, and to expand understandings of others' experiences, we selected these texts to serve as windows and mirrors (Bishop, 1990). The majority of texts used are illustrated biographies; however we did include traditional biographies as well as videos so students could learn how to research from different biography text types and media.

Community, Cultural, and Social Connections: Grades 3 to 5

As emerging bilingual learners continue on their trajectory for developing biliteracy, they continue to expand their understandings of themselves and their capacity to engage more fully not only within their communities but also in the larger social context. In the biliteracy unit presented in this chapter, students are learning to think about community and social issues in a more expansive way that builds toward serving as agents of social justice. Emerging bilingual students need to learn about the struggles and triumphs of people from their own and others' backgrounds to raise essential issues of social justice. Biliteracy instruction that is inclusive of students' linguistic, cultural, and experiential knowledge honors and expands their potential in creating contexts in which students are engaged and promotes social transformation.

LECTO-ESCRITURA	**LITERACY-BASED ELD**
La estudiante mayor: Cómo Mary Walker aprendió a leer/The Oldest Student: How Mary Walker Learned to Read by Rita Lorraine Hubbard and Oge Mora, Vintage Español, 2022. Esta biografía ilustrada cuenta la historia de Mary Walker, la estudiante mayor que a los 116 años aprendió a leer. Nació en la esclavitud y aunque fue liberada, hubo muchos obstáculos para aprender, pero siguió soñando. Nos enseña que nunca es demasiado tarde para aprender a leer.	*Child of the Flower-Song People: Luz Jiménez, Daughter of the Nahua* by Gloria Amescua (author) and Duncan Tonatiuh (illustrator). Harry N. Abrams, 2021. This is an illustrated biography of how Luz Jimenez, a Nahua from Mexico, realized her dream to become a teacher after suffering many obstacles. We learn how Luz shared her knowledge, honor, and love of the Nahua culture and language and how it was preserved and written into history.
Gabriela, la poeta viajera by Alejandra Toro (author), and Isabel Hojas (illustrator). Editorial Amanuta, 2015. Esta biografía ilustrada de Gabriela Mistral, nos explica la vida de una niña que era distinta de los demás cuando era pequeña. Quería ser maestra y en su vida escribió mucho y viajó por el mundo. Esta biografía tiene un lenguaje elevado para los estudiantes emergentes bilingües.	*Xiuhtezcatl Martinez: Compilation* (video)—Xiuhtezcatl Martinez is an environmental activist who began his advocacy at the age of six. His activism involves examining the impacts of climate change on indigenous and minoritized communities. (*Xiuhtezcatl Age 16, 2016*. BigSpeak Speakers Bureau. Retrieved from https://www.youtube.com/watch?v=97a-WhYpFfE&ab_channel=BigSpeakSpeakersBureau.)

Figure 6.4. Paired texts for biography unit.

Writing Exemplars to Plan Instruction

Working with teachers over time, we have heard the benefits of taking the time to deconstruct the texts that will be used to teach the genre as well as writing exemplars in both languages based on the CCSS and unit objectives. We recognize the amount of time it may take to engage in this activity; however, the investment made provides a roadmap for attending to the Holistic Biliteracy Framework, with particular attention given to the planning of oracy and metalanguage instruction.

In beginning this work, it is important to become familiar with the texts that will be used for whole group instruction as either interactive read-alouds or shared reading. When reading texts, pay attention to how the texts are structured, what language is used, and the overall complexity because they serve as mentor texts for writing. Then access the writing rubric used in your school, district, or curriculum and read through the descriptors of the grade-level expectations and the level above. The exemplar you create should at least meet grade-level expectations or reflect the CCSS. As you engage in this analysis, keep in mind your students' abilities and needs across languages, and think of their biliterate potential, full linguistic repertoire, and cultural wealth.

We provide a model of exemplars we wrote for the unit and describe how we used the exemplars to identify specific teaching points (see Figure 6.5 and Table 6.2). Chronological order is the dominant text structure used in the biographies and autobiographies read in this unit. Paragraphs are used to group events to distinguish the subject's childhood and adolescence, adulthood, and late life. Note in the following examples how each section conforms to this rhetorical pattern. Finally, culturally and linguistically responsive teaching requires teachers to be vulnerable and share who they are to deepen the sociocultural classroom-community, and to invite a multitude of voices, experiences, and knowledge to affirm the identities of marginalized students and create *confianza* (trust). Thus, we recommend you share yourself and experiences with your students.

After writing the exemplars, it becomes clear what needs to be taught explicitly for oracy as well as metalanguage. For the text to be organized chronologically and linguistically, explicit instruction is provided to expand language to use across languages. Metalanguage instruction within Spanish attends to how the preterite tense indicates when an event/action took place at a specific point in time and requires an accent, while using the imperfect tense has no definitive beginning or ending (see Figure 6.5). Within English, teaching will need to focus on how to transform biographical information written in the third person to the first person. Many metalinguistic connections can be made between languages, such as differences in how commas are used in a series and the writing of dates. See Table 6.2 for more details.

After you write the exemplars, score them with the rubric you used to generate them. Remember the exemplar should be at or above grade-level benchmark. Then work through how you will scaffold and support your students to be successful. Remember the process you took to write them, as that will support how you model the process for your students. Creating exemplars is a messy process, so remember to work with your colleagues collaboratively and keep the work to share with your students. Through the creation of biliterate exemplars, planning for writing is more efficacious and provides a model to work from as you plan your day-to-day lessons. In what follows, we delineate how to use the various pedagogical approaches in the different language environments.

Spanish Literacy

The writing objective in Spanish is for students to write a three- to five-paragraph biography of a family member based on questions that will be asked through an interview. Students will consider the purpose for collecting this information and what point of view they want to use to present the information collected. As the unit is introduced, so are the expectations. Thus, the exemplar created can be presented to the students alongside the rubric that will be used to evaluate the written products. It can also be a good time to collect a prewriting sample to observe

Spanish Exemplar	English Exemplar
Mi papá: Juan	Luz Jiménez: Living Link to the Aztecs
Juan nació el 8 de diciembre en un pueblo pequeño en Argentina. Era el séptimo hijo de 12 hermanos y hermanas y vivía en una finca donde se criaban pollos.  *Juan era un niño muy inteligente, curioso y dedicado. Le encantaba escuchar a sus familiares hablar en diferentes idiomas. En su casa se hablaba el español y el alemán, y Juan aprendió los dos idiomas con gran facilidad. Hasta aprendió el latín en la iglesia y en la escuela. En ese entonces, los papás decidían qué carrera deberían tomar sus hijos. Como había tantos hermanos en la familia, su papá decidió que él iría a la escuela para ser un maestro. Después de la primaria, lo mandaron a un internado de secundaria. A él no le gustó estar tan lejos de su familia, pero allí aprendió otro idioma más, el inglés.* *A los 20 años, Juan se fue a la India y trabajó en una escuela por 10 años. En la India, Juan aprendió su quinto idioma, el hindi. Al volver a Argentina, él conoció a su esposa, María, y se casaron. Después de uno años, tuvieron una hija y emigraron a los Estados Unidos donde Juan enseñó español. Tuvieron dos hijos más. Juan era un buen hombre de negocios. Iba a misa todos los días y toda la congregación lo reconocía por su voz encantadora. Juan, mi papá, fue un hombre dedicado y me enseñó a apreciar el bilingüismo.*	My name is Luz Jiménez, child of the flower-song people, the Aztecs, who call themselves Nahua. I was born in Milpa Alta, Mexico, on January 28, 1897. My people lost their land to Cortés and the Spaniards, but we did not disappear. As a child, I learned the way of the Nahua. My mother taught me how to grind corn in a metate, how to twist yarn with my toes, and how to weave on a loom. I was curious and words swirled in my head in Nahuatl, the Aztec language. I wanted to learn in school, but the Nahua were not allowed. One day, the government required all native children to go to school. We had to learn Spanish, how to bake bread, and draw. We had to dress in modern clothes. I did well in school. Although we were not allowed to speak Nahuatl, I told Nahua stories in secret. Even though everyone was changing, I longed to carry the traditions of the Nahua. When I was thirteen, I knew I wanted to be a teacher but the Mexican Revolution came to Milpa. My father was killed and my mother, sisters, and I fled to Mexico City. Instead of selling *atole* and tamales, I found work as a model for artists. As a model, I taught the artists about Nahua traditions. In my thirties, I returned to Milpa Alto to be a teacher, but was rejected. I did not give up on teaching though. I returned to the city and taught artists and scholars all about Nahua culture and the Nahuatl language. I love my culture and language and was able to keep it alive by sharing it with others that recorded what I knew.

Figure 6.5. Fourth-grade biliterate exemplars for biography unit.

Table 6.2. Instructional Foci/Teaching Points to Address in Biography and Autobiography Writing

	Spanish		English
Text Structure	**Orden cronológico** (Chronological order)—*niñez/adolescencia, educación, profesión, madurez*		**Chronological order**—childhood, adolescence, adulthood, profession
	Punto de vista—*tercera persona— narración (él, ella, ell@s)*		**Point of view**—first person (I, we, our)
Oracy	**Frases que indican sucesión** *(En ese entonces, Después de, A los 10 años)*		**Temporal language to demonstrate time** (As a child, One day, When I was thirteen, In my thirties)
	Frases adverbiales para indicar lugar *(en su casa, en la __)*		
Metalanguage within Language	**Tiempos verbales**—*diferencia entre el uso del tiempo imperfecto (hablaba, cantaba) con el pretérito (nació)*		**Pronoun use**—"I" vs. "me" when speaking of a group (my mother, sisters, and I)
Metalanguage Cross-language connections	**Fechas**—*nombre del mes sin mayúsculas (diciembre)*		**Written dates**—How to read/write dates and years. Capitalize month (January). Read years as eighteen ninety-seven (1897).
	Puntuación—*comas—en español no se incluye coma en una serie antes de "y"; Se usa una* **coma para frases adverbiales** *que indican tiempo y lugar en ambos idiomas.*		**Punctuation**—Commas in a series—comma before "and" and last item
	En español no se escribe el **nombre de idiomas** *con mayúscula, pero en inglés sí (alemán/German)*		**Languages** are capitalized in English and not in Spanish (Nahuatl/*nahuatl*).

growth from the beginning to the end of the unit. (This is what the teacher did in collecting the English writing samples analyzed in Figure 6.2.)

The book, *La estudiante mayor: Cómo Mary Walker aprendió a leer/The Oldest Student: How Mary Walker Learned to Read* by Rita Lorraine Hubbard (2022), will be used as the first text to demonstrate the author's point of view in writing the text as well as to show how the text is organized and narrated chronologically. To establish this, the teacher created an anchor chart to highlight the purpose, point of view, and features of biographies (see Figure 6.6). As the book is read, the

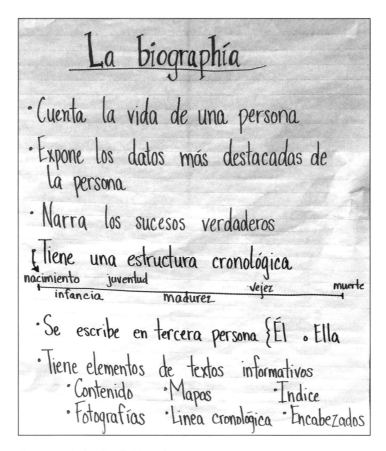

Figure 6.6. Anchor chart for biography.

different features of the text are identified both explicitly and by engaging students in meaningful planned dialogues. Some examples of open-ended dialogue questions for oracy include:

- *¿Por qué fue escrita esta biografía?* [Why was this biography written?]
- *¿Cuáles son algunas cualidades de la persona? ¿Cómo es qué la autora/el ilustrador las demuestra?* [What are some of this person's qualities? How does the author/illustrator demonstrate them?]
- *¿Cuál era el sueño de Mary Walker? ¿Que barreras le impidieron ser verdaderamente libre?* [What was Mary Walker's dream? What barriers prevented her from being truly free?]
- *¿Cómo fue que Mary Walker llegó a hacer su sueño realidad?* [How did Mary Walker make her dream come true?]
- *¿Qué sueño tienes tú? ¿Qué necesitas para lograrlo?* [What dream do you have? What do you need to achieve it?]

In Spanish more time is spent on teaching text structure, while in English more attention is given to point of view. Because of this planning, connections between environments are more efficacious and redundancy of teaching is minimized, thus developing and accessing knowledge within the bilingual brain is activated. In addition, an anchor chart (Figure 6.7) containing temporal language is started and students add to it as they find different examples in other biographical texts. In this way, reading and writing serve a reciprocal purpose.

To capture the major events of Mary's life, a timeline or graphic organizer can be created so students can see that biographies are organized chronologically by life stages (e.g., *nacimiento*/birth, *adolescencia*/adolescence, *educación*/education, *profesión*/professional life, *legado*/legacy, *la madurez*/maturity, *razón por ser reconocid@*/why person became famous; see Figure 6.8). This same graphic organizer will be used for literacy-based ELD not only to deconstruct the books/texts, but also to serve students as they write their biographies and autobiographies in each environment. Always include the author's note or any additional material in illustrated biographies. The author's note is traditionally structured as traditional informative texts.

Although writing was part of analyzing the biography on Mary Walker, dedicated time must be allocated to modeling the writing standards expectations. In many intermediate grade levels, modeled writing is sometimes omitted. However, for emerging bilingual learners, it is imperative to ensure students see a written text modeled for them, including the processes (e.g., planning, drafting, revising, and editing) and thinking about what the teacher goes through to produce it.

LECTO-ESCRITURA	**LITERACY-BASED ELD**
La estudiante mayor (Hubbard & Mora, 2022) • *Durante los años siguientes* (p. 8) • *Al final de la semana* (p. 9) • *Cuando Mary se casó* (p. 12) • *Mary tenía 20 años cuando tuvo su primer hijo* (p. 13) • *Durante las siguientes cuatro décadas* (p. 15) *Gabriela la poeta viajera* (Torro, 2011) • *El viaje duró una semana.* (p. 22) • *Poco tiempo después del fin de la guerra,* (p. 31)	*Child of the Flower-Song People* (Amescua, 2021) • But at thirteen, her dreams whirled away in a storm (p. 18). • After the Revolution, Luz returned to Milpa (p. 26). • So, Luz at last became a teacher (p. 27). • Into the early twentieth century Luz still spoke Nahuatl (p. 34). *Kamala Harris: Rooted in Justice* (Grimes, 2020) • Sadly, when Kamala was seven, (p. 8). • After Howard, California called Kamala home (p. 22).

Figure 6.7. Temporal language taken from books.

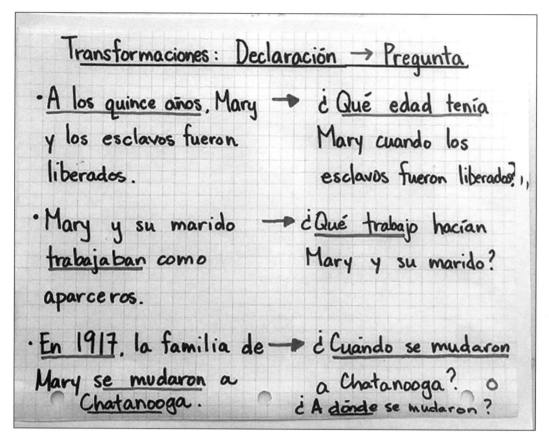

Figure 6.8. Transforming statements to questions. (Provided by Ms. Hilary Barthel from Columbine Elementary.)

In this unit, it is necessary to transform some of the statements from the book or from the exemplar so that students can begin formulating their own questions for their family member/friend they will interview. Similar to the oracy transformation activity in Chapter 2, the teacher pulls statements or summaries from the book and models how to transform them to questions. For example:

- *"No se debía enseñar a los esclavos a leer o escribir, ni hacer algo que los ayudará a aprender." → ¿Por qué no se debía enseñar a los esclavos a leer o escribir?*

  ["The enslaved were not to be taught to read or write, or do anything that would help them learn." → **Why were the enslaved not permitted to learn to read or write?**]

- *Mary tenía 114 años cuando empezó una clase de lectura. → ¿Cuándo empezó Mary a aprender a leer?*

  ["Mary was 114 years old when she started a reading class." → **When did Mary start learning to read?**]

Another approach to transforming declarations with questions, could involve sharing a prior student's writing and making annotations in the text (see Figure 6.9) by turning declarative statements into questions. Regardless of the manner in which the transformations occur, students should have a model and be working collaboratively by talking and the teacher giving feedback.

As students are guided through this transformation activity, they begin identifying the questions they want to ask of their family member. As a class, questions will be collected to interview a school staff or community member to practice conducting the interview as well as note-taking. This will be a shared writing activity as the person to be interviewed comes to class physically or

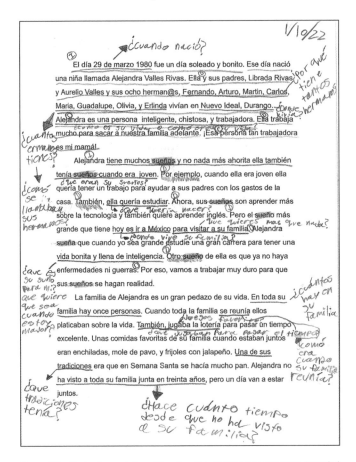

Figure 6.9. Student's annotation of transforming statements to questions. (Provided by Ms. Hilary Barthel from Columbine Elementary.)

remotely. Before engaging in the classroom interview, students will rehearse asking the interview questions to one another. Some possible interview questions include:

- *¿Cuándo naciste? ¿Dónde?* [When you were born? Where?]

- *¿Cómo era tu familia cuando eras niñ@?* [What was your family like when you were a child?]

- *¿Cómo eras de niñ@? ¿Qué te gustaba hacer?* [What were you like as a child? What did you like to do?]

- *¿Qué estudiaste? ¿Dónde fuiste a la escuela?* [What did you study? Where did you go to school?]

- *¿Qué deseo/sueño tenías/tienes? ¿Qué querías/quieres hacer?* [What wish/dream did/do you have? What did you/do you want to do?]

- *¿Cómo es tu vida como adulto? ¿Cómo es tu trabajo/familia? ¿Qué te gusta hacer como pasatiempos?* [How is your life as an adult? What is your work/family like? What do you like to do in your free time?]

- *¿Hay alguna otra cosa que te gustaría compartir?* [Is there anything else you would like to share?]

After collecting responses from the interview, a shared writing will take place to demonstrate how the ideas can be organized into a graphic organizer that provides a schema for grouping ideas into paragraphs and to address the other aspects of metalanguage and oracy instruction. Because the interview was a shared experience, the teacher guides the thinking, and the students collectively participate to fill in the graphic organizer. In the intermediate grades, especially in the fourth and fifth grades, it may be beneficial to conduct shared writing with an electronic document, wherein students are in a shared Google document co-constructing the text with the teacher. As ideas are negotiated into sentences, students can provide their ideas in the document, and the teacher discusses selecting which sentences/ideas to include *with* the students. This form of shared writing allows everyone to not only *hear* and *see* but also *write* the text being produced and revised.

While the biographies being read are about uncommon people, we often neglect to ask and record the rich experiences and stories our family members possess and share them with others. As students prepare to interview their family members, it is important to emphasize the purpose for collecting these responses and with whom they will share their biography. Have students reflect on their relationship with this person and think about what more they can ask and learn from them. Thus, the questions they choose need to meet their purpose and audience. By engaging in this work, we emphasize biliteracy as a way to teach for social justice by honoring students' and families' linguistic, cultural, historical, and familial wealth (Yosso, 2005) and bringing that knowledge into the classroom.

As students conclude their interviews, they begin the process of organizing their ideas and begin composing their paragraphs. Ms. Barthel, a teacher in Colorado, scaffolded the interview notes into determining how to organize the information into aligned paragraphs as illustrated in Figure 6.10. In some instances, the notes did not contain complete information and the students had to return and ask more questions to build their ideas. While this may seem tedious, the students understand the importance of developing topics with facts, details, and examples related to the topic to create grade-level informative texts. It is noteworthy how much time and effort the teacher and students put into this published work. The translation of Mateo's notes and outline for the second paragraph of the biography (see Figure 6.10) reads as follows:

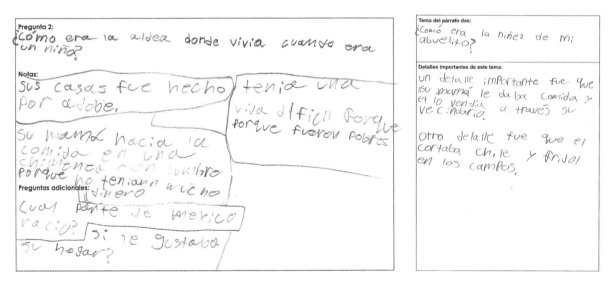

Figure 6.10. Mateo's notes and outline for the second paragraph of the biography. (Provided by Ms. Hilary Barthel from Columbine Elementary.)

Question 2

What was your village like when you were a child?

- ▶ The houses were made from adobe.
- ▶ I had a hard life because we were poor.
- ▶ His mom made food in a wood burning stove because they did not have money.

Additional questions:

▶ Where in Mexico were you born?

Did you like your home?

Topic for Paragraph 2

▶ What was my grandfather's childhood like?

Important details for this topic:

▶ An important detail was that his mom would give him food to sell around the neighborhood.

▶ Another important detail is that he cut chiles and beans in the fields.

As the teacher continues to provide individual and small-group support to students, there is continued work on the shared writing biography to model the processes of writing. Of course, more biographies are read and explored to understand the structure of biographies. Additionally, the teacher can provide support with language structures and work around grammar to support the students as a whole and make cross-language connections when necessary. Keep in mind as well, that students are broadening their understanding of biographies simultaneously in literacy-based ELD.

The biography that appears at the end of this chapter in Figure 6.11 was produced by Mateo, the same student who produced the samples in Figure 6.2. As can be seen, Mateo not only increased the amount of text but also grouped similar ideas into paragraphs and wrote a clear introduction and conclusion.

Just as demonstrated in Chapters 4 and 5, with the appropriate objectives, teaching foci, pedagogical approaches, and explicit instruction, bilingual students can achieve grade-level standards while also incorporating culturally and linguistically sustaining practices.

The Biliterate Writing Trajectory: Grades 3–4

Mateo's writing illustrates what a biliterate writing trajectory might look like for an EB child in the intermediate grades. In the third and fourth grades, students are able to express their ideas and knowledge with increased facility including more details and varied sentences across languages. Because of the amount of writing students can produce, greater attention is given to organization and cohesion. With consistent attention to the integration of oracy and metalanguage instruction, the linguistic quality of the writing increases and students take greater risks. If not for the side-by-side analysis, we would not see the totality of the students' abilities, because some abilities appear in one language and not the other.

Literacy-Based ELD

Within this biliterate genre unit, students will continue to read biographies in literacy-based ELD but write an autobiography. As we have worked with intermediate teachers implementing Literacy Squared, we recognize how hard it is to make time to teach writing in English and Spanish. What is important to remember is not to teach the same thing in both languages but rather to think strategically in how to organize instruction across languages so that students can extend their knowledge across languages. Thus, many of the skills and concepts taught in

Spanish literacy will be built upon in English literacy. For example, the same graphic organizer will be used across languages, as autobiographies are organized chronologically. Furthermore, we paired the first two books because they have similar themes related to dreams and aspirations. What is different in literacy-based ELD, is that students will be researching a person of interest through books and other media sources (e.g., internet searches, videos, etc.) and using first person to share their learning. Students will be reading and writing; however the final product is presented orally through a living wax museum event where the student will present and answer questions about their researched person. We were motivated to have students work on producing an autobiography because it is an effective way to teach point of view and work metalinguistically in transforming information written in biographies from third person to first person. Remember, as you work in both environments, be sure to make the connections obvious. Ask students to reflect on how what they are learning in each environment is helping them meet the biliteracy objectives.

Unlike the Spanish literacy lesson, the teacher will produce the exemplar as a modeled writing to show the many steps involved in researching, note-taking, drafting and presenting. The teacher will introduce the book *Child of the Flower-Song People, Luz Jiménez, Daughter of the Nahua* by Amescua (2021), which is an illustrated biography, and set up the expectations for the end-of-unit presentation/product which are similar to the Spanish assignment, but different because of the oral presentation. The text can be shared with the whole class so students can pay attention and analyze the chronological order of the text. Focus must also be given to prioritizing the representation of people of minoritized communities, their struggles, their legacies, and activism. Prior to beginning the reading, share the quote from Luz Jimenez in the Author's note, also included at the beginning of this chapter: "I have seen many good things and many bad things in my life, but what I loved most was when I was a little girl and started going to school" (Amescua, 2021). This quote can serve as the purpose for reading. While we read, think about how the author presents the good and bad things Luz experienced, and how school impacted her life. This purpose can center several oracy dialogues for the students. During and after reading the text, the teacher asks students to engage in dialogue related to learning about Luz Jiménez. Some open-ended dialogue questions could include:

- What was Luz like before she went to school?
- What did she know and learn about her Nahua culture? Why was that important to her?
- How did Luz learn to read? How did the school attempt to take the Nahua children's culture and language from them?
- What was Luz's dream?
- How did she make her dream a reality?
- How does the author show that the Nahua culture is important to Luz?
- What is meant when the author says, "Luz was a 'living link' to the Aztecs?"
- **Connect to family:** The author includes different Nahua legends, customs, stories in the biography. Ask your family to share customs, stories, legends that are important to their identity. Ask why. Perhaps you can include these in your biography.

After engaging deeply in the meaning of the book, the teacher begins modeling how to extract the important events of Luz's life to fill in the graphic organizer. While the students are helping identify the information, the teacher is *modeling the writing* after the idea is negotiated. While much writing in the intermediate grades can be done electronically, when modeling, it is important to have the text put up on chart paper for students to reference.

Once the important ideas are in the graphic organizer, the teacher shows how to transform the statements from third person to first, engaging students in a metalinguistic discussion. After modeling a few ideas from the graphic organizer, the teacher can release responsibility to the students to work in collaborative groups so that they can practice with teacher feedback.

Once the students begin to understand the transformations from third to first person, the autobiography writing is modeled using the transformed sentences. Although the graphic organizer groups ideas chronologically, explicit attention is given to temporal language and expanding upon the ideas in the graphic organizer. In the intermediate grades, it is essential to teach students how to elaborate on simple sentences by using precise language. For example, the sentence, "In the city, the Nahua struggled to make money." A more sophisticated and expansive sentence can be written by providing specificity, "In Mexico City, the Nahua widows and children struggled to earn money and survive." We cannot take for granted the importance of teaching this explicitly to emerging bilingual learners across languages. As the writing of the autobiography is being completed over a few days, students can begin exploring biographies of people of interest to research and present for the living wax museum.

To guide students in their independent work of research, note-taking, and writing that will go on over the next week or so, the teacher can continue modeling the processes with different types of texts on a different person or focus on other aspects of writing, oracy, or vocabulary development. Through the teacher's observations of the students' progress, different teaching can occur.

Finally, students should transfer their autobiography to notecards for the living wax museum event and practice. Students can be paired to ask questions and rehearse with one another. Provide students with explicit feedback. To ensure the Living Wax Museum event involves dialogue and not just the presenter reading their index cards, proposed questions for dialogue are suggested:

- Why did you select this person?

- What did you learn about this person's legacy? In what way does their legacy relate to you or to someone you know?

- What can you take away from this person's life?

- What questions do you have? Or what else would you like to know?

- How was what you learned in Spanish literacy similar and different from literacy-based ELD?

SUMMARY: BILITERATE WRITING AND GENRE STUDY IN GRADES 3 TO 5

Final teacher-led dialogues and evaluation can include reflections on learning about two main text types, biography and autobiography, within the genre of informative/explanatory texts and most importantly the incorporation of the wealth of knowledge from underrepresented and minoritized communities. Every effort must be made to ensure biliteracy instruction is social-justice oriented. In this unit, we included opportunities for students to learn more from respected elders and family members. Furthermore, emphasis is given to including a variety of texts representing members of minoritized communities and models of linguistic sophistication. Examples of how to backward plan are included by analyzing a student's biliterate writing samples prior to the unit, selecting culturally and linguistically diverse books/texts/various media, and most importantly including all these aspects to create biliterate developmentally and grade-level appropriate exemplars to plan for writing, oracy and metalanguage instruction in both language environments.

Mi Abuelito
Por: Mateo

El día 16 de abril de 1960 nació un niño llamado Luis Miguel que nació en Zacatecas, México con sus padres Abel y Regina. Fue un día muy bonito. Él es un hombre muy amable, trabajador y amable. Él vivía con sus 9 herman@s Carlos, Raúl, Juan, Jose, Abel, Sara, Marta, y Eugenia. Él tenía un sueño y ese sueño es aprender inglés y usar la tecnología. También tenía un sueño para su nieto y eso fue para que crezca para ser un hombre inteligente y que descubriera el mundo.

La niñez de Luis Miguel no fue fácil. Cuando él era un joven él mandaba comida que le dio su mamá y lo vendía a través de su vecindario. También cuando él era un jovencito su mamá le cocía comida y le compraba un bolio y una coca. Cuando él era un addolescente el trabajaba en el campo cortando chile y frijol. La niñez de mi abuelito no ha sido fácil pero él nunca se ha sido de vencida.

Mi abuelito tiene un trabajo difícil pero a él no le importa. Mi abuelito vende comida en su camioneta. Él vende comida que a mucha gente le gusta, el vende tacos, empanadas, quesadillas, gorditas, y más. Su mamá le enseñó cómo cocinar y su esposa también. Él tiene su propio restaurante donde puede ir la gente. Mi abuelito tiene un trabajo difícil pero le gusta poner una sonrisa en las caras de la demás gente.

Mi abuelito es una persona a la que le gusta viajar. Mi abuelo viajaba más al norte en especifico Monterrey. Él viajaba allí porque le gustaba la playa y toda la fruta. Él y su esposa viajaban allí porque es una parte muy bonita y una parte buenísima para viajar. Monterrey es una parte muy bonita para viajar y por eso mi abuelito y su esposa tienen muchas memorias allí.

Yo elegí hacer esta biografía de mi abuelito porque él es alguien muy especial para mi y yo lo quiero con todo mi corazón y lo cambiaría por el mundo.

Biography of Jimi Hendrix

Jimi Hendrix was a very good musician who wrote a lot of music and really changed the world of rock and roll. Jimi was born in 1942 in Seattle, Washington. He played the guitar and people loved it when he did. Also, he liked to dance to not only his music, but others' music, too. Jimi is a musician unlike any other who ever lived, and will be remembered in history as one of the best rock musicians.

Jimi Hendrix is someone who changed rock music and put in so much effort to accomplish his dream and he wants everybody to do the same. Jimi played his own style of what he thought rock and roll was, which led people to keep practicing his music. He also inspired many people to follow their dreams and never give up. Jimi is a very important person in the world of rock and roll and inspired many people.

Jimi was a very happy and delightful person. Jimi loved to smile around people. No matter where or when Jimi passed by someone he brightened their day. Jimi never mistreated anyone in his life and was always nice to everyone. Jimi was an activist who never used violence to bring people together, but instead he used his words and kindness. Jimi was a very kind and non violent person and I think we need more people like him. Jimi spoke for people who did not have a voice. Most importantly, he spoke for people of color. Jimi was a very inspirational person. He will go down in history as one of the greatest activist musicians in the world.

I chose Jimi for my biography because he was a very inspirational person and overall an amazing human being. Also, I really enjoy his music because it makes me happier throughout my day. I hope that you can find some joy while listening to Jimi Hendrix's music, too.

Figure 6.11. Mateo's fourth-grade biliterate writing pieces for the biography genre study unit: "*Mi Abuelito*," written in Spanish, and "Jimi Hendrix," written in English.

Questions for Reflection and Action

- ▶ Why is it important to include a multitude of voices to understand different points of views and experiences? How can you or do you attend to this in biliteracy instruction?
- ▶ How can you ensure your biliteracy instruction, particularly biliterate writing instruction, is drawing upon your EB students' cultural, linguistic, familial, and experiential wealth?
- ▶ The samples in Figure 6.11 were produced by Mateo, the same student who produced the samples in Figure 6.2. Take time to evaluate if the student met the CCSS standards for this genre unit. How are the student's abilities the same or different between languages? Did the student meet the standards?

7 Furthering Biliteracy via Genre Studies in Grades 3 to 5

Social Justice

"... what just is, isn't always justice."

—The Hill We Climb, *Amanda Gorman (2021)*

Key Terms

Diverse literature	**Social Justice Standards**
Humanizing curricula	

Guiding Questions

- How can we expand our vision of the purposes for writing as students proceed through the grades?
- How can the **Social Justice Standards** complement the goals of the Common Core State Standards and other State-/District-based standards?
- How do teachers plan holistically to use resources creatively to help students to develop the tools to express themselves through biliterate writing?

State and district standards often define what writing genres students should write, but rarely do they specify the content of that writing. The CCSS, for example, specify that third-, fourth-, and fifth-grade students should:

1. Write opinion pieces on topics or texts, supporting a point of view with reasons and information;
2. Write informative/explanatory texts to examine a topic and convey ideas and information clearly; and
3. Write narratives to develop real or imagined experiences or events using effective technique, descriptive details, and clear event sequences.

In the vagueness of the standards lie possibilities! It invites educators to determine the range and variety of topics their students explore. Schools should be places to learn how to advocate for oneself and others. They should provide spaces where students reimagine the world and begin to understand the power they have to transform it. Writing instruction can provide opportunities for students to explore topics that matter to them.

FOSTERING ENGAGED WRITING IN GRADES 3 TO 5

By expanding upon what can be accomplished within the parameters of the standards, we engage upper-grade students to use all of their languages to explore topics like immigrant justice, linguistic freedom, ableism, structural oppression, self-determination, inclusive and accepting spaces, food justice, erasure politics, environmental protection, civil rights, and cultural equity. The possibilities are only limited by our understanding of the vast universe of human needs and struggles.

If you have been educating bilingual learners for any amount of time, you know that what we do is inherently political. Every time we choose to teach or elevate a language other than English, we are engaging in a fight for linguistic and social justice. We are fighting for a more just world—for everyone. The pluralistic democracy we aspire to uphold requires that we disrupt and dismantle systems of oppression and that we do so to the benefit of all. The mirrors and windows that we provide with our inclusion of **diverse literature** decenter whiteness and create educational experiences that affirm identity, build empathy, and value diversity. While some imagine these changes as being adult driven, we know that at a very young age, children can distinguish right from wrong, fair from unfair. We need their voices and their actions in our quest to create a more just world. We open this chapter, therefore, with a quote by the first National Youth Poet Laureate, Amanda Gorman. It reminds us that the status quo, or what "just is", does not encompass what could be (i.e., justice). The goal of education must be broader than instruction that is confined to a single isolated disciplinary component such as writing. We do not advocate teaching writing for writing's sake, but in service to a broader vision of what the world could be. Paulo Freire taught us that children should learn to read the word and the world (2000). Not only do they read the world, they shape it, they live it, they write it. Children should learn to use words to imagine the world as it could be rather than how it is. Perhaps we should have begun with a nod to the idea that "the pen is mightier than the sword." With the stroke of a pen, laws are changed, and governments dismantled or reconfigured. Writing allows us to touch others' hearts and souls. It is a means of sparking innovation and inciting transformation. We need to apprentice our students into these traditions.

We understand and recognize that schools often focus on teaching students the art of writing in ways that inform, persuade, and explain. We hope, too, that students are encouraged to use writing to explore ideas, express their feelings, and to argue for or against a position. In this chapter, we will argue that the content of students' writing is as important as the decontextualized skills that anchor that content. We are committed to advocating for school systems that develop student activists who see writing as a tool that can be used to give voice to the excluded, to argue for justice, to broaden our collective understanding of whose experiences matter, to challenge the status quo and to pose important dilemmas while exploring creative solutions. In this respect, this chapter will deviate from the chapters that preceded it.

Throughout this book, we have advocated collecting and analyzing students' biliterate writing samples with intentionality and purpose. We have prioritized students' messages over attention to structural elements and spelling. We have offered examples of how to collect evidence and use it to inform and drive your instruction. What we hope has become apparent is that writing outcomes are sensitive to instruction and that success breeds success. We begin from an assets-based approach and use data and research to integrate writing instruction into a holistic approach to literacy that ties together Spanish and English and emphasizes the interconnectedness of reading, writing, oracy, and metalinguistic awareness. Once again, we feel compelled to reiterate that writing should not be taught in isolation. Just as languages should not be siloed, neither should individual language and literacy domains. As we transition children from elementary to middle school, we deviate a bit from our earlier examples of dissecting and analyzing specific pieces of writing, to provide a broader perspective of what to expect in the upper grades. We do this assuming that the reader will consult earlier chapters to understand how to apply and interpret the Literacy Squared Writing Rubric (see Chapters 1, 4, 5, and 6).

USING A BILINGUAL LENS TO PROMOTE A DEVELOPMENTALLY APPROPRIATE TRAJECTORY

We know that learning to express oneself bilingually is a difficult task. It is further exacerbated by the fact that most assessments and rubrics used to examine the writing of bilingual learners are based on monolingual views of writing development. This results in deficit framings of children and their abilities. Collecting and analyzing writing samples systematically in Spanish and English while applying a holistic biliteracy lens not only allows us to understand how students are currently able to express themselves, but also helps us understand their potential. Throughout the nearly 20 years that we have engaged in this work, we have collected and analyzed many thousands of writing samples across the elementary grades. This has helped us to envision a writing trajectory that is sensitive to instruction and that provides insights into how students' languages are developing as part of a unified whole.

Our research indicates that students apply their full linguistic repertoires when writing, and that these behaviors are sometimes misinterpreted by teachers as evidence of linguistic interference rather than strategic deployment of an expansive repertoire. Further, students' Spanish and English writing are highly correlated, such that students who are strong writers in one language tend to be strong writers in the other and vice versa. This is particularly true in content communication and the use of structural elements. In other words, languages serve as scaffolds and supports for one another rather than as sources of interference. For some students, there is a near perfect one-to-one correspondence across languages with regard to content and form, particularly as they reach the fourth and fifth grades. In fact, as we have argued throughout this book, if students demonstrate a skill or strategy in one language, they should be held accountable for applying it or approximating it in the other. These expectations ensure that students' languages and literacies develop in parallel.

Our hope is that by the end of elementary school, because of focused and explicit instruction, biliterate students produce comparable writing pieces in each of their languages with thoughtful organization, high accuracy, and appropriate rhetorical strategies. In terms of our rubric, we want to see the majority of our students with overall scores of 18 to 20 in both Spanish and English. This is the equivalent of scoring an 8 to 9 in content, a 5 in structural elements, and a 4 to 5 in spelling. To score at this level, students must write well-organized, multiparagraph pieces that include effective transitions, vivid examples, and have a sense of completeness in each of their languages. These benchmarks can be demonstrated and taught using a wide variety of themes and can be developed through the examination of well-crafted and diverse mentor texts.

BEYOND THE COMMON CORE: SOCIAL JUSTICE STANDARDS AND HUMANIZING CURRICULA

Academic standards define and articulate consistent learning goals about what students should know and be able to do at the end of each grade level. They ensure some level of consistency in expectations. They also, whether intentionally or not, point to what we value and whose histories and voices are included or elevated in most schooling experiences. We contend that the Common Core State Standards do not go far enough in **humanizing curricula** and promoting culturally and linguistically sustaining pedagogies that favor anti-racist and anti-bias values. Therefore, we suggest that teachers also consider incorporating into their academic instruction the K–12 Social Justice Standards developed by the Southern Poverty Law Center and *Learning for Justice*, formerly known as *Teaching Tolerance* (2022).

The twenty anchor Social Justice Standards are organized into the four domains of *Identity*, *Diversity*, *Justice* and *Action*. (See Figure 7.1 for a list of the standards arranged by each domain.) The developers have provided kid-friendly, grade-specific outcomes and scenarios that contribute to the development of knowledge and skills that reduce prejudice and induce collective action. For example, in *justice outcomes* for third through fifth grade, students are expected to affirm,

Social Justice Anchor Standards

Learning for Justice & The Southern Poverty Law Center

https://www.learningforjustice.org/frameworks/social-justice-standards

IDENTITY

1. Students will develop positive social identities based on their membership in multiple groups in society.

2. Students will develop language and historical and cultural knowledge that affirm and accurately describe their membership in multiple identity groups.

3. Students will recognize that people's multiple identities interact and create unique and complex individuals.

4. Students will express pride, confidence and healthy self-esteem without denying the value and dignity of other people.

5. Students will recognize traits of the dominant culture, their home culture and other cultures and understand how they negotiate their own identity in multiple spaces.

DIVERSITY

6. Students will express comfort with people who are both similar to and different from them and engage respectfully with all people.

7. Students will develop language and knowledge to accurately and respectfully describe how people (including themselves) are both similar to and different from each other and others in their identity groups.

8. Students will respectfully express curiosity about the history and lived experiences of others and will exchange ideas and beliefs in an open-minded way.

9. Students will respond to diversity by building empathy, respect, understanding and connection.

10. Students will examine diversity in social, cultural, political and historical contexts rather than in ways that are superficial or oversimplified.

JUSTICE

11. Students will recognize stereotypes and relate to people as individuals rather than representatives of groups.

12. Students will recognize unfairness on the individual level (e.g., biased speech) and injustice at the institutional or systemic level (e.g., discrimination).

13. Students will analyze the harmful impact of bias and injustice on the world, historically and today.

14. Students will recognize that power and privilege influence relationships on interpersonal, intergroup and institutional levels and consider how they have been affected by those dynamics.

15. Students will identify figures, groups, events and a variety of strategies and philosophies relevant to the history of social justice around the world.

ACTION

16. Students will express empathy when people are excluded or mistreated because of their identities and concern when they themselves experience bias.

17. Students will recognize their own responsibility to stand up to exclusion, prejudice and injustice.

18. Students will speak up with courage and respect when they or someone else has been hurt or wronged by bias.

19. Students will make principled decisions about when and how to take a stand against bias and injustice in their everyday lives and will do so despite negative peer or group pressure.

20. Students will plan and carry out collective action against bias and injustice in the world and will evaluate what strategies are most effective.

Figure 7.1. Social Justice Standards. *Learning for Justice* and The Southern Poverty Law Center. (Reprinted with permission of Learning for Justice, a project of the Southern Poverty Law Center https://www.learningforjustice.org/frameworks/social-justice-standards.)

"I know that life is easier for some people and harder for others based on who they are and where they were born" or "I know that words, behaviors, rules and laws that treat people unfairly based on their group identities cause real harm." Relatedly, in the *action outcomes* for third through fifth grade, students affirm, "I know it's important for me to stand up for myself and for others, and I know how to get help if I need ideas on how to do this." Are these not values and ideas worth incorporating into our educational settings? Ironically, while most states have taken up the Common Core with regard to writing, few, if any, have adopted the Social Justice Standards. Many of the teachers we encounter tell us that they do not even know they exist. Sadly, we know that there are those who fear the introduction of standards and topics that examine societal inequities and would ban teachers from introducing them into the curriculum. They describe honest and critical examinations of our storied history to be divisive and they suggest that books and ideas should be eliminated and swept aside. We argue that our country's increasing racial and linguistic diversity commands that we elevate and highlight them while engaging in honest age-appropriate, historically accurate discussions that name past and continued injustices. We cannot solve problems we cannot name, and the generation we are currently educating needs to be prepared to understand the world that is in contrast to one they might create.

Linking the writing standards to the Social Justice Standards asks teachers and students to recognize and name injustices, to problem solve, to think critically, to advocate effectively, to analyze resources and arguments, and to commit to the betterment of communities. In short, the skills and knowledge that are developed through these types of investigations and writing foster leadership. Further, students develop the ability to examine and expose problematic and entrenched patterns that cause harm. They nurture the seeds for empathy, political activism, and civic engagement. At their core, these standards personalize and humanize the larger educational project. They affirm for children that the kind, just, right, and humane thing to do is to care for one another and the world we occupy. It is what responsible human beings do.

Choosing to teach in humanizing and affirming ways, for the ultimate betterment of society, means beginning with the students. We must develop safe spaces in which students can bring their full selves. Our learning environments and our approach to teaching must be organized so that we can answer the questions: Who are the students in our classrooms? Where do they come from? What languages do they speak? What do they care about? Students bring an array of lived experiences into the classroom. We must learn to value and tap into them. In the next few pages, we will suggest ways to pair texts and to develop themes that affirm students' identities while also helping them to learn about others. Combining the CCSS with the Social Justice Standards, we will suggest how to organize texts around a theme while differentiating tasks by language.

Guiding Questions

Problem solving and inquiry begin with a sense of curiosity and wonder. What are students noticing? How can you get them to question why things are the way they are? When we teach children to ask and explore meaningful questions, we create stimulating environments in which students have authentic reasons to read, speak, write, view, and think. Employing a social justice lens, we encourage "how" and "why" questions that are not easily answered. Some examples include:

- How do our identities and upbringings influence what we read, write, and view?

- How do our identities and upbringings influence how we interpret what we read, write, and view and how others will interpret our writing?

- What is the history of people who look and sound like me? How does this history impact me and my community today?

- How are language and power intertwined and what does this mean for me and my family?

- Why do some people stand up to prejudice and unfairness while others do not?
- In what ways are all narratives influenced by bias and perspective?[1]

Beyond broad questions related to students' lived experiences and issues of social justice, we can organize and develop questions related to a theme—for example, immigration. Questions students might explore include:

- Why and how do families and individuals immigrate? From where do they originate and where do they settle?
- What are the experiences of immigrants to the United States?
- How might we promote a greater sense of belonging for immigrants?

Beyond grade level foci, we have seen entire schools adopt a theme of societal importance (i.e., Black Lives Matter). The hallways, the library, and the classrooms all find ways to display learning and work that is connected to the school-wide focus.

Planning, therefore, includes a consideration of the questions you want students to explore and be able to answer at the end of a unit of study. Leave space for students to propose topics, but ground the work in the big ideas you want to explore collectively. Recognize these as the "essential questions" and share them with your students from the beginning of a unit. Explain to students that they will be talking and writing extensively as they formulate answers to these questions. Be sure students understand that it is always okay to change their minds as they gather new information and listen carefully to one another. As they read, talk, write, and view, refer them back to the essential questions and teach them how to gather evidence to support their new understandings. Students need guidance on where and how to focus their attention. Use these questions to plan your oracy lessons and to guide your materials selection. By beginning with a group of essential questions that are linked closely to your content, language, and justice standards, you assist your bilingual students to focus their attention and provide concrete guidance about expectations.

Collaborative Writing

Writing is often a communal act, yet in schools we hurry students to work in solitude on independent projects. Bilingual learners are acquiring the same knowledge and skills as monolingual students while simultaneously developing linguistic proficiency in two languages. As discussed in Chapter 2, a critical component of language development in relation to overall literacy growth is oracy. When working in pairs or groups, students must articulate their inner dialogue, express content-related ideas, and co-navigate language problem-solving tasks. One means of developing opportunities for purposeful oracy work is to engage students in collaborative writing tasks.

In our first book, *Biliteracy from the Start*, we suggested that there is much value for bilingual learners in co-authorship, or collaborative writing (Escamilla et al., 2014). Collaborative writing requires extended talk, thoughtful negotiation, and a reliance upon the collective wisdom and abilities of the group members. One student may excel in organization, another may demonstrate a more sophisticated command of expressive language, while a third exudes a creative spirit and approach. Collaboration requires planning, coordination, and compromise. All group members are expected to contribute equally; therefore, we recommend that teachers organize the task so that tasks are distributed fairly and individual students cannot dominate. Some teachers assign roles or employ collaborative structures. Importantly, collaborative writing should not look like side-by-side independent work. There should be a sense of collective responsibility to the product and to the intended audience. Success often depends upon a strong plan with systemic check-in opportunities for feedback. Research indicates that bilingual

---
[1] Some of these questions are taken from *Learning for Justice*.

students who engage in collaborative writing solve more language-related problems and transfer their learning to other contexts (Jang & Cheung, 2020). Further, collaborative writing is particularly valuable for novice and passive learners who benefit from seeing how others engage in composition.

At the upper grades, collaborative writing takes the form of meaningful inquiry projects, script writing, web-page design and production, performance art, imaginative narratives, poetry for multiple voices, traditional essays/reports, and dramatic reenactments. Critical to a successful collaborative experience is the establishment of a real or imagined audience and the necessity for the pair or group to present their work to others. Guidelines should include the caveat that all members must have a speaking role when their product is shared with a broader public, even if that public is simply the teacher or their classmates.

The Biliterate Writing Trajectory: Grade 5 and Up

Beyond the elementary school years, as students continue to develop their biliteracy at the secondary level, it is imperative that students have numerous opportunities to continue to expand their understanding about how to write in a variety of genres employing what they know and can do across languages. Explicit oracy instruction, coupled with opportunities to work collaboratively, results in more sophisticated and complex writing. Continue to integrate reading and writing, encouraging students to think expansively about the materials and resources available to them. In other words, students should be encouraged to gather information in all languages even if the final product will be restricted to one language. The opportunities to write for change and in service to themes of social justice will only be expanded as students' life experiences grow. Students should be guided to understand that writing is not just a school-based exercise. It is a tool to engage with the greater social world. As they come into their own as writers, we want them to see that they can engage this tool in service to the creation of a more just world.

SAMPLE UNIT SKETCH: READING AND WRITING ABOUT RACISM

By way of example, we offer the following fifth-grade unit sketch focused on anti-racism to demonstrate how one might plan and organize a bilingual unit of study that culminates in a powerful display of collaborative writing across two languages. It is grounded in oracy and foregrounds both the CCSS and the Social Justice Standards. We refer to this as a unit sketch because it will not name every minilesson or oracy structure that would be necessary to guide students to the final product. Completing the unit would require many individual sessions, and those will not be outlined or presented here. Rather, this sketch will provide a broad brushed template for planning that is guided by critical questions and offers a glimpse into the thought process for planning a holistic lesson that considers carefully what will take place in each language. While it is focused on the upper grades, the process can be applied to any grade level. Our planning is intentional in focus, but like everyone, we sometimes need reminders to be sure we have not steered too far astray from our primary purpose. Because of this, we review any unit we develop with a series of questions. We have included this list of questions in Table 7.1. Because we are focused here on only one aspect of a paired biliteracy unit, writing, we will not address all of the questions, but we will strive to indicate which ones guide our thinking as we flesh out the writing component of the unit. Importantly, these questions map onto the lesson plan template that we use in our biliteracy model. The questions, however, can be applied to any lesson plan format that you use. In a biliteracy teaching and learning model, it is important that any unit considers what will be learned and demonstrated in Spanish (or a language other than English) and what will be learned and demonstrated in English. This unit sketch is unusual in that the final product will combine work and learning from both languages.

Table 7.1. Guiding Questions

	Guiding Questions Literacy Squared Lesson Planning
Standards (Content, language, and social justice)	• What will students know and be able to do at the end of this unit? • How will I hold them accountable for these skills across languages? • Are the learning goals in each language environment similar and complementary?
Literacy objectives	• What text and language-specific goals will help you to meet the standards? • What genre and/or skills will you develop so that the students can meet the standards? • What big ideas and enduring understandings will students exhibit? • What essential questions will guide students' reading, discussions, and writing? • Can you begin to identify some evidence the students will produce?
Materials	• Which texts will you use in each language environment? • Are the texts appropriate for the standards selected? • Are the texts grade-level appropriate? • Have you considered text complexity and linguistic demands? • Are there supplemental texts that should be used?
Connection between literacy environment	• How are the two language environments connected? (Theme, Genre, Bilingual Book, Comprehension Strategy, Metalinguistic Awareness, Oracy Structures...)
Cross-language connections	• How will you raise metalinguistic awareness? (Either across languages or within a single language). • How are you being explicit about the similarities/differences between Spanish and English? (Cognate instruction, Así se dice, Anchor charts)
theDictado	• Are the teaching points relevant to the standard? • Have you weighed quality versus quantity? • Will you be able to administer theDictado in less than 20 minutes while spending at least ½ the time reconstructing the text, attending to teaching points, and guiding students to self-correct? • Are your Spanish and English dictados complementary without being duplicative?
Oracy	• Do the oracy objectives support the literacy objectives and the standards? • Do the language structures and opportunities for dialogue support language development? • Is the vocabulary both general and specific? • Are the language structures sufficiently complex? • Will the language taught during oracy ensure students' successful demonstration of mastery of standards and objectives?
Assessment	• Are all domains assessed (reading, writing, speaking, listening)? • Are the learning goals evident? • Is it clear how the learning goals are measured or evaluated (checklist, rubric, etc.)?
Session planning	• Is the "heavy lifting" occurring in Spanish? • Is literacy-based ELD less cognitively demanding and sufficiently focused on language? Is literacy-based ELD directly and explicitly connected to Spanish language literacy? • Is there a gradual release of responsibility—across the lessons? • Is there more shared and collaborative work in English? • Are reading and writing lessons evident in both languages? Are reading and writing connected? • Do the lessons ensure that students will master the standards and objectives? • Do the lessons provide a strong foundation for literacy-based ELD? • Is the sequence of activities clear (1., 2., 3.,)? Does each lesson build upon what was previously learned?

The Standards: What Will Students Know and Be Able to Do?

Our lesson planning and implementation should always be guided by grade-appropriate standards. As articulated previously, standards set uniform expectations for what students should know and be able to do at any particular grade level. Bilingual students learn and apply these standards across language environments. A continuum of standards that spirals across curricula, subject matters, and grade levels ensures that students develop a solid foundation in the skills and knowledge we have established as important and that subsequent lessons build upon these previously attained proficiencies and abilities.

The key question we pose when we begin any unit is: *What will students know and be able to do at the end of this unit?* We then turn to the standards to see what is expected. At the point that we have determined the key standard guiding the lesson, we begin the backward planning process by asking: *How will I invite students to apply skills and knowledge across languages?* and *How will students demonstrate their learning in meaningful ways?*

Writing Standards   While the standards addressed in the broader unit on racism and antiracism will span many domains of literacy, here we focus on our thematic approach to writing development and how the standards guide not only the process students will follow, but provide guidance on how they will be assessed.

The core writing standard to be addressed in this fifth-grade unit is:

> *CCSS.ELA-Literacy.W.5.2: Write informative/explanatory texts to examine a topic and convey ideas and information clearly.*

According to the CCSS, successful completion of this standard includes the following substandards:

> CCSS.ELA-LITERACY.W.5.2.A: Introduce a topic clearly, provide a general observation and focus, and group related information logically; include formatting (e.g., headings), illustrations, and multimedia when useful to aiding comprehension.
> CCSS.ELA-LITERACY.W.5.2.B: Develop the topic with facts, definitions, concrete details, quotations, or other information and examples related to the topic.
> CCSS.ELA-LITERACY.W.5.2.C: Link ideas within and across categories of information using words, phrases, and clauses (e.g., *in contrast*, *especially*).
> CCSS.ELA-LITERACY.W.5.2.D: Use precise language and domain-specific vocabulary to inform about or explain the topic.
> CCSS.ELA-LITERACY.W.5.2.E: Provide a concluding statement or section related to the information or explanation presented.

One can see how these substandards could easily be incorporated into a rubric that students and teachers use to evaluate final products. Note, too, that these standards align closely to the Literacy Squared Writing Rubric and our previous statement that in the intermediate grades we expect students to write well-organized, multiparagraph pieces that include effective transitions, vivid examples, and have a sense of completeness in each of the students' languages.

Social Justice Standards   Once we have determined the Common Core (or district/state) standards that will anchor our teaching, we turn to the Social Justice Standards. If our goal is to examine racism, which standards might help us to create essential questions and learning outcomes? Returning to Figure 7.1, we see that the standards in the justice domain are particularly relevant. Further, we want to invite students to use their newly gained knowledge to envision and inspire change. Therefore, we also consult the action domain. For this unit, we choose justice anchor standards numbers 13 and 14, and action anchor standard number 20 to guide the planning of the overall unit:

> *Justice Domain*:
> 13. Students will analyze the harmful impact of bias and injustice on the world, historically and today.
> 14. Students will recognize that power and privilege influence relationships on interpersonal, intergroup and institutional levels and consider how they have been affected by those dynamics.

Action Domain:
20. Students will plan and carry out collective action against bias and injustice in the world and will evaluate what strategies are most effective.

The choice of these Social Justice Standards will help us to evaluate the books, texts, and materials that we select to make available to students. The information contained within must help students gather enough information to affirmatively meet these standards. We recognize, too, that there may be social studies standards that overlap and can be included in a teacher's approach to a unit such as this. The standards we have selected here are not exhaustive. We advocate thematic approaches that allow students and teachers to accomplish multiple goals and standards within the biliteracy component of their academic day.

The Final Product: How Will Students Be Accountable for These Skills Across Languages?

Once we have determined the knowledge and skills students will demonstrate as a result of our unit, we need to consider what products students will deliver and how these will complement one another across languages. Will students be responsible for all standards in both languages, or will they demonstrate some standards in one language and other standards in another? Keep in mind that once a standard is mastered, no matter what language students use to demonstrate it, it does not have to be retaught in the other language. It is not necessary, therefore, to ensure that all standards are taught in all languages. We simply do not have time for such inefficiencies.

In light of the standards selected, we determined that students would demonstrate their mastery and understanding through the collaborative creation of a *2 to 4 minute video*, to be recorded in Spanish, that summarized or provided a commentary on their understanding or experiences of racism, including suggestions for anti-racist actions elementary-aged children could embrace and enact in their day-to-day lives. The information to be presented in the videos would be scripted (i.e., written) collaboratively and include a summary of the relevant issues that reference evidence gleaned from their reading/viewing opportunities. Creative approaches would be encouraged and suggestions would include creating a vignette of how one might interrupt racism, designing a video around an artistic performance (spoken word, rap song, poetry), or telling a story through puppets and props. Each person in the pair or group would be responsible for taking on a speaking role and contributing to the final production. Prior to production, groups would exchange texts and translate one another's work into English, so that subtitles could be included in the final productions. We envision that this process would lead to further discussion and the pointed inclusion of oracy structures and targeted vocabulary to ensure clarity of message and appropriate language complexity. Further, students will negotiate how ideas are expressed differently across languages, engendering elevated metalinguistic awareness. The intended outcome provides students with opportunities to use expressive language in both Spanish and English and flips the script in terms of the typical YouTube video composite in which pertinent information is presented in English with subtitles provided for speakers of other languages. It also provides an opportunity to research, read, talk, and write that honors holistic biliteracy and asks students and teachers to combine information into a single final product. The video format (i.e., honoring Spanish and providing access in English) challenges the primacy and hegemony of English while offering students an opportunity to authentically access and apply their expansive linguistic repertoire.

Returning to the standards, we would ask that groups verify that they have written a clearly introduced and focused piece that demonstrates information logically using graphics and visual media to emphasize key points. Language would be refined to ensure that ideas were linked and connected appropriately and that the conclusion tied everything together. In this way, we ensure that students demonstrate grade-appropriate standards-based learning. By starting with the standards and considering the enduring understandings students will exhibit in their final products, we lay the foundations for selecting materials, articulating essential questions, and developing oracy work that intentionally provides students with language experiences that inform their final written products.

Materials

Materials selection begins by taking stock of what is available related to the proposed theme and determining how those materials correspond to each language environment. When seeking materials, we think beyond print-based materials (e.g., books, magazines, newspapers) to include multimedia and electronic sources. As bilingual teachers, we know that what is available in a language other than English is often limited, so when we locate and identify as many pertinent materials as possible, it is critically important that we consider which are available in other languages and we consider their use wisely. When exploring materials, it is important to consider the following:

Which texts will you use in each language environment?

Are the texts appropriate for the standards selected?

Are the texts/materials grade-level appropriate?

We understand the need to have materials to accommodate a range of language proficiency levels, but we worry that upper-grade students are consistently exposed only to texts that do not represent grade-level expectations. If you choose to use a book at a lower reading level, can you justify its inclusion? Does it offer something that other texts do not? Consider tapping into the knowledge and expertise of your local media specialist. It is likely that they can help you to locate additional resources that reflect the standards, are grade appropriate, and are available in languages other than English.

Core Text: *Stamped (For Kids): Racism, Anti-Racism, and You* For the unit on racism, we begin with a core text that is available in Spanish and English, knowing that individual schools and districts have access to a wide variety of materials. If you were to teach a similar lesson, you might assemble a different collection of core materials related to the theme. The importance is not in any particular group of materials; rather, it is that reading, writing, speaking, and metalanguage are nurtured in two languages in a holistic manner that allows students to demonstrate and develop complex productive language abilities. Because we want students to be challenged, it was important to us to select a sophisticated chapter book that was rich in information while also presenting that information with mature language. We selected *Stamped (For Kids): Racism, Anti-Racism, and You* as the primary core text.

This chapter book is available in Spanish and English and is adapted for children from the award-winning, best-selling, adult-level book also titled *Stamped: Racism, Anti-racism, and You*[2] (Cherry-Paul, 2021) that explores the history of racism and anti-racism in the United States and helps readers to understand the impact of racism on their current lived experiences. The idea of using a single text in both languages is not to engage in duplicative reading, but to disperse the reading experiences and knowledge acquisition across languages. Here teachers have the opportunity to explore ideas and language simultaneously, calling students' attention to how ideas and language are similar or different when expressed in different languages. Different chapters can be read and discussed in different languages and connections across environments are necessary. To fully grasp the concepts, students will need to discuss topics they read in Spanish while working in English and vice versa. It requires that teachers think carefully about how to scaffold the language students will need to acquire and use to talk and write about experiences that were initiated in a different language.

Supplementary Texts Once we have selected the core text, we assemble supplementary texts. These texts may include picture books, electronic materials, or photographs and illustrations. We have chosen to include the picture books *Something Happened in Our Town: A Child's Story*

---

[2] According to the American Library Association *Stamped* and *Something Happened in Our Town* were two of the top ten books challenged most often by parents and community members in 2020.

about Racial Injustice (Celano et al., 2018) and *Race Cars: A Children's Book About White Privilege* (Devenny, 2021). These books, on their own, would not meet the criteria for grade-level reading; however, their presentation of issues related to race and white supremacy are complex and used in conjunction with *Stamped (For Kids)*, they help to tell a fuller story and serve as wonderful catalysts for students to engage in deep discussion. Unfortunately, they are not available in Spanish. It is important to balance materials so we expand our search so as not to appear to privilege English over Spanish. The subtle and not-so-subtle messages we send when we provide access to texts and materials only in English are not lost on our bilingual students and families.

Because many of the texts we located related to racism and anti-racism were English-centric and not available in Spanish, we turned to the internet to see what multimedia materials might be available in Spanish. These resources provide us not only with ways to generate and develop students' thinking about racism and anti-racism, but they provide examples for the kinds of videos students will produce as part of the unit. We noted as we explored materials that racism as a concept is not exclusive to the United Sates. The universality of this issue opened up the range of materials available. With regard to this theme, some videos that stood out to us included:

Estudiante Puma rapea contra la discriminación (UNAM Global TV, YouTube, 3/15/22)

Jovenes Latinos Opinan Sobre Racismo (El Minnsesota de Hoy, YouTube, 6/3/20)

Racismo vs. Clasismo (AJ + Español Presenta, Facebook, 5/14/18)

¿Qué significa raza? (Sesame Street in Communities, YouTube, 4/14/21)

In each of these short videos, students are exposed to ideas and language that can inform their video scripts.

At this point in our planning, we have our standards. We know what we want kids to read, write, and produce. We have identified a core collection of reading and viewing materials in Spanish and English that will anchor the unit. What more should we be thinking about? Without getting into individual sessions, or minilessons related to the craft of writing, we want to think about oracy.

Oracy

In planning this component of the unit, we ask ourselves, "What oral language opportunities will students need to support their development and mastery of the content and literacy standards?" As we begin to think about oracy, we return to our standards and the importance of essential questions. The Social Justice Standards lend themselves nicely to question formation. For example, Social Justice Standard #13 gets reworded from "Students will analyze the harmful impact of bias and injustice on the world, historically and today" to "What are some of the harmful impacts and injustices on the world, historically and today?" The action statement, "Students will plan and carry out collective action against bias and injustice in the world and will evaluate what strategies are most effective" becomes "How can I (we) plan and carry out collective action against bias and injustice in the world?" Once you have formulated the essential questions, consult the materials students will be reading, viewing, and experiencing. Use the information contained within the materials to attempt to produce written answers. It is important that you engage at this level so that you can analyze and understand the complexity of what you are asking students to do. What language (vocabulary and language structures) did you use? How did you connect and link ideas? What open-ended questions could be posed to students that would provide opportunities for students to express the ideas you have included in your response? These are what will need to be taught during oracy instruction. Remember, it is not enough to do this in one language. How are the same ideas expressed across languages and at a variety of levels? It is important that as you navigate these questions and make instructional decisions, you consider your students' language proficiencies and offer language goals that allow all students to participate while also providing them with linguistic challenges. Remember, we are teaching to the potential not to the current ability.

Once we have identified the vocabulary, language structures, and dialogue opportunities that will support our students' reading and writing related to the theme, we check ourselves by asking:

Do the oracy objectives support the literacy objectives and the standards?

Do the language structures and opportunities for dialogue support language development?

Are the language structures sufficiently complex?

Is the vocabulary both general and specific?

Will the language taught during oracy ensure students' successful demonstration of mastery of standards and objectives?

If we can answer these questions in the affirmative, we are ready to build out the day-to-day sessions that will happen in each language, thinking carefully about all of the skills and lessons students will need to successfully produce a video that demonstrates in both Spanish and English that they have mastered the writing standards while deepening their understanding of an issue of social justice.

SUMMARY: BILITERATE WRITING IN GRADES 3–5 AND BEYOND

As we near the end of this book, we hope we have offered a vision of what genre-based planning and writing entails within a holistic biliteracy framework for students in the upper grades. It is our sincere wish that students be provided opportunities to write about important topics in ways that are engaging and help them to imagine a more just world. Biliterate students' potential is astounding, and as biliterate educators, we have an obligation to help them to realize this potential and to understand how their writing and their words can have real-world impacts. We hope we demonstrated the value in combining the Social Justice Standards with state and district standards to engage students in thinking critically about the world they are living in and creating, and we hope we have illustrated sufficiently the importance of connecting oracy and metalinguistic awareness to writing instruction through formats that encourage collaboration. In this chapter, we used a unit sketch on racism to demonstrate the process for fleshing out a standards-based grade-appropriate biliteracy unit that is holistic, identifies and distributes multilingual resources related to a theme, and maintains high expectations in two languages for our upper-grade students. This process and the accompanying questions can be followed to develop any number of appropriate theme-based units.

Questions for Reflection and Action

▶ Given your district mandates and state curricula guidelines, what opportunities are there for students to write about issues of social justice?

▶ Imagine you are designing a unit on immigrant justice (or any topic related to human rights). How might you organize learning so that some tasks are accomplished in Spanish and others are accomplished in English?

Glossary

Note: Definitions marked with an asterisk (*) are reprinted or adapted from Biliteracy from the Start: Literacy Squared in Action *(Escamilla et al., 2014).*

Bilingualism as a First Language This term refers to children who acquire two languages at the same time from birth or, as some researchers propose, before 5 years of age. This is also known as simultaneous bilingualism. These children do not have a distinct dominant language or a distinct L1 and L2—bilingualism is their first and dominant language.

Biliterate pedagogy, biliterate pedagogies Biliterate pedagogies are created from applying bilingual perspectives on biliteracy development that include but go beyond monoliterate pedagogies in either Spanish or English and consider, in the development of biliterate language and literacy programs, how two languages interact and converge as individuals become biliterate. Biliteracy is a special form of literacy that must be understood as distinct from that of monolinguals. Biliteracy practices call for rethinking of assumptions about first and second language and literacy to perspectives that emanate from a bilingual perspective including the role that context, as well as the sociolinguistic and sociocultural environment plays in the acquisition of biliteracy. A biliterate pedagogy develops students' biliterate abilities that result in the development of key linguistic and cultural tools that result in intellectual development not readily available in monolingual English classrooms. Unlike monolinguals, this biliterate development enables individuals to interact with two literate worlds, thus amplifying their resources for thinking and learning.

Biliterate writing* A complex process to develop and produce texts that involves bilingual competencies, strategies, and knowledge in two languages.

Collaborative writing* An approach to teaching writing in which children write with their peers and the teacher monitors their work, providing further assistance as needed. It encourages greater student involvement in the actual encoding, revising, editing, and publishing processes. It is also an opportunity for students to talk about what they intend to write.

Concept of word The ability to match the spoken word to print and the knowledge that written words have spaces between them.

Cross-language connections* The ability to use one language to analyze and understand a second language. Cross-language connections enable children to develop metacognitive abilities and knowledge about their two languages and how they are the same and different. Cross-language connections are bidirectional. The Literacy Squared project used two types of cross-language connections. The first cross-language connection referred to specific methods the model adapted from Mexico and modified for use in U.S. English/Spanish literacy programs. The second focused on teaching children the metacognitive linguistic skills of cross-language expression in reading and writing. See also, *Literacy Squared*.

Cross-language metalinguistic awareness The capacity to analyze the similarities and differences one encounters when examining two or more languages concurrently.

Cross-language strategy An instructional approach that can be used in either language and that raises metalinguistic awareness about the similarities and differences in the languages students are acquiring.

Cuaderno A notebook where children can record their ideas with teacher support and that also serves as a resource to be referenced again and again.

Diverse literature Literature that centers on nondominant experiences, identities, languages, ethnicities, cultures, and protagonists.

Early biliterate writing development This term refers to the early writing development of bilingual children. Within alphabetic languages, children pass through a typical sequence, though each child does so with great variability. Emerging bilingual learners go through nearly the same progressions in both languages, demonstrating their ability to draw upon their writing knowledge and applying it across languages.

Expressive language skills Expressive language skills are also known as productive skills because they involve the production of language. Speaking and writing are known as the productive skills because they involve producing words, phrases, sentences, and paragraphs either orally or in writing.

Foundational skills (monoliterate English pedagogy): In monolingual English pedagogy, there are five aspects to the process of reading: phonics, phonemic awareness, vocabulary, reading comprehension, and fluency. These five aspects work together to create the reading experience. As children learn to read they must develop skills in all five of these areas in order to become successful readers.

Foundational skills (biliterate pedagogy): A Spanish/English biliterate pedagogy also includes the five aspects to the process of reading defined by the monoliterate pedagogy, but also includes oracy, writing, and metalinguistic development.

Genre studies Genre studies within biliteracy/paired literacy expand upon the three main writing genres of persuasive, informational/explanatory, and narrative writing by diversifying text types within each genre and privileging emerging bilingual learners' knowledge and experiences within these genres. Doing so means biliterate writing instruction is authentic and meaningful and thus is culturally and linguistically sustaining.

Holistic biliteracy framework* A framework that includes recommended teaching approaches and time allocations across the grades intended to foster development and learning in two languages through paired literacy instruction. This instructional framework is unique in that it intentionally and purposefully connects Spanish and English environments.

Humanizing curricula Humanizing curriculum centers students and strives to create the conditions for students to reach their full potential in service to the collective good and the creation of a more socially just world for all.

Linguistic, cultural, experiential knowledge The concept of linguistic, cultural, and experiential knowledge offers a way in which to honor emerging bilingual children's linguistic and cultural knowledge as well as their life experiences. Supporting this knowledge within biliteracy classrooms is particularly important for Latinx children from marginalized communities as it incorporates this knowledge (e.g., family stories) within biliteracy instruction to challenge dominant ideologies.

Literacy Squared Literacy Squared is a program that was developed around a Spanish/English biliterate pedagogy for Spanish-speaking and simultaneous (Spanish/English) bilingual children in the U.S. The program consists of four major components—research, instruction, professional development, and assessment. It has been in existence for 20 years and is both research based and research tested.

Literacy Squared Writing Rubric* A rubric designed for the analysis of biliterate writing for the purposes of informing instruction and measuring growth.

Lotta Lara Teaching strategy that focuses on developing oracy through explicit planning and increasing reading fluency through repeated reading. The teacher uses the same book or text three times over a one-week period, in sessions of 20–40 minutes, with students reading the book a total of nine times. The teacher selects a text that is personally and culturally relevant, prereads the book and plans oracy objectives and instruction, and then does the multiple readings of the text, starting with one completed read-aloud and then using echo reading, choral reading, and partner reading, with explicit oracy and comprehension instruction throughout.

Metalanguage* Thinking and talking about language and, in the case of biliteracy, understanding the relationships between and within languages. It is the language used to talk about language, and its mastery allows students to analyze how language can be leveraged to express meaning. The development of metalanguage includes the ability to identify, analyze, and manipulate language forms and to analyze sounds, symbols, grammar, vocabulary, and language structures within and between languages. It has been identified as one of three fundamental skills, along with the psycholinguistic abilities, necessary to decode and to comprehend.

Metalinguistic awareness The ability to see and understand language as a process and as an artifact. See also *within-language metalinguistic awareness; cross-language metalinguistic awareness.*

Metalinguistic development The strategy of explicit teaching of metalinguistic awareness during the course of biliteracy development that includes both within-language and cross-language metalinguistic awareness.

Modeled writing* A teaching approach where the teacher demonstrates for students the process of writing a text and multiple uses of writing as a communicative and learning tool. In modeled writing, the teacher encodes the message and students watch as they participate orally in the composition of the written piece. The text the teacher produces is at a higher level than what the students would be able to compose independently.

Oracy* The development of oral skills in formal education. Oracy is an important form of communication between human beings. It has many purposes and functions, including talking to learn and the capacity to understand speech and use it to express oneself. Oracy skills assist children in expressing their reading and writing comprehension. Oracy has three main components: language structures, vocabulary, and dialogue.

Oral language Spoken language, which includes speaking and listening. Oral language skills provide the foundation for word reading and comprehension. They are at the heart of listening and reading comprehension, serving as a predictor for both.

Paired literacy instruction* A holistic approach to teaching reading and writing where students learn to read and write in two languages simultaneously, beginning in kindergarten. Paired literacy approaches are not duplicative and do not involve concurrent translation.

Phonemic awareness A sub-set of phonological awareness that involves the ability to hear and manipulate the smallest units of sounds (phonemes) in spoken words. This includes blending sounds into words, segmenting words into sounds, and deleting and playing with the sounds in spoken words.

Phonological awareness The ability to recognize and manipulate the spoken parts of sentences and words. Examples include being able to identify words that rhyme, recognizing alliteration, segmenting a sentence into words, identifying the syllables in a word, and blending and segmenting onset-rimes. This continuum of skills develops over time and is crucial to reading and spelling success, because these skills are central to learning to decode and spell printed words.

Receptive language skills Receptive skills in language are those skills that involve receiving information and include reading and listening.

Self-extending linguistic system The development of metalinguistic awareness through explicit attention to patterns, analogies, and connections across languages that allows students to make educated guesses or approximations in new and unknown language situations.

Shared writing* An instructional approach in which the teacher and students take turns constructing a written text together. All the students in the class participate in the writing of the text by sharing the pen with the teacher, copying from the board, or encoding the text in their own notebooks.

Social Justice Standards The Social Justice Standards (Learning for Justice & The Southern Poverty Law Center, Inc., 2022) are age-appropriate, K–12, anti-bias focused guidelines for K–12 educators. They encompass four domains: Identity, Diversity, Action, and Justice. They are available here: https://www.learningforjustice.org/frameworks/social-justice-standards

Talk-through Crucial step in theDictado procedure in which the teacher uses direct and explicit instruction to teach about language, conventions, grammar, and spelling. During this step the teacher models and generates metalinguistic awareness and helps students to make cross-language connections.

Teaching for social justice Social justice is the view that everyone deserves equal economic, political, and social rights and opportunities. Teaching for social justice involves teaching the principles of access, equity, diversity, participation, and human rights. Teaching for social justice involves teaching respect and moral responsibility. Approaches to teaching for social justice are embodied in the Social Justice K–12 Teaching Standards (Learning for Justice & The Southern Poverty Law Center, Inc., 2022).

Teaching points The grammar, vocabulary, spelling, and structural elements that are intentionally included in theDictado because students have demonstrated that they do not yet control them or because they are required according to the standards or a district-level scope and sequence.

theDictado A method to teach content, conventions, grammar, and spelling in an integrated way. It involves having the teacher dictate a series of phrases or sentences to the students. The students and teacher then collaborate to create a corrected model of the focus text. Students amend their sentences using a two-color system to draw attention to errors. The same phrases or sentences are repeated throughout the week, giving students multiple opportunities to practice and learn the targeted content, conventions, grammar, and spelling. TheDictado is adapted from Latin American schools and provides multiple opportunities for within-language and cross-language metalinguistic development.

Trajectories toward biliteracy* A framework for documenting patterns of development and growth in Spanish and English for emerging bilingual children who are receiving paired literacy instruction. Children's achievement is expressed in terms of biliteracy development rather than by grade level or other monolingual norms that separate the two languages. Spanish literacy outcomes may be slightly ahead of English literacy outcomes in this trajectory.

Within-language metalinguistic awareness The ability to look at a single language and understand how it functions in both its oral and written forms.

References

Amescua, G. (2021). *Child of the flower-song people: Luz Jiménez, daughter of the Nahua*. Harry N. Abrams.
Ancona, G. (2005). *Mi familia/My family*. Children's Press.
Aukerman, M., & Schuldt, L. (2021). What matters most? Toward a robust and socially just science of reading. *Reading Research Quarterly, 56*(S1), S85–S103.
August, D., & Shanahan, T. (2006). *Developing literacy in second language learners: Report of the National Panel on language-minority children and youth*. Mahwah, NJ: Erlbaum.
Bauer, E., & Gort, M. (2011). *Early biliteracy development: Exploring your learners' use of their linguistic resources.*: Routledge, Taylor and Francis Group.
BigSpeak Speakers Bureau. (n.d.). *Xiuhtezcatl Martinez: Compilation* [Video]. YouTube. https://www.youtube.com/watch?v=97a-WhYpFfE&ab_channel=BigSpeakSpeakersBureau
Bishop, R.S. (1990). Mirrors, windows, and sliding glass doors. *Perspectives, 6*(3), ix–xi.
Britton, J. (2019). Spoken language: The importance of oracy. In Clements, J. (Ed.). *Teaching English by the book* (pp. 145–154). Routledge.
Browne, A. (1989). *Things I like*. Dragonfly Books.
Butvilofsky, S., Escamilla, K., Silva, E., & Gumina, D. (2021). Beyond monolingual reading assessments for bilingual learners: Expanding the understanding of biliteracy assessment. *Reading Research Quarterly, 56*(1), 53–70.
Butvilofsky, S., Fine, C., & Silva, E. (2016). Literacy Squared® Technical Report: Adams 14, 2015–2016.
Butvilofsky, S., Hopewell, S., Escamilla, K., & Sparrow, W. (2017). Shifting deficit paradigms of Latino students' literacy achievement: Documenting emerging bilingual students' biliterate trajectories. *Journal of Latinos and Education, 16*(2), 85–97.
Cabell, S. Q., Tortorelli, L. S., & Gerde, H. K. (2013). How do I write . . .? Scaffolding preschoolers' early writing skills. *The Reading Teacher, 66*(8), 650–659.
Celano, M., Collins, M., & Hazzard, A. (2018). *Something happened in our town: A children's story about racial injustice*. Magination Press.
Center for Applied Linguistics. (2017). Directory of two-way immersion programs in the U.S. https://www.cal.org/twi/directory/twigrow.htm (accessed Apr. 23, 2018).
Cherry-Paul, S. (With contributors Kendi, I. X., & Reynolds, J.). (2021). *Stamped (for kids): Racism, antiracism, and you*. Little, Brown and Company.
Clay, M. (1975). *What did I write? Beginning writing behavior*. Heinemann.
Clay, M. (1991). *Becoming literate: The Construction of inner control*. Heinemann.
Colorado Department of Education. (2020). 2020 Colorado Academic Standards—Family and Community Guide for 2nd Grade. Retrieved from https://www.cde.state.co.us/standardsandinstruction/guidestostandards
Costales, A. (2009). *Sundays on fourth street/Los domingos en la calle Cuatro*. Arte Publico Press.
Devenny, J. (2021). *Race cars: A children's book about white privilege*. Quarto Publishing.
Durán, L. (2017). Audience and young bilingual writers: Building on strengths. *Journal of Literacy Research, 49*(1), 92–114. https://doi.org/10.1177/1086296X16683420
Ehri, L. The science of learning to read words: A case for systematic phonics instruction. *Reading Research Quarterly, 55*(S1), S45–S60.
Escamilla, K. (2006). Semilingualism applied to the literacy behaviors of Spanish speaking emerging bilinguals: Emerging biliteracy or biliteracy? *Teachers College Record, 108*(11), 2329–2353.
Escamilla, K., Butvilofsky, S., & Hopewell, S. (2017). What gets lost when English-only writing assessment is used to assess writing proficiency in Spanish-English emerging bilingual learners? *International Multilingual Research Journal, 12*(4), 221–236. https://doi.org/10.1080/19313152.2016.1273740
Escamilla, K., Fine, C., & Hopewell, S. (2019). Enhancing writing outcomes in Spanish/English biliteracy programs. *Bilingual Review/Revista Bilingüe. 34*(1). Retrieved from https://www.bilingualreviewjournal.org/index.php/br/article/view/303

Escamilla, K., & Hopewell, S. Transitions to biliteracy: Creating positive trajectories for Emerging Bilinguals in the U.S. (2010). In J. Petrovic (Ed.). *International perspectives on bilingual education: Policy, practice and controversy.* Information Age Publishing.

Escamilla, K., Hopewell, S., Butvilofsky, S., Sparrow, W., Soltero-González, L., & Escamilla, M. (2014). *Biliteracy from the start: Literacy Squared in action.* Caslon.

Escamilla, K., Olsen, L., & Slavick, J. (2022). *Toward comprehensive effective literacy policy and instruction for English learners/emergent bilingual students.* www.multilingualliteracy.org

Ferreiro, E. (1991). *Haceres, quehaceres y deshaceres: con la lengua escrita en la escuela primaria.* México. Secretaría de Educación Pública.

Ferreiro, E. (2002). *Relaciones de (in)dependencia entre oralidad y escritura.* Mexico City: Gidesa Editorial.

Ferreiro, E. (2017). *9 frases de Emilia Ferreiro sobre el aprendizaje de los niños y la lectoescritura.* Retrieved from https://eligeeducar.cl/acerca-del-aprendizaje/9-frases-de-emilia-ferreiro-sobre-el-aprendizaje-de-los-ninos-y-la-lectoescritura/

Ferreiro, E., & Teberosky, A. (1979). *Los Sistemas de escritura en el desarrollo del niño.* México: Siglo XXI.

Ferreiro, E., & Teberosky, A. (1982). *Literacy before schooling.* Heinemann.

Flesch, R. (1955). *Why Johnny can't read—and what you can do about it.* New York: Harper & Row.

Freire, P. (2000). *Pedagogy of the oppressed* (30th anniversary ed.). Continuum.

García, O., Ibarra Johnson, S., & Seltzer, K. (2017). *The translanguaging classroom: Leveraging student bilingualism for learning.* Caslon.

García, O., & Kleifgen, J. (2018). *Educating emergent bilinguals: Policies, programs, and practices for English learners (Language and Literacy Series)* (2nd edition). Teachers College Press.

Garcia, O., & Wei, L. (2014). *Language, bilingualism and education.* Springer.

Gardner, D. (1983). *A nation at risk: The imperative for educational reform.* National Commission on Excellence in Education.

Gaunt, A., & Stott, A. (2018). *Transforming teaching and learning through talk: The oracy imperative.* Rowan & Littlefield.

Genesee, F., & Riches, C. (2006). Literacy instruction issues. In F. Genesee, K. Lindholm-Leary, W. Saunders, and D. Christian (Eds.). *Educating English language learners: A research synthesis* (pp. 109–176) Cambridge University Press.

Gentile, L. (2004). *The oracy instructional guide.* Dominic Press.

Goldenberg, C. (2020). Reading wars, reading science, and English learners. *Reading Research Quarterly, 55*(S1), S131–S144.

Good, R.H., III, & Kaminski, R.A. (Eds.). (2002). *Dynamic Indicators of Basic Early Literacy Skills* (6th ed.). Institute of the Development of Educational Achievement.

Gort, M. (2006). Strategic Codeswitching, interliteracy, and other phenomena of emergent bilingual writing: Lessons from first-grade dual language classrooms. *Journal of Early Childhood Literacy, 6*(3), 323–354. https://doi.org/10.1177/1468798406069796

Graham, S. (2020). The sciences of reading and writing must become more fully integrated. *Reading Research Quarterly, 55*(S1), S35–S34.

Hopewell, S. (2017). Pedagogies to challenge monolingual orientation to bilingual education in the United States. In B. Paulsrud, J. Rosén, B. Strazer, & A. Wedín (Eds.) *New perspectives on translanguaging and education.* Multilingual Matters.

Hopewell, S., & Abril-González, P. (2019). ¿Por qué estamos code-switching? Understanding language use in a second-grade classroom. *Bilingual Research Journal, 42*(1), 105–120.

Hopewell, S., & Butvilofsky, S. (2016). Privileging bilingualism: Using biliterate writing outcomes to understand emerging bilingual learners' literacy achievement. *Bilingual Research Journal, 39* (3–4), 324–338. http://dx.doi.org/10.1080/15235882.2016.1232668

Hopewell, S., Butvilofsky, S., & Escamilla, K. (2016). Complementing the Common Core with holistic biliteracy. *Journal of Education, 196*(2), 89–100.

Hopewell, S., & Escamilla, K. (2014). Struggling reader or emerging biliterate student? Reevaluating the criteria for labeling emerging bilingual students as low achieving. *Journal of Literacy Research, 46*(1), 6889.

Hopewell, S., Slavick, J., & Escamilla, K. (in press). Toward a biliterate pedagogy. In Freire, J.A., Alfaro, C., & DeJong, E. (Eds). *The handbook of dual language bilingual education.* Routledge.

Howard, E., Lindholm-Leary, K., Rogers, D., Olague, N., Medina, J., Kennedy, B., Sugarman, J., & Christian, D. (2019). *Guiding principles for dual language education.* Center for Applied Linguistics.

Hubbard, R.L., & Mora, O. (2022). *La estudiante mayor: Cómo Mary Walker aprendió a leer / The oldest student: How Mary Walker learned to read.* Vintage Español.

Jang, H. & Cheung, Y. L. (2020). Impacts of dyadic interaction on second language writing: A study with eight bilingual primary school students in Singapore. *Education 3-13, 48*(5), 527–540.

Jiménez, R. T., Smith, P. H., & Martínez-León, N. (2003). Freedom and form: The language and literacy practices of two Mexican schools. *Reading Research Quarterly, 38*(4), 488–508.

Kaufman, A. M., & Rodríguez, M. E. (1993). Hacia una tipología de los textos. *La escuela y los textos,* 19–27.

Kilpatrick, D. (2015). *Essentials of assessing, preventing and overcorrecting reading difficulties.* Wiley.

Learning for Justice and The Southern Poverty Law Center. (2022). *Social Justice Standards: The Learning for Justice anti-bias framework*, 2nd edition. The Southern Poverty Law Center, Inc. https://www.learningforjustice.org/frameworks/social-justice-standards

Lewis, G., Jones, B. & Baker, C. (2012). Translanguaging: Developing its conceptualisation and contextualisation. *Educational Research and Evaluation: An International Journal on Theory and Practice.* 18(7), 655–670.

Lopez, M., Butvilofsky, S.A., Le, K., & Gumina, D. (2022). Project *Recuerdo*: Honoring Mexican families' knowledge within the school. *The Reading Teacher, 75*(4), 429–440. https://doi.org/10.1002/trtr.2062.

Moats, L. (2020). *Teaching reading is rocket science*. American Federation of Teachers.

Moll, L. C., Amanti, C., Neff, D., & Gonzalez, N. (1992). Funds of knowledge for teaching: Using a qualitative approach to connect homes and classrooms. *Theory into practice, 31*(2), 132–141.

Montaño-Harmon, M. R. (1991). Discourse features of written Mexican Spanish: Current research in contrastive rhetoric and its implications. *Hispania, 74*(2), 417–425.

National Center for Education Evaluation and Regional Assistance. (2008). *Reading First impact study: Final report*. National Center for Education Evaluation.

National Governors Association Center for Best Practices & Council of Chief State School Officers. (2010). Common Core State Standards for English language arts. http://www.corestandards.org/ELA-Literacy/

National Institute of Child Health and Human Development (NICHD). (2000). *Report of the National Reading Panel. Teaching children to read: An evidence-based assessment of the scientific research literature on reading and its implications for reading instruction* (NIH Publication No. 00-4769). U.S. Department of Health and Human Services.

Nguyen-Le, K. (2021). What is a Refugee Unit. Presented at the Annual La Cosecha Conference, Albuquerque, NM

No Child Left Behind Act of 2001, P.L. 107-110, 20 U.S.C. § 6319 (2002).

Norman, C. (1992). *Thinking voices: The work of the national oracy project*. Hodder & Stoughton.

Paris, D., & Alim, H. S. (2014). What are we seeking to sustain through culturally sustaining pedagogy? A loving critique forward. *Harvard Educational Review, 84*(1), 85–100.

Paris, D., & Alim, S. (2017). *Culturally sustaining pedagogies: Teaching and learning for justice in a changing world*. Teachers College Press.

Rosa-Mendoza, G. (2001). *My family and I / My familia y yo* (4th ed.). Me+mi Publishing.

Saéz, F.T. (2003). Culture in writing: Discourse markers in English and Spanish student writing. Eds, Departamento de Didáctica de la Lengua y la Literatura. *Tadea seu liber de Amicitia Granada*, pp. 345–364.

Serrano, R., & Howard, E. (2007). Second language writing development in English and in Spanish in a two-way immersion programme. *International Journal of Bilingual Education and Bilingualism, 10*(2), 152–170.

Share, D. (2021). Is the science of reading just the science of reading English? *Reading Research Quarterly, 56*(S1), S391–S402.

Snow, C., & Tabors, P. (1993). Language skills that relate to literacy development. In B. Spodek & O. Saracho (Eds.). *Yearbook in early childhood education.* (Vol. 4, pp. 1–20). Teacher's College Press.

Snow, M., Eslami, Z. R., & Park, J. H. (2015). Latino English language learners' writing during literacy-enriched block play. Reading Psychology, 36, 741–784. https://doi.org/10.1080/02702711.2015.1055872.

Soltero-González, L., & Butvilofsky, S. (2015). The early Spanish and English writing development of simultaneous bilingual preschoolers. *Journal of Early Childhood Literacy, 16*(4), 473–497.

Soltero-Gonzalez, L. Escamilla, K., & Hopewell, S. (2011). Changing teachers' perceptions about the writing abilities of emerging bilingual students: Towards a holistic bilingual perspective on writing assessment. *International Journal of Bilingual Education and Bilingualism, 15*(1), 71–94.

Toro, A. (2015). *Gabriela, la poeta viajera*. Editorial Amanuta.

U.S. Department of Education. (2018). Number of English learners born in the U.S. https://www.ncela.ed.gov/files/fast_facts/FastFacts-HispanicELs-2018.pdf

Vernon, S., & Ferierro, E. (1999). Writing development: A neglected variable in the consideration of phonological awareness. *Harvard Educational Review,* 69, 395–415.

Weill, C. (2013). *Mi familia calaca / My skeleton family*. Cinco Puntos Press.

Yosso, T. J. (2005). Whose culture has capital? A critical race theory discussion of community cultural wealth. *Race Ethnicity and Education, 8*(1), 69–91.

Index

Note: Page numbers followed by *f* and *t* indicate figures and tables, respectively.

Accountability, TheDictado, 50
Achievement gaps, 20
Alphabetic writing, learning of, 58, 60*f*, 61
Anti-racism, 121–127, 122*t*
Approximations, 6–7, 7*f*, 8
Audience for writing, 62, 96

Backward planning for biliterate writing, 98–100, 99*f*
Bilingual instruction, 5–6
    phonological awareness in, 62–63
Bilingual pedagogy, 5–6
Bilingual/biliterate lens
    rubric analysis using, 79
    trends from qualitative analysis using, 79–81
Bilingualism as a First Language, 3
Biliteracy from the Start: Literacy Squared in Action, 38, 40, 63, 82
Biliterate pedagogies, 5
Biliterate writing, 5, 6–9, 13–14
    about racism, 121–127, 122*t*
    backward planning for, 98–100, 99*f*
    collaborative, 84–86*f*, 85–86
    considerations for developing, 32–35, 33*f*
    example of, in grade 1, 75–77, 76*f*
    expanding upon main writing genres to develop, in grades 3 to 5, 94–98, 95*t*, 97*f*
    general trends in grades 1 and 2, 77–78, 77*t*, 78*f*
    independent, 86, 87*f*
    kindergarten instruction in, 54–55, 54*t*
    literacy-based ELD, 61–65, 64*t*, 65*f*, 88–90*f*, 88–91, 91*t*
    Lotta Lara reading strategy and, 81
    modeled, 82–83*t*, 82–85, 83–84*f*
    potential in grade 1, 79–80, 79*f*
    rubric analysis using bilingual/biliterate lens, 79
    shared, 90–91, 91*t*
    See also Writing
Britton, James, 22

CCSS, *See* Common Core State Standards
Clay, Marie, 39
Collaborative writing, 65, 65*f*, 73, 73*f*
    social justice standards and humanizing curricula and, 120–121
    Spanish, 84–86*f*, 85–86
Common Core State Standards (CCSS), 6, 66, 66*t*, 81, 94
    reading and writing about racism and, 123–124
    on social justice standards and humanizing curricula, 117–121, 118*f*
    text genres and, 95, 95*t*
    writing standards for fourth grade, 101

Comprehension and oracy, 26–27, 26–27*f*
Concept of word, 58
Cross-language connections, 2, 4, 4*f*, 5
    approximations in, 6–7, 7*f*
Cross-language metalinguistic awareness, 39
Cross-language strategy, 38

Dialogue, 28–29
DIBELS, *See* Dynamic Indicators of Basic Early Literacy Skills
Differentiation with TheDictado, 48
Drawing representing writing, 55, 56*f*
Dynamic Indicators of Basic Early Literacy Skills (DIBELS), 11
Dyson, 75
Dyson, Anne Haas, 93

Early biliterate writing development, 55–61
    stage 1: drawing representing writing in, 55, 56*f*
    stage 2: child producing string of letters, 55, 57*f*, 58
    stage 3: child writing salient and beginning sounds or representing syllables, 58, 59*f*
    stage 4: child learning alphabetic writing, 58, 60*f*, 61
EB (Emerging Bilingual) learners, 1–2, 94
    achievement gaps and, 20
    deeper, assets-based understanding of, 3
    in kindergarten (*See* Kindergarten)
    narrowing of literacy curriculum and, 21, 21*f*
    research reports on, 20–21
ELD, *See* English-language development
Empathy, oracy for, 31–32
English-language development (ELD), 4, 4*f*
    daily writing instruction in literacy-based, 61–65, 64*t*, 65*f*
    literacy-based, 71–74, 71*f*, 73–74*f*, 88–90*f*, 88–91, 91*t*, 110–112
English-only assessments, 11
Expressive language skills, 23

Ferreiro, Emilia, 1, 53
Flesch, Rudolph, 2
Formative assessment, 32–33, 33*f*
Foundational skills in writing, 62–63
Fourth-grade biliteracy unit, 100–112
    overview of, 100
    Spanish literacy and, 103–109, 104–109*f*, 105*t*
    text selection and exemplar creation for, 101–102
    writing exemplars to plan instruction in, 103
    writing standards for, 101, 101*f*

Genishi, Celia, 93
Genres, text, 95–96, 95t
Google Classroom, 49
Gorman, Amanda, 115
Grades 1 and 2, 75, 91, 112
    biliteracy in, 75–77, 76f
    biliterate writing potential in, 79–80, 79f
    community, cultural, and social connections in, 87–88
    general trends in biliterate writing in, 77–78, 77t, 78f
    instructional implications for, 81–91
    modeled, shared, and independent writing approaches for, 82–83t, 82–85, 83–84f
    Spanish collaborative writing in, 85–86, 85–87f
Grades 3 to 5, 93–94, 115
    backward planning for biliterate writing in, 98–100, 99f
    community, cultural, and social connections in, 102
    expanding upon the main writing genres to develop biliteracy in, 94–98, 95t, 97f
    fostering engaged writing in, 116
    literacy-based ELD in, 110–112
    reading and writing about racism in, 121–127, 122t
    sample fourth-grade biliteracy unit and, 100–112
    social justice standards and humanizing curricula for, 117–121, 118f
    using bilingual lens to promote developmentally appropriate trajectory in, 117
Gravel, E., 25
Guiding Principles for Dual Language Education, 5

High states testing, 6, 11
Hill We Climb, The, 115
Holistic biliteracy framework, 4, 4f, 9

Independent writing, 69, 70f, 73–74, 74f
    Spanish, 86, 87f
Institute of Educational Research, 2

Jiménez, Luz, 93

Kindergarten, 53–54, 74
    biliterate writing trajectory in, 61
    daily writing instruction in both Spanish literacy and literacy-based ELD in, 61–65, 64t, 65f
    instructional implications for, 61
    literacy-based ELD in, 71–74, 71f, 73–74f
    nuanced analysis of biliterate writing in, 55–61
    paired literacy lesson in, 65–69, 66f, 66t, 67–70f
    pedagogical approaches in writing for, 63–65, 64t, 65f
    research supporting biliterate writing instruction in, 54–55, 54t

Literacy Squared Holistic Biliteracy Model
    bilingual instruction from the beginning, focused on quality and bilingual pedagogy and, 5–6
    brief history of, 2–6
    broader definition of literacy and, 3–5, 4f
    deeper, assets-based understanding of EB children and, 3
    greater focus on writing and, 6
    Lotta Lara reading strategy and, 81
    oracy in, 24–25, 24f
    research findings to guide development of, 9–12, 10t, 11f
    Science of Reading (SOR) and, 2–3
Literacy Squared Research Project, 10, 10t, 11f
Literacy Squared Writing Rubric, 9, 10, 11, 12, 15–17, 54
Literacy-based ELD, 71–74, 71f, 73–74f
    in grades 1 and 2, 88–90f, 88–91, 91t
    in grades 3 to 5, 110–112
Lotta Lara reading strategy, 81

Metalanguage, 4
Metalinguistic awareness, 38–40
Modeled writing, 63–64, 64t, 68–69, 69f, 72, 73f, 89–90, 89f
    Spanish, 82–83t, 82–85, 83–84f

Nation at Risk, A, 20
National Committee for Effective Literacy, 20
National Literacy Panel, 2, 21
National Reading Panel, 21
Nguyen-Le, K., 25, 30
No Child Left Behind (NCLB), 20
Note taking, 29–31, 30f

Online accommodations with TheDictado, 48–50
Oracy, 4
    for comprehension objectives, 26–27, 26–27f
    considerations for developing biliteracy, 32–35, 33f
    for dialogue objectives, 28–29
    for empathy, 31–32
    in Literacy Squared, 24–25, 24f
    oral language development and, 22–24, 23f
    to prepare for writing, 89
    reading and writing about racism and, 126–127
    What Is a Refugee? unit, 25–27f, 25–32, 30f
    for writing, 29–31, 30f
Oral language development
    oracy and, 22–24, 23f

Paired literacy instruction, 3, 65–69, 66f, 66t, 67–70f
Pear Deck, 49
Pedagogical approaches in writing for kindergarten, 63–65, 64t, 65f
Phonemic awareness, 23–24
Phonological awareness, 23, 62–63
Purpose for writing, 62

Racism, reading and writing about, 121–127, 122t
Reading First Program, 2–3, 20–21, 21f
Reading Recovery, 39
Receptive language skills, 23
Remediation, 8

Science of Reading (SOR), 2–3, 21, 21*f*
SeeSaw, 49–50
Shared writing, 64–65, 67–68, 67*f*, 71–72, 71*f*, 90–91, 91*t*
Sobrato Early Academic Language (SEAL), 40
Social justice and humanizing curricula, 116
   collaborative writing and, 120–121
   guiding questions on, 119–120
   standards for humanizing curricula and, 117–121, 118*f*
Social justice standards and humanizing curricula and sample unit sketch for, 121–127, 122*t*
SOR, *See* Science of Reading
Sounds, beginning, 58, 59*f*
Spanish collaborative writing, 84–86*f*, 85–86
Spanish independent writing, 86, 87*f*
Spanish modeled writing, 82–83*t*, 82–85, 83–84*f*
Spanish-English biliteracy, 12–13
   daily writing instruction in, 61–65, 64*t*, 65*f*
   in fourth-grade biliteracy unit, 103–109, 104–109*f*, 105*t*
Strings of letters, 55, 57*f*, 58
Syllables, 58, 59*f*

Talk-through, TheDictado, 47–48
Teaching for social justice, 25
TheDictado, 91
   accountability and, 50
   analytic framework for planning, 41–43, 42*f*
   conducting talk-through of, 47–48
   content of, 41
   creating, 41–43, 42*f*
   definition of, 38
   determining teaching points in, 47
   developing metalinguistic awareness, 38–40
   differentiation with, 48
   how to analyze student's writing systematically using, 43–47, 44*f*, 45–46*f*
   implementation of, 40–41
   online accommodations with, 48–50
   in practice, 41–50
   summary of, 50
   using the analytic framework to create, 43
Transformations, 26

Weill, Cynthia, 66
What Is a Refugee? unit, 25–26, 25*f*
   oracy for comprehension objectives, 26–27, 26–27*f*
   oracy for dialogue objectives, 28–29
   oracy for empathy, 31–32
   oracy for writing, 29–31, 30*f*
Why Johnny Can't Read, 2, 20
Writing, 37–38
   approximations in, 6–7, 7*f*, 8
   asset-based, holistic, bilingual interpretation in, 9
   audience for, 62, 96
   collaborative, 65, 65*f*, 73, 73*f*, 84–86*f*, 85–86, 120–121
   daily instruction in both Spanish literacy and literacy-based ELD, 61–65, 64*t*, 65*f*
   drawing representing, 55, 56*f*
   foundational skills in, 62–63
   goals and instructional scaffolds in, 63, 64*t*
   greater focus on, 6
   independent, 69, 70*f*, 73–74, 74*f*, 86, 87*f*
   loss of information with English-only assessments of, 11
   meaningful and authentic purpose for, 62
   modeled, 63–64, 64*t*, 68–69, 69*f*, 72, 73*f*, 82–83*t*, 82–85, 83–84*f*
   no delay in English literacy acquisition due to learning two language, 12
   note taking, 29–31, 30*f*
   pedagogical approaches in, for kindergarten, 63–65, 64*t*, 65*f*
   salient and beginning sounds or syllables, 58
   samples of, 7, 8*f*, 45–46*f*
   shared, 64–65, 67–68, 67*f*, 71–72, 71*f*, 90–91, 91*t*
   Spanish-English biliteracy and, 12–13
   strings of letters and, 55, 57*f*, 58
   systematic analysis of student, 43–47, 44*f*, 45–46*f*
   utilizing children's Spanish and English writing as formative assessment in teaching oracy and, 32–33, 33*f*
   See also Biliterate writing

Zoom, 49